CONTENTS

INTRODUCTION 10

ESSENTIALS OF TRAGER WOOD PELLET GRILL 11

    What Is Traeger Wood Pellet Grill 13

    Components of Traeger Wood Pellet Grill 13

    How It Works 14

    Traeger Wood Pellet Grill Vs. Charcoal and Wood Grills 15

    Pellets to Use 15

TIPS AND TRICKS 18

HOW TO CLEAN YOUR TRAEGER WOOD PELLET GRILL 20

    Cleaning the Water Pan 20

    Cleaning the Firepot 20

    Cleaning Your Traeger Grill Oven Without a Clean Panel 21

    Cleaning your Traeger Pellet Grill Oven with a Clean Panel 21

TROUBLESHOOTING 22

EASY AND EASY TO FIND RECIPES 24

BAKED GOODS, CHEESE, NUTS 24

    Quick Yeast Dinner Rolls 24

    Baked Cornbread with Honey Butter 24

    S'Mores Dip with Candied Pecans 25

    Brown Sugared Bacon Cinnamon Rolls 26

    Traeger Soft Gingerbread Cookie 26

    Sweet Pull-Apart Rolls 27

    Baked Pulled Pork Stuffed Potatoes 27

    Banana Walnut bread 28

    Peach Blueberry Cobbler 28

    Baked Wild Sockeye Salmon 29

    Pizza dough roll 29

    Twice-Baked Spaghetti Squash 29

    Take and Bake Pepperoni Pizza 30

    Classic Apple Pie 30

    Crusty Artisan Dough Bread 30

    Red Chile and Lime Shortbread Cookies 31

    Kahluá Coffee Brownies 31

Twice- Baked potatoes with Smoked Gouda and grilled scallions.................................32
Chocolate Pecan Bourbon Pie 32

RUBS, SAUCES..**33**
Smoked Tomato Cream Sauce 33
Smoked Mushroom Sauce 33
Smoked Cranberry Sauce 34
Smoked Sriracha Sauce 34
Smoked Soy Sauce 35
Smoked Garlic Sauce 35
Smoked Cherry BBQ Sauce 35
Smoked Garlic White Sauce 36
Texas-Style Brisket Rub 37
Pork Dry Rub 37
Texas Barbeque Rub 37
Barbeque Sauce 37
Steak Sauce 38
Bourbon Whiskey Sauce 38
Chicken Marinade 38
Carne Asada Marinade 39
Grapefruit Juice Marinade 39
Steak Marinade 39

POULTRY **40**
Herb Roasted Turkey 40
Turkey Legs 40
Turkey Breast...41
Hellfire Chicken Wings..42
Spicy BBQ Chicken..43
BBQ Half Chickens 43
Teriyaki Wings 44
Korean Chicken Wings 44
Garlic Parmesan Chicken Wings..45
Rosemary Orange Chicken 46
Lemon Chicken Breast 46
Smokey Fried Chicken 47
Maple and Bacon Chicken...48
Paprika Chicken 48
Sweet Sriracha BBQ Chicken..49
Smoked Chicken Drumsticks 49

Chicken Cordon Bleu 50
Smoked Whole Duck 50
Chicken Fajitas on a Wood Pellet Grill 51
Smoked Cornish Chicken in Wood Pellets 52
Wild Turkey Egg Rolls 52
BBQ Chicken 53
Chicken Tortillas with Tzatziki Sauce 53
Spicy Chipotle Chicken Kabobs 54
Louisiana Hot Apple-Smoked Turkey 55
Spicy Turkey Cheeseburgers 56
Whole Maple-Smoked Turkey 56
Smoked Whole Chicken 57
Smoked Whole Chicken with Carolina Glaze 58
Cajun Smoked Chicken Wings 58
Smoked Chicken 59
Chicken, Applewood Smoked 59
Glazed Smoked Chicken 60
Chicken Brined with Lemon 61
BBQ-Seasoned Chicken Breast 62
Spicy Chicken Thighs 62

MEAT (BEEF, LAMB, RIBS AND PORK) **63**
Grilled Bloody Mary Flank Steak 63
Smoked Tomahawk Steak 63
Cocoa-Rubbed Steak for Two 64
Smoked Rib-Eye Caps 64
Spiced Tomahawk Steaks 65
Beef Tenderloin with Cherry Tomato Vinaigrette 65
Grilled Beef Short Ribs 66
Smoked Beef Brisket with Mop Sauce 66
Steak Skewers with Cherry BBQ Sauce 66
Seared Strip Steak with Butter 67
Seared Rib-Eye Steaks 67
Garlic-Mustard Roasted Prime Rib 68
Grilled Lamb and Apricot Kabobs 69
Spicy Braised Lamb Shoulder 69
Grilled Lamb Leg 70
Roasted Breaded Rack of Lamb 70
Garlicky Grilled Rack of Lamb 71

Grilled Stuffed Turkey Breast..71

BBQ St. Louis-Style Ribs..72

Balsamic Smoked Pork Chops..72

Juicy BBQ Ribs...73

Traeger Smoked Queso 73

BBQ Honey Pork Belly..74

Spicy Smoked StLouis Ribs...74

Chile Verde Braised Pork Shoulder 75

Traeger Grilled Pork Chops 75

Butter-Sugar Glazed BBQ Pork Ribs...76

Traeger Braised BBQ Ribs...76

Apricot BBQ Smoked Pork Tenderloin 77

Brown Sugar Baked Pork Belly..77

Fajita Favorite Pork Shoulder 78

Simplest Pork Belly..78

Beautiful Christmas Ham 79

Backyard Cookout Sausages...79

Elegant Lamb Chops...80

Easy-to-Prepare Lamb Chops...80

Foolproof Lamb Chops 81

Deliciously Spicy Rack of Lamb...81

Aromatic Herbed Rack of Lamb 82

Holiday Dinner Leg of Lamb 82

Fancy Gathering's Lamb Shoulder..83

Spicy & Tangy Lamb Shoulder 83

Wine Braised Lamb Shank..84

Cheesy Lamb Burgers...84

Grilled Lamb Burgers 85

Traeger Stuffed Burgers..85

Grilled Lamb Sandwiches...86

Lamb Chops..86

Lamb Ribs Rack 87

Lamb Shank..87

Leg of a Lamb 87

Lamb Breast..88

Smoked Lamb Shoulder Chops...88

Lamb Skewers...89

Brown Sugar Lamb Chops 89

Bacon-Wrapped Sausages in Brown Sugar 90
Sweet and Hot BBQ Ribs 90
Lemon Pepper Pork Tenderloin 91
Chinese BBQ Pork 91
Smoked Sausages 92
BBQ Baby Back Ribs 93

FISH & SEAFOOD **94**
Juicy Smoked Salmon 94
Peppercorn Tuna Steaks 94
Stuffed Shrimp Tilapia 94
Togarashi Smoked Salmon 95
BBQ Oysters 96
Grilled Shrimp 96
Teriyaki Smoked Shrimp 97
Jerk Shrimp 97
Lobster Tails 98
Lemon Garlic Scallops 98
Halibut in Parchment 99
Wine Infused Salmon 99
Citrus Salmon 100
Omega- Rich Salmon 100
Enticing Mahi-Mahi 101
Super-Tasty Trout 101
No-Fuss Tuna Burgers 102
Lively Flavored Shrimp 102
Flavor-Bursting Prawn Skewers 102
Yummy Buttery Clams 103
Crazy Delicious Lobster Tails 103
Baked Steelhead 104
Whole Vermillion Snapper 104
Grilled Clams with Garlic Butter 105
Simple but Delicious Fish Recipe 105
Crab Legs on the Grill 105
Seared Tuna Steaks 106
Roasted Shrimp Mix 106

VEGETABLES, SIDES AND MEATLESS DISHES **107**
Roasted Parmesan Cheese Broccoli 107
Cajun Style Grilled Corn 107

Grilled Cherry Tomato Skewers 108
Roasted Vegetable Medley 108
Smokey Roasted Cauliflower 109
Smoked Deviled Eggs 109
Crispy Maple Bacon Brussels Sprouts 110
Sweet Jalapeño Cornbread 110
Grilled Broccoli 111
Smoked Healthy Cabbage 111
Garlic and Rosemary Potato Wedges 112
Smoked Tomato and Mozzarella Dip 112
Feisty Roasted Cauliflower 113
Green Beans with Bacon 113
Vegetable Sandwich 114
Cauliflower with Parmesan and Butter 115
Roasted Butternut Squash 115
Roasted Sheet Pan Vegetables 115
Smoked Hummus 116
Baked Cheesy Corn Pudding 116
Grilled Corn on The Cob with Parmesan and Garlic 117
Grilled Asparagus with Wild Mushrooms 117
Smoked -Bean Salad 118
Grilled Artichokes 118
Grilled Scallions 118
Butter Braised Green Beans 119
Smoked Baked Kale Chips 119
Smoked Pickles 119
Grilled Zucchini Squash 120
Smoked Balsamic Potatoes and Carrots 120
Grilled Potato Salad 121
Grilled Zucchini 121
Grilled Sugar Snap Peas 122
Grilled Carrots and Asparagus 122
Kale Chips 123
Roasted Root Vegetables 123
Vegetable Skewers 124

VEGETARIANS **125**
Traeger Smoked Mushrooms 125
Grilled Zucchini Squash Spears 125

Grilled Asparagus & Honey-Glazed Carrots...125

Traeger Grilled Vegetables 126

Smoked Acorn Squash 126

Vegan Smoked Carrot Dogs 127

Stuffed Grilled Zucchini 127

Smoked Stuffed Mushrooms 128

Bacon-Wrapped Jalapeno Poppers 128

Roasted Green Beans with Bacon 128

Smoked Watermelon 129

Grilled Corn with Honey Butter 129

Smoked Mushrooms 130

Smoked Cherry Tomatoes 130

Smoked and Smashed New Potatoes 130

Smoked Brussels Sprouts 131

Apple Veggie Burger..131

Smoked Tofu 132

Easy Smoked Vegetables..132

Zucchini with Red Potatoes...132

Shiitake Smoked Mushrooms 133

Coconut Bacon 133

Garlic and Herb Smoke Potato 134

Smoked Baked Beans 134

Smoked Cauliflower 134

Smoked Peppers...135

Smoked Aubergines 135

Smoked Mackerel 136

Grilled Sweet Potatoes...137

Grilled Yellow Squash 137

DESSERTS & COCKTAILS **138**

Traeger Marinated Chicken Kabobs 138

Bacon-Wrapped Jalapeño Poppers 138

Bacon-wrapped Chicken Tenders...139

Traeger Smoked Italian Meatballs 139

Traeger Steak Kabobs 140

Traeger Apple cake 140

Traeger Beef Pot Pie..141

Traeger Apple Crisp 141

Berry Cobbler 142

Traeger Smoked Mac and Cheese 143

Smoked Bananas Foster Bread Pudding 143

Grilled Pound Cake with Fruit Dressing 144

Grilled Pineapple with Chocolate Sauce 145

Nectarine and Nutella Sundae 145

Cinnamon Sugar Donut Holes 146

Pellet Grill Chocolate Chip Cookies 147

Delicious Donuts on a Grill 147

Smoked Pumpkin Pie 148

Wood Pellet Smoked Nut Mix 148

Grilled Peaches and Cream 149

Smoked Peach Parfait 149

Grilled Fruit and Cream 150

Apple Pie Grill 150

Fall Season Apple Pie 150

Sweet Tooth Carving Rhubarb Crunch 151

North American Pot Pie 152

Decadent Chocolate Cheesecake 152

Traditional English Mac n' Cheese 153

Satisfying Veggie Casserole 154

Potluck Favorite Baked Beans 155

Amazing Irish Soda Bread 155

Native Southern Cornbread 156

RECIPE INDEX **157**

INTRODUCTION

Traeger Wood Pellet Grill is a fascinating type of wood Grills that burns wood in the grill using the firewood pellets. Traeger Wood Pellet grill is one of the most common among the top 10 wood pellet grills. It is a perfect match for the warm seasons because they grill any kind of meat, fish, vegetables, chocolate, and fruit to be delicious. For meat lovers, it is a perfect option to turn on the grill to enjoy their favorite meat on the grill. The way to enjoy the grill in any weather with grillers is truly amazing. While using it, all the greasy, smoky, and meat smell will vanish away. It is an open grill, clean, and environment friendly. Using the white oak wood pellets, you can make your favorite meal truly delicious. Every day, you will definitely enjoy your food with the grillers.

Traeger grill and smoker cookbook is your complete guide to use your Traeger grill and smoker to make your home cooking masterpieces, from appetizers to desserts. Traeger grills feature a wood flavoring system that makes the invisible air around you taste as good as if you were eating in a log cabin. This book is a guide to take full advantage of using your Traeger grill or smoker.

We have put this book together with the intent to make you knowledgeable on how to use your Traeger grill to the maximum. We want everything in this book to be as easy as possible for you to achieve. That's why Jack has included her recipes and cooking techniques for you to learn from.

Working:

As it is an electronic grill, so it has several features for us. It has surprising features that are not found in any other product. It has wood pellets. These wood pellets are the main feature of this grill. It has inbuilt fans in it, and it does not need a man to operate. You can easily experience this grill while sitting or standing in your drawing-room. Little efforts are required from your side such as controlling the temperature. It is truly applicable to you because you are the only person who controls the temperature. The fan filter system will automatically seal the air inside the grill so it will never smell of food or any other odor. The controlled temperature is the most unique feature of the grill that will give you the best result at the end of the meal.

ESSENTIALS OF TRAGER WOOD PELLET GRILL

It is not necessary for anyone to say how important an easy griller is. Anyone can use it without much involvement along with professional help. It is a convenient, compact, and comfortable griller. It is very versatile and can be used for creating a BBQ Menu in a relatively short time. You don't require any freestanding gas or propane tanks which makes it very friendly to the environment. It requires very little effort for light, temperature, and comfort. It is the best answer for easy grilling and it is the appetizing kind of grill.

Here are some essentials for every grill owner's tool kit.

1. Gourmet Rubs & Spices

If you've ever slathered a pork roast in a grocery-store BBQ sauce and stuck your meat with a bunch of flavorless, loaded with sugar, trade-name spikes, then you instantly understand the importance of making your rubs and sauces.

While it's awesome to have access to the authentic, high-quality ingredients (and cheap, too!), you don't have to give up your everyday cheat list either.

2. Premium Wood Pellets

There are two big reasons why wood pellets are at the top of the food chain: A) They have zero additives, and B) they smoke up like a pro. It might look like hard work, but woods like hickory, oak, apple, cherry, and maple are the best breeds of trees for the tastier grilling you can get. Never settle for convenience store chips again!

3. Pink Butcher Paper

The light-colored surface of Signature pink butcher paper acts as a natural pad for protecting the meat from the direct heat source. It has a low permeability, dissolves quickly, and can reflect infrared rays to prevent excessive drying. The difference is that you'll eat more of the meat you paid for instead of throwing away a dry crusty surface.

4. Flexible Stainless-Steel Skewers

Looking to master your kebab game? Then your grill shouldn't be without stainless-steel skewers. They're almost odorless, won't scratch your grill like wooden ones, and the flavor-converting ability is way better than regular metal skewers. Plus, building your own kebabs will allow you to master your creative side.

5. Stainless Steel Meat Shredding Claw

Get that juicy pulled chicken and pork meat you've been dreaming about, every time. The meat claw is the ultimate bathroom staple, making it easy to use your hands (and fingers) to finish shredding a huge amount of meat, veggies, cheese, noodles or whatever else the situation calls for.

6. Drip Tray Liners

When it comes to charcoal or wood grilling, you can't go wrong with a drip tray liner. It's not like you have to be a genius to know it helps a lot. It's basically like a mini, removable grill rack for easy cleanup. These liners are great for any grill that doesn't have a removable rack, whether it's a huge monster offset BBQ or a small, compact tabletop electric grill.

7. Stuffed Burger Press

You're barbecuing sick burgers, but have you tried to make bacon-stuffed burgers? Wait-there are hamburgers stuffed with blue cheese? Burger stuffing options are limitless, and they're delicious! But, whether you're a meatloaf-stuffer, a taco-stuffing-whiz, or a burger-ball-flinger, the Ball Stuffer Burger Press makes it easy to add all the deliciousness that's already inside the meat.

8. Dexter Large Cut Slicing Knife

So, carving up a brisket is no easy task -especially if you opt for a single-point blade. More than likely, you'll end up sawing from side to side and hacking up your meat wherever you see fit. That's why we love Dexter's Large Cut Slicing Knife. It's got a serrated edge and a comfortable grip that will make the toughest cuts look like a piece of cake.

9. Barbecue, Smoking & Grilling Cookbooks

Barbecue cookbooks are not one-size-fits-all, but we rounded up a list of the best barbecuing titles out there. Whether you're a smoker-meister or a rotisserie-rager, you'll find something that suits your preferences for how you like your meat to be cooked.

10. Spray Bottles

If you want value-added to your food, then you need a spray bottle. Whether you're spraying a fresh burst or a light mist of flavor, these bottles are the perfect tools for nailing your perfect meal.

11. Vacuum Sealer

Vacuum sealers keep your food wholesome and tasty. It locks in all the juices that are lost when wrapped in plastic wrap or aluminum foil and makes keeping meats, veggies, and snacks fresh and delicious.

12. Magnetic & Clamp Grill Light

If you're a grill-master, then you're a daytime grill-master. This explains why you need a clamp light.

13. Food Saver Jar Sealer

If you vacuum seal your food, then you're also a day-time vacuum sealer. The Food Saver Jar Sealer lets you expand the shelf life of your meats, veggies, and snacks with an airtight, watertight seal. It locks deep flavors in and keeps air, bacteria, and other contaminants out.

14. High Heat Baking Pans + Lids

Bring out the grill master in you. High heat baking pans and lids are two tools that work great for grilling food indoors. You can even stack your pans for a unique presentation.

15. Grill-Shaped Cake Pan

Cake for dinner anyone? A grill-shaped cake pan is perfect for sweeping up all the flavors of your favorite grilled meats.

What Is Traeger Wood Pellet Grill

Traeger Wood Pellet Grill is a wood pellet grill that has a set of manual controls that allows the user to control the cooking temperature. It differs from other smoker grills such as the Traeger electric smoker and the pellet grills that use a digital control to adjust the temperature. The grill uses a wood pellet fuel that causes it to smoke. The different types of wood pellets that the grill uses to smoke food are Apple wood pellets, Hickory wood pellets, Mesquite wood pellets, Cherry wood pellets, and Alder wood pellets. The wood pellets can be used to smoke chicken, turkey, fish, oysters, cow beef, and many other types of poultry.

The wood pellets can be used to smoke other foods such as pizza, vegetables, and other foods. The wood pellets are made using recycled wood materials. The wood pellet grill can also be used to grill foods and bake foods. The grill is easy to use because it's made of a simple design and it doesn't have any complicated elements. The Traeger wood pellet grill is easy to use and can be used indoors as well as outdoors. The user can check the temperature to make sure that the food is cooked perfectly. Most types of grill can be used both as gas grills and charcoal grills.

One of the popular features of the Traeger wood pellet grill is the result of its smoke from the wood pellet. Many customers are amazed by the wood pellet smoker. There are hundreds of positive and amazing testimonials about the grill. The grill allows users to smoke and grill their food and the meat can be smoked for up to 15 hours. The grill is easy to use, functional, and reliable. The Traeger grill is also very durable because of its body. The body of the grill is made of cast iron. The BBQ grill is easy to install and is easy to maintain.

The grill can create smoke by using wood pellets and it can be adjusted to a temperature of about 225 degrees Fahrenheit. The food cooked on the grill has a consistent smoky flavor because of the wood pellets. The grill is an automatic cooker, meaning it conserves the heat that it produces and doesn't lose it.

Components of Traeger Wood Pellet Grill

Traeger makes a few additions to most of their models including the firebox, heat exchanger, side shelf, and cabinet. Each model has a specific focus the allows the customer to decide which grill will fit their needs. Below is a brief description of what makes each model different. Some components are shared among the models. The firebox and heat exchanger are shared among Traeger's entire line of grills.

The firebox is the heart of every Traeger grill. The wood pellets are loaded into the firebox from the front of the grill. The firebox is a rectangular box with the fires for the grill in it. After the wood pellets are loaded in, the lid is closed, igniting the pellets. First, as the wood pellets ignite, they begin to release smoke. As the fire burns, smoke carries the heat to the heating element inside the grill where it is turned into heat that is used to cook the meat, and then convection that distributes the heat evenly throughout the grill.

The heating element is what does most of the work. It is made of aluminum blocks stacked to create a column and is covered in Therma-cast which is insulation that prevents heat from exiting the grill too much. When a customer grills on the Traeger Pellet grill, they are grilling on the heating element, which slowly cooks the meat evenly.

The side shelf is where most of the tools and wood pellets are kept on the Traeger Pellet grill. It has a coated surface to prevent the tool and pellets from damaging the finish of the grill. Tools are kept on the side shelf while the grill is in use don't need quick access. If a tool does need to be used in mid grilling, it can be placed in the warming drawer with the wood pellets.

The warming drawer is found on all of Traeger's grills except for one. On all of Traeger's grills except for the RecTec, the warming drawer can be found on the side table on the front of the grill. The warming drawer is more of a compartment than a drawer. It provides a place where the tools that need to be kept hot can stay warm while their job is being finished. It also provides a place where novices can keep wood pellets until they are ready to be put into the firebox.

The secondary cooking chamber is used on the 4-burner grill and the 4-burner grill with the side burner. The extra space on the firebox is left open for maximum heat exposure. The customer can place their meat on the exposed grates in the secondary cooking chamber to give them more options in how to cook their food.

The cabinet holds accessories for Traeger Pellet grills. Every Traeger pellet grill has its specific accessories that can be purchased from Traeger's website and applied to the grill. The accessories are ranging from back up wire to protect and insulate the electronics to the cabinet, allowing more accessories and attachments to be added. The cabinet on Traeger's pellet grill is offered for extra smoke when cooks desire more smoke or if the grill is in an outdoor environment where the temperature fluctuates a lot, waterproofing the firebox can add protection to the grill.

The rear-mounted fill tray is unique to Traeger Pellet grills. It can be folded and used as a table or can be set up in the back of the grill. The rear-mounted fill tray is equipped with a Velcro latch that can hold the tray in an upright position. The rear-mounted fill tray allows for easier and more accessible adding of wood pellets.

A general purpose of Traeger, from inception, was to cook food with the wood pellets. Almost all Traeger models have the capability of smoking and grilling. However, all of Traeger's grills are capable of grilling and smoking except for the smaller Traeger Junior Elite.

How It Works

Many people try to grill using real firewood methods while grilling in the Traeger grill. But they do not know how to use Traeger grill with wood pellets. Let's first see how Traeger pellet grill works.

To start with Traeger grill, the user has to open the lid and set the temperature at 250 and make the grill smoke by turning it on. It has to be set as 250 for the first 30 mins. The user also has to turn on the heat of the grill and grill meat or food, which you want to use. The smoke has to be essential for cooking with pellets. If Traeger grill is not important to work with, then the user can also set the smoker for working with the Traeger pellets.

It will not work without smoke. So, the first thing to do is get the griller hot and the smoker working. The temperature will rise up to 260. The grill grates are placed on the grill to let the smoke pass through the meat while cooking. The temperature will rise up to 260, if one is not able to control it, be sure to turn off the barbecue grill. The Traeger grill is very simple to use and it is quite easy to control the temperature. Once you want to know how to use Traeger grill and smoke, you will be able to find it quite easy and all you need to do is to open the lid and then set the temperature. Switch on the smoke for the first time so that smoke can come out and cook the food.

It is the same as the way how to use Traeger pellet grill for smoking

So, if you want to do BBQs for your family, then Traeger grill is the best choice to use. It has the capacity to hold about seventeen burgers. So, one can easily do a party or BBQ night for a quite large crowd. The food will be very tasty, once it is ready with Traeger pellet grill.

Traeger Wood Pellet Grill Vs. Charcoal and Wood Grills

Traeger wood pallets have numerous benefits that other charcoal and gas grill cannot provide. Barbecuing is a great gathering excuse and outdoor activity, but it is a hassle to set. In this day and age where everything is becoming more convenient, this activity should also become easier to deal with as well.

It is easy to start:

To get a charcoal or gas grill to ignite is a hassle, but the fire inside the firepot is easy to turn on. It also is much safer as you don't have to stick your hands inside the grill to start the fire.

It's versatile

This grill is not only used for grilling but can be used for different processes of cooking as well. You can bake, roast, smoke, and braise using this device. This also increases the menu at your barbecue gathering.

No burnt areas

Because the cooking process happens by convection mechanism, the entire piece of meat, or whatever, your cooking gets cooked evenly. There is also no need to flip around the meat constantly. Also, the drip tray prevents direct fire from hitting your food, so no charring occurs.

More flavor in your dishes

In grilling, nothing beats all-natural hardwood flavor. Professional chefs use them, and now, with ease, so could you. It is not hard to produce a much more delicious juicy meat steak at your home anymore.

Pellets to Use

The dark charcoal type of wood pellets is used to cook food. They are burned to cook food inside it. It is made of a variety of woods like beech, maple, and cherry that has a composition of 15 - 20 percent mesquite, it burns at 1400 degrees. The process to burn wood pellets is very simple. You need to pour it into a box, add in the grill, and light it with a matchstick, then it will burn to give you the best flavor. The burning wood pellets will provide you the warmth and keep you surrounded by the great and the best natural flavor.

This is the burning pellets or the logs that make the grills unique.

Wood Pellet Reference Chart

Wood	Flavor Profile	Use With
Apple	Mild, subtle sweet and fruity flavor	Pork, Poultry, Lamb, Wild Game, Beef, Some Seafood
Cherry	Light and sweet. Delicate, not overpowering	Pork, Poultry, Wild Game, Beef, Some Seafood
Hickory	Sweet, yet strong flavor. Not overpowering. Versatile	Pork, Poultry, Wild Game, Beef, Fish
Alder	Delicate, earthy, with a hint of sweetness	Fish, Shellfish, Pork, Beef, Lamb, Poultry, Veggies
Maple	Mild and slightly sweet flavor	Pork, Poultry, Beef, Small Game Birds, Cheese, Veggies
Oak	Medium smoky flavor. Versatile. Milder than Hickory, stronger than Cherry	Pork, Poultry, Beef, Some Wild Game, Fish
Mesquite	Strong and earthy flavor. One of the hottest burning woods	Red Meats, Dark Meats, Wild Game
Peach	Sweet, fruity flavor	Pork, Poultry, Small Game Birds
Pecan	Stronger than most fruitwoods, but milder than Hickory and Mesquite	Pork, Poultry, Beef

Most Popular Pellet Blends

Wood	Brand(s)	Flavor Profile	Use With
BBQ Blend	Pit Boss	Sweet, savory, and tart blend of maple, hickory, and cherry	All foods
Apple Mash Blend	CookinPellets	Lightly sweet blend of apple mash and hard maple	Chicken, Pork, Muffins, Cold-Smoked Dishes
Bourbon Brown Sugar	Cabela's	Seasoned oak blend of bourbon, smoke flavor, and sweetness	Chicken, Beef, Pork
Competition Blend	Traeger	Blend of sweet, savory, and tart (maple, hickory, cherry)	Chicken, Beef, Pork
Pellet Pro Exclusive Charcoal Blend	Smoke Daddy Inc.	Charcoal blended with red oak.Mix with any flavor of wood pellets and use to enhance smoke ring	All meats

Perfect Mix Blend	CookinPellets	Blend of cherry, hickory, maple, and hard maple	Short cooks for any foods
Texas Blend	Green Mountain	Blend of oak, mesquite and hickory	All meats
Turkey Pellet Blend with Brine Kit	Traeger	Hickory, oak, maple, and rosemary	Turkey
Realtree Big Game Blend	Traeger	Blend of hickory, rosemary, red and white oak	Venison, Pheasant, Game Meats
Tennessee Whiskey Barrel	Big Poppa Smokers	Aged oak from Jack Daniel's Whiskey	Most meats

TIPS AND TRICKS

It's been two years since we bought our Traeger grill, and I have a few suggestions to help new users with pellet smokers avoid any issues—usually due to inexperience or negligence. Let's start on the right foot.

Pellet Storage

You have to be vigilant in storing your pellets, especially if you live in a humid climate. Damp or wet pellets will not lead to the best grilling experience—you won't be able to get a fire going. What's worse, damp or wet pellets will damage the auger since it won't be able to rotate and will burn out the motor.

I bought some 5-gallon pails, and my husband went on the hunt for sealing lids, since storing your pellets in an open container is counterproductive. We found that screw-on covers work best to keep moisture out, and they're convenient—you won't have to break your fingers trying to pry them open.

Temperature Readings

After using your grill a few times, you may notice that the temperature starts to fluctuate quite a bit. This is because of grease and soot build-up on the temperature probe used to regulate the temperature. An effortless way to stop this from happening is to clean the probe and cover it with foil. Consequently, cooking temperature readings will be more accurate.

Cover Your Grill

You may think a grill cover isn't necessary, but believe me, it's crucial. Your Traeger grill is an appliance and one with electronics inside to boot! If you want to ensure your pellet smoker's durability, protect it from the elements. If you can, move your grill under a rooftop after having a barbeque and use a grill cover. You don't want your pellet smoker to stop working suddenly due to water damage.

Clean Your Grill

A lot of people fail at keeping their grill clean. This step is crucial to guard against overfilling the firepot and protect against flare-ups. Not to mention that your grill will look brand-new for longer if you care for it in this simple way. I recommend cleaning your Traeger grill after cooking something for an extended period, or after you're done using it for the weekend. If you love cooking greasier foods, you'll have to clean your grill more often. Here are the steps you should follow:

1. Use an all-natural degreaser/cleaner to spray the grill grate and the inside of the chimney.
2. Remove and clean the sides of the grill grates.
3. Throw away the old foil and drip tray liners.
4. Remove the drip tray and heat baffle.
5. Use a vacuum inside the grill and firepot to remove any food particles.
6. Clean the inside of the chimney.
7. Again, use an all-natural degreaser/cleaner to spray the inside and outside of the grill. Wait a few minutes before wiping clean.

8.   Put all components back in their place, including the heat baffle, drip tray, and foil liners. You're all set for your next barbeque!

Tip: Avoid using wire brushes as it will scratch your Traeger grill. Heavy-duty paper towels or a cleaning cloth will work nicely.

Be Adventurous

This is vital to your grilling success—you won't enjoy your Traeger grill for long if you have to make the same recipes over and over. What's more, you own a 6-in-1 appliance, and you can't let that versatility go unused. In the beginning, as you get used to a pellet grill, you may end up cooking simple meals, but once you feel confident in your grilling abilities, try new things! Don't limit yourself to cook only traditional barbeque foods—what about making a smoky bean stew in your Traeger grill? Don't worry, later on in this cookbook, you'll see recipes that will spark your adventurous side.

These aren't the only elements that will contribute to your grilling success, but they cover some of the rookie mistakes many people, myself included, make. It put a real downer on my grilling plans!

HOW TO CLEAN YOUR TRAEGER WOOD PELLET GRILL

You will have to give your Trager grill a deep clean every few months. Think of it as spring cleaning your pellet smoker. You should give your Traeger grill a fairly good cleaning before firing it up for the first time in the spring. The manufacturer recommends cleaning the water pan and the firepot. Depending on how much you use the grill, you may want to give it a good cleaning before the season ends in the fall. A good cleaning before the first fire-up in the spring or a cleaning before you store it in the fall will ensure that your Traeger grill starts the season or the next season with a clean slate. Cleaning the interior of the smoker is fairly close to cleaning your oven. It's a bit messy, and it will probably leave you smelling like a campfire, but it's fairly easy to do, and it's the only way to maintain a perfectly clean pellet smoker. Here is a step-by-step instruction on how to clean your Traeger wood pellet grill. Tools and Supplies Needed:
Clean your Traeger pellet grill thoroughly.

Cleaning the Water Pan

1. Empty the water tray and dump the water down the drain. Be sure not to fill up the drain with water.
2. Wash the water pan with warm, soapy water. Be sure to check for burnt-on stuff. Use a sponge or a soft-bristled brush, and make sure to soak into all corners of the pan.
3. Dry with a towel. This is very important.
4. If you have a pellet grill with a solid water pan, you will have to add water to the pan after cleaning it. You don't want a large gap between the bottom of the pan and the base of firepot.
5. If you have a pellet grill with a slotted water pan, you will be fine as is, or instead of adding water to the pan, fill the empty space with the unused pellets.

Cleaning the Firepot

1. Remove all of the grates and the heat deflector.
2. Empty the ash pan and remove all of the ashes.
3. Spray the ash pan with a degreaser and scrub with a brush. Rinse and dry.
4. Spray the firepot with a degreaser and scrub with a brush. Rinse and dry.
5. If you have a pellet grill with a hopper, empty the hopper and clean it.
6. Be sure to clean all of the areas around and under the pellet hopper and the firepot with a degreaser. Run water through the pellet hopper and firepot. This is especially important if you use a lot of pellets. Be sure all traces of the degreaser and water are out.
7. Clean the burner compartment and the chimney using a brush. Don't forget to clean the drip plate above the firepot.
8. Inspect all hardware before proceeding. If necessary, tighten the screws.

9. Reinstall the burners, heat deflector, and water pan. Make certain you have a tight connection between the burners and the water pan.

10. Fill the grill with pellets.

Cleaning Your Traeger Grill Oven Without a Clean Panel

1. Remove the cooking racks and place them in the sink.

2. Spray the racks, the interior of the grill, and the inside of the screened vents with a degreaser. This is very important. You don't want residual grease and ash on the cooking racks.

3. Scrub the cooking racks with a brush and rinse.

4. Scrub the interior of the grill and the inside of the screened vents with a brush and rinse.

5. Scrub the interior of the grill and the inside of the screened vents with a brush and rinse.

6. Scrub the interior of the grill and the inside of the screened vents with a brush and rinse.

7. Repeat until the racks are completely clean.

8. Be certain not to get the grill overheated with open flames.

9. Inspect all hardware before proceeding. If necessary, tighten the screws.

10. Fill the grill with pellets.

Cleaning your Traeger Pellet Grill Oven with a Clean Panel

1. Remove all the racks and the cooking grates. Place them in the sink.

2. Spray the racks, the interior of the grill, and the inside of the screened vents with a degreaser.

3. After using the cleaner, wipe the grill with a cloth to remove any stains or streaks. Dry with a clean cloth.

4. Spray the interior of the grill and the inside of the grilled vents with a degreaser.

5. Scrub the racks and the interior of the grill with a brush and rinse.

6. Spray the interior of the grill and the inside of the screened vents with a degreaser.

7. Scrub the racks and the interior of the grill with a brush and rinse.

8. Scrub the interior of the grill and the inside of the screened vents with a brush and rinse.

9. Scrub the interior of the grill and the inside of the screened vents with a brush and rinse.

After cleaning, you may want to season your new Traeger grill with a fresh coat.

TROUBLESHOOTING

Troubleshooting a Traeger grill is not an easy task. Most of the time unless you are well-versed with the internal workings of the grill, you will not be able to fix it yourself. Here is a troubleshooting guide for your Traeger pellet grill:

Problems caused by food:
1) Pellets are not igniting

Solution:
1) Clean the grill.
2) Change the pellets to another brand.
3) Replace the drip tray.
4) Check the settings and adjust the temperature.
5) Reset the grill (press the program button).
6) Check the grease tray.
If your Traeger grill has a problem igniting, do not panic. Just remember to keep calm and try the above solutions one by one. You may find that a single solution will do the trick.
2) Grill is not warm enough

Solution:
1) Clean the grill.
3) Check the location of the grill, make sure it is getting sufficient radiant heat from the sun, the room, nearby furniture, etc.
4) Check the nuts on the wheels.
5) Check the foil covering, chicken wire, and the lid.
6) Replace the drip pan.
7) Check the air intake.
8) Low Fuel
6) Food is not browning
7) Smoke is coming out of the exhaust
8) Weak flame
9) Smoky, bitter taste to food

Problem: Heat is not sufficient
1) Check location of the grill, scorched food, etc.
2) Loose or damaged cord.
3) Press the PROGRAM button on the grill outbox to reset the unit (press the button a couple of times longer than you normally would).
4) Check the grease tray and clean it.
5) Check the Set-It and forget-it box, lid, food temp, air intake tube, meat scoop, and the steps.
6) Make sure the cord is undamaged and connected to the light inside the grill.
7) Clean the wires and check for loose nuts.
8) Clean the coils and the air intake valve.
9) Clean off the food.
10) Replace the drip pan.
12) Turn the air intake valve several times to remove the burned insulation.
13) Check the lid to see if it is making good contact with the flame.
The Traeger Pellet Grill can be a great tool for anyone who is fond of grilling. It is perfect for people who spend a lot of time outside. It is indeed the best way to cook your food when you are on a camping trip or preparing yourself for a barbecue party. Troubleshooting these problems may be a bit frustrating but it can also be very enjoyable because you can save yourself the trouble of calling for repairmen.

EASY AND EASY TO FIND RECIPES
BAKED GOODS, CHEESE, NUTS

Quick Yeast Dinner Rolls

Preparation time: 5 minutes
Cooking time: 30 minutes
Servings: 8
Method of Preparation: Grilling

Ingredients:

2 tablespoons yeast, quick rise

1 cup water, lukewarm

3 cups flour

¼ cup sugar

1 teaspoon salt

¼ cup unsalted butter, softened

1 egg

Cooking spray, as needed

1 egg, for egg wash

Directions:

Combine the yeast and warm water in a small bowl to activate the yeast. Let sit for about 5 to 10 minutes, or until foamy.

Combine the flour, sugar and salt in the bowl of a stand mixer fitted with the dough hook. Pour the water and yeast into the dry ingredient with the machine running on low speed.

Add the butter and egg and mix for 10 minutes, gradually increasing the speed from low to high.

Form the dough into a ball and place in a buttered bowl. Cover with a cloth and let the dough rise for approximately 40 minutes.

Transfer the risen dough to a lightly floured work surface and divide into 8 pieces, forming a ball with each.

Lightly spritz a cast iron pan with cooking spray and arrange the balls in the pan. Cover with a cloth and let rise for 20 minutes.

When ready to cook, set Traeger temperature to 375ºF (191ºC) and preheat, lid closed for 15 minutes.

Brush the rolls with the egg wash. Place the pan on the grill and bake for 30 minutes, or until lightly browned.

Remove from the grill. Serve hot.

Baked Cornbread with Honey Butter

Preparation time: 10 minutes
Cooking time: 35 to 45 minutes
Servings: 6
Method of Preparation: Grilling

Ingredients:

4 ears whole corn

1 cup all-purpose flour

1 cup cornmeal

⅔ cup white sugar

1½ teaspoons baking powder

½ teaspoon baking soda

½ teaspoon salt

1 cup buttermilk

½ cup butter, softened

2 eggs

½ cup butter, softened

¼ cup honey

Directions:

When ready to cook, set Traeger temperature to High and preheat, lid closed for 15 minutes.

Peel back the outer layer of the corn husk, keeping it attached to the cob. Remove the silk from the corn and place the husk back into place. Soak the corn in cold water for 10 minutes.

Place the corn directly on the grill grate and cook for 15 to 20 minutes, or until the kernels are tender, stirring occasionally. Remove from the grill and set aside.

In a large bowl, stir together the flour, cornmeal, sugar, baking powder, baking soda and salt.

In a separate bowl, whisk together the buttermilk, butter and eggs. Pour the wet mixture into the cornmeal mixture and fold together until there are no dry spots. Pour the batter into a greased baking dish.

Cut the kernels from the corn and sprinkle over the top of the batter, pressing the kernels down with a spoon to submerge.

Turn Traeger temperature down to 350ºF (177ºC). Place the baking dish on the grill. Bake for about 20 to 25 minutes, or until the top is golden brown and a toothpick inserted into the middle of the cornbread comes out clean.

Remove the cornbread from the grill and let cool for 10 minutes before serving.

To make the honey butter, mix the butter and honey until combined. Serve the cornbread with the honey butter.

S'Mores Dip with Candied Pecans

Preparation time: 10 minutes
Cooking time: 37 to 45 minutes
Servings: 4
Method of Preparation: Smoking

Ingredients:
Candied Smoked Pecans:
½ cup sugar
½ cup brown sugar
1 tablespoon ground cinnamon
1 teaspoon salt
¼ teaspoon cayenne pepper
1 egg white
1 teaspoon water
1-pound (454 g) pecans
S'mores Dip:
1 tablespoon butter
2 cups milk chocolate chips
10 large marshmallows, cut in half
Graham crackers, for serving

Directions:
When ready to cook, set Traeger temperature to 300ºF (149ºC) and preheat, lid closed for 15 minutes.

In a small bowl, stir together the sugars, cinnamon, salt and cayenne pepper. In a medium bowl, whisk together the egg white and water until frothy.

Pour the pecans into a large bowl. Pour in the egg white mixture and sugar mixture and toss to coat well.

Spread the coated pecans on a sheet tray lined with parchment paper. Place the tray directly on the grill grate. Smoke for 30 to 35 minutes, stirring often.

Remove from the grill and let cool. Break apart and roughly chop. Set aside.

When ready to cook, set Traeger temperature to 400ºF (204ºC) and preheat, lid closed for 15 minutes.

Place a cast iron skillet directly on the grill grate while the grill heats up.

When the cast iron skillet is hot, melt the butter in the skillet and swirl around the skillet to coat. Add the chocolate chips to the skillet, then top with the marshmallows. Cook for 7 to 10 minutes, or until the chocolate is melted and marshmallows are lightly browned. Remove from the grill.

1.   Spread a handful of the candied pecans over the top and serve with the dip with the graham crackers.

Brown Sugared Bacon Cinnamon Rolls

Preparation time: 5 minutes
Cooking time: 25 to 35 minutes
Servings: 6
Method of Preparation: Grilling

Ingredients:
12 slices bacon, sliced
1/3 cup brown sugar
8 cinnamon rolls, store-brought
2 ounces (57 g) cream cheese, softened

Directions:
When ready to cook, set Traeger temperature to 350ºF (177ºC) and preheat, lid closed for 15 minutes.

Dredge 8 slices of the bacon in the brown sugar, making sure to cover both sides of the bacon.

Place the coated bacon slices along with the other bacon slices on a cooling rack placed on top of a large baking sheet.

Place the sheet on the grill and cook for 15 to 20 minutes, or until the fat is rendered, but the bacon is still pliable.

Open and unroll the cinnamon rolls. While bacon is still warm, place 1 slice of the brown sugared bacon on top of 1 of the unrolled rolls and roll back up. Repeat with the remaining rolls. Turn Traeger temperature down to 325ºF (163ºC). Place the cinnamon rolls in a greased baking dish and cook for 10 to 15 minutes, or

until golden. Rotate the pan a half turn halfway through cooking time.

Meanwhile, crumble the cooked 4 bacon slices and add into the cream cheese.

Spread the cream cheese frosting over the warm cinnamon rolls. Serve warm.

Traeger Soft Gingerbread Cookie

Preparation time: 10 minutes
Cooking time: 10 minutes
Servings: 8
Method of Preparation: Grilling

Ingredients:
1¾ cups all-purpose flour
1½ teaspoons ground ginger
½ teaspoon ground cinnamon
½ teaspoon baking soda
¼ teaspoon ground cloves
¼ teaspoon kosher salt
⅓ cup brown sugar
¾ cup butter
½ cup plus 4 tablespoons granulated sugar, divided
¼ cup molasses
1 egg

Directions:
When ready to cook, set Traeger temperature to 325ºF (163ºC) and preheat, lid closed for 15 minutes.

In a medium bowl, stir together the flour, ginger, cinnamon, baking soda, cloves and salt. Set aside. In the bowl of a stand mixer, cream together the brown sugar, butter and ½ cup of the granulated sugar until light and fluffy. Stir in the molasses and egg and mix on medium speed until combined, scraping down the sides of the bowl.

Add the flour mixture to the bowl and mix on low speed until combined. Scrape the sides again and mix for 30 seconds longer.

Roll the dough into balls, 1 tablespoon at a time, and then roll the balls in the remaining 4 tablespoons of the sugar.

Place the dough balls on a baking sheet lined with parchment paper, leaving a couple inches between each cookie.

Place the sheet directly on the grill grate and cook for about 10 minutes, or until lightly browned but still soft in the center.

Remove from the grill and let cool on a wire rack. Serve.

Sweet Pull-Apart Rolls

Preparation time: 5 minutes
Cooking time: 10 to 12 minutes
Servings: 8
Method of Preparation: Grilling

Ingredients:
⅓ cup vegetable oil
¼ cup warm water
¼ cup sugar
2 tablespoons active dry yeast
1 egg
3½ cups all-purpose flour, divided
½ teaspoon salt
Cooking spray, as needed

Directions:
When ready to cook, set Traeger temperature to 400ºF (204ºC) and preheat, lid closed for 15 minutes.

Spritz a cast iron pan with cooking spray and set aside.

In the bowl of a stand mixer, combine the oil, warm water, sugar and yeast. Let sit for 5 to 10 minutes, or until frothy and bubbly.

With a dough hook, mix in the egg, 2 cups of the flour and salt until combined. Add the remaining flour, ½ cup at a time.

Spritz your hands with cooking spray and shape the dough into 12 balls.

Arrange the balls in the prepared cast iron pan and let rest for 10 minutes. Place the pan in the grill and bake for about 10 to 12 minutes, or until the tops are lightly golden.

Serve immediately.

Baked Pulled Pork Stuffed Potatoes

Preparation time: 10 minutes
Cooking time: 50 minutes
Servings: 6
Method of Preparation: Grilling

Ingredients:
4 russet potatoes
Canola oil, as needed
Salt, to taste
2 tablespoons butter, melted
3 cups pulled pork
1 cup Cheddar cheese
1 cup Mozzarella cheese
4 tablespoons Traeger Sweet & Heat BBQ Sauce
Topping:
Sour cream
Chopped bacon
Chopped green onion

Directions:
When ready to cook, set Traeger temperature to 450ºF (232ºC) and preheat, lid closed for 15 minutes.

Rub the potatoes with canola oil and sprinkle evenly with salt. Place the potatoes directly on the grill grate and cook for 45 minutes, or until fork tender.

Cut the potatoes in half and scoop the flesh out, leaving ¼ inch of the potato on the skin. Brush the inside of the skins with the melted butter and place on a baking tray. Place the tray on the grill and cook for 5 minutes, or until golden brown.

In a bowl, stir together the pulled pork, cheeses and Traeger Sweet & Heat BBQ Sauce.

Fill the potato skins with the mixture and return to the grill. Cook for 30 seconds, lid closed, or until the cheese is melted.

Serve topped with the sour cream, bacon and green onion.

Banana Walnut bread

Preparation time: 1 hour 15 minutes
Servings: 1
Method of Preparation: Smoking

Ingredients:
2-1/2 cup of all-purpose flour
1 cup of sugar
2 eggs
1 cup ripe banana, mashed
1/4 cup whole milk
1/4 cup walnut, finely chopped
1 tsp salt
3 Tbsp of Vegetable oil
3 tsp baking powder

Directions:
Set the wood pellet smoker-grill for indirect cooking at 3500 F.

Combine all the ingredients in a large bowl. Using a mixer (electric or manual), mix the ingredients. Grease and flour the loaf pan. Pour the mixture into the loaf pan.

Transfer loaf pan to the grill and cover with steel construction. Bake for 60-75 minutes. Remove and allow to cool.

Nutrition:
Calories: 548, Carbs: 69g, Fat: 36g, Protein: 14g

Peach Blueberry Cobbler

Preparation time: 1hour15 minutes
Servings: 4
Method of Preparation: Smoking

Ingredients:
2 cups of peaches, peeled and sliced
1 cup of fresh blueberries
1 cup of all-purpose flour
1 cup of milk
1/2 cup of melted butter, salted
2 tsp Baking powder
1-1/2 cup sugar
1/2 tsp salt
1/2 tsp vanilla extract

Directions:
Set the wood pellet smoker-grill to indirect cooking at 3750Ϝ

In a bowl, add blueberry, peaches, and ¾ cup sugar. Stir the mixture until the blueberry is coated. Set aside.

In another bowl, combine the other ingredients with the remaining sugar and mix well. Be careful not to over stir the mixture.

Pour into the baking dish, add the blueberry-peach mixture on top. Do not stir.

Transfer baking pan to the grill and cover with steel construction. Bake for 45-60 minutes, remove and allow to rest before serving.

Nutrition:
Calories: 474, Carbs: 41g, Fat: 25g, Protein: 21g

Baked Wild Sockeye Salmon

Preparation time: 45 minutes
Servings: 6
Method of Preparation: Smoking

Ingredients:

6 sockeye salmon fillets
3/4 tsp Old bay seasoning
1/2 tsp Seafood seasoning.

Directions:

Set the wood pellet smoker-grill to indirect cooking at 4000 F
Rinse the fillet and pat dry with a paper towel. Add the seasoning, then rub all over the fillets.
Arrange fillets in a baking dish with the skin facing down, then transfer the dish to the cooking grid. Cover grill and bake for 15-20 minutes or until fillets begin to flake.
Serve.

Nutrition:

Calories: 294, Carbs: 10g, Fat:1g, Protein: 26g

Pizza dough roll

Preparation time: 1hour 15 minutes
Servings: 6
Method of Preparation: Smoking

Ingredients:

1 tsp Yeast
1 cup of warm water
2-1/2 cups of all-purpose flour
1 tsp Kosher salt
Tbsp Virgin olive oil
1 tsp Sugar

Directions:

Set the wood pellet smoker-grill to indirect cooking at 4000 F
Combine all your ingredients and mix until the mixture is sticky and has a shaggy texture. Knead the dough for 3-5 minutes, then set aside and cover. Keep for 1 hour at room temperature or until it doubles in size.
Divide the dough into six equal parts and roll into a ball using a floured hand. Cover the baking pan with a parchment paper, place the roll on it, then cover and allow to rise for 30 minutes. Transfer the baking pan to the cooking grid, then cover. Bake for 15-20min or until the rolls are golden brown. Allow to cool before serving.

Nutrition:

Calories: 506, Carbs: 46g, Fat:251g, Protein: 10.1g

Twice-Baked Spaghetti Squash

Preparation time: 1 hour 15 minutes
Servings: 2
Method of Preparation: Smoking

Ingredients:

1 medium spaghetti squash
1/2 cup of parmesan cheese (grated and divided)
1/2 cup of mozzarella cheese (shredded and divided)
1 tsp Salt
Tbsp Extra-virgin olive oil
1/2 tsp Pepper

Directions:

Set the wood pellet smoker-grill to indirect cooking at 3750 F
Using a knife, cut the squash into half lengthwise and remove the seed and pulp. Rub the inside of the squash with olive oil, salt, and pepper. Place on the hot grill with the open part facing up and bake for 45 minutes or until the squash can be easily pierced with a fork. Remove and allow to cool.
Place on a cutting board. Using a fork, scrape across the surface in a lengthwise direction to

remove the flesh-in strand (to look like spaghetti). Transfer to a bowl, add parmesan and mozzarella cheese, then stir well. Stuff back into the shell, sprinkle cheese on the toppings.

Increase the pellet smoker-grill to 4250 F, place the stuffed squash on the hot grill and bake for 15 minutes or until cheese starts to brown.

Remove and allow to cool, serve.

Nutrition:

Calories: 294, Carbs: 10.1g, Fat:12g, Protein: 16g

Take and Bake Pepperoni Pizza

Preparation time: 15 minutes
Servings: 4
Method of Preparation: Smoking

Ingredients:

Take and bake pizza bread
Pepperoni toppings of your choice

Directions:

Set the wood pellet smoker-grill to indirect cooking at 4000 F

If refrigerated, remove pizza bread from the refrigerator 20-30 minutes before baking. Add the toppings and place the bread directly on the cooking grates for a crispier crust.

Bake for 10-15 minutes. Remove pizza with a pizza paddle, and allow to cool before cutting into slices and serving.

Nutrition:

Calories: 324, Carbs: 31.2g, Fat: 10g, Protein: 14g

Classic Apple Pie

Preparation time: 2 hours
Servings: 8
Method of Preparation: Smoking

Ingredients:

2 Tbsp all-purpose flour
2 pie dough rounds
6 cups of apple, peeled and sliced
1 Tbsp lemon juice
3/4 cup of sugar
1/4 tsp powdered nutmeg
1/2 tsp powdered cinnamon
1/2 tsp salt

Directions:

Set the wood pellet smoker-grill to indirect cooking at 4250 F

In a large bowl, combine all your ingredients (except for the pie dough) and mix well. Gently press one of the pie doughs unto a 10-inch pie dough plate. Make sure it is firm and covers the sides.

Pour in your apple mixture. Cover the filling with the second pie dough, gently clip the two doughs together. Make a crosshatch slit on the top with a knife—transfer dough plate to the cooking grid. Bake for 45-60 minutes or until the crust browns. Allow to cool for 1 hour before serving.

Nutrition:

Calories: 542, Carbs: 41g, Fat: 20g, Protein: 10g

Crusty Artisan Dough Bread

Preparation time: 2 hours
Servings: 6
Method of Preparation: Smoking

Ingredients:

3 cups all-purpose flour
1/2 tsp Yeast
1-1/2 cups of warm water
1-1/2 tsp salt

Directions:

In a large bowl, combine all your ingredients and mix until it is sticky and has a shaggy texture.

Cover with plastic wrap and allow to rest for 12 hours

After 12 hours, set the wood pellet smoker-grill to indirect cooking at 4250 F, using any pellet. Preheat the Dutch oven.

Transfer prepared mixture to a dry, floured surface and mold into a ball. Open the Dutch oven and place the dough in the middle—cover and bake for 30 minutes.

Remove the lid and bake for an additional 20 minutes.

Remove and allow to cool.

Nutrition:
Calories: 462, Carbs: 41g, Fat: 18g, Protein: 5g

Red Chile and Lime Shortbread Cookies

Preparation time: 30 minutes
Servings: 8
Method of Preparation: Smoking

Ingredients:
2 tsp lime zest
8 Tbsp unsalted butter
1 cup of all-purpose flour
1/2 tsp Salt
1 tsp Red Chile rub
1/4 cup of sugar

Directions:
Set the wood pellet smoker-grill to indirect cooking at 3000 F

In a large bowl, combine all the ingredients (except flour). Mix thoroughly until the butter is creamy but not smooth. Gradually add the flour until it forms a ball.

Transfer the dough onto a floured surface, roll until about 1/4-inches thick. Cut into eight equal parts, but do not cut through.

Arrange in a cake pan, bake for 10 minutes. Allow to cool before serving.

Nutrition:
Calories: 478, Carbs: 46g, Fat: 8g, Protein: 2g

Kahluá Coffee Brownies

Preparation time: 60 minutes
Servings: 12
Method of Preparation: Smoking

Ingredients:
4 oz. pure chocolate, unsweetened
1 cup of white chocolate chip
1 cup of bittersweet chocolate chip
4 eggs
1/8 Tsp of salt
Tbsp instant coffee
1-1/2 cup all-purpose flour
cups of sugar
1 cup unsalted butter

Directions:
Set the wood pellet smoker-grill to indirect cooking at 3500 F

Place a small pot on the cooking grid, then add the butter and coffee. Stir until it melts completely. Remove the pot from heat and stir in the unsweetened chocolate, stir until it is smooth. Add the eggs one at a time, mix well. While still mixing, add the sugar, flour, and salt. Gently fold the white chocolate and bittersweet chocolate into the mixture.

Pour the mixture into a baking pan and bake on the grates for 20 minutes or until a toothpick comes out clean.

Remove and allow to cool.

Nutrition:
Calories: 589, Carbs: 60g, Fat: 42g, Protein: 24g

Twice- Baked potatoes with Smoked Gouda and grilled scallions

Preparation time: 1hours 15 minutes
Servings: 6
Method of Preparation: Smoking

Ingredients:

3 large potatoes
8 Tbsp Unsalted butter
Tbsp Of barbeque rub
1-1/2 cup of smoked gouda cheese (grated)
1/4 cup of extra-virgin olive oil
3/4 cup heavy cream
Salt and pepper to taste
1/4 cup chopped scallions

Directions:

Set the wood pellet smoker-grill to indirect cooking at 4000 F

Brush the potatoes with olive oil, make incisions with fork and season with salt. Wrap with aluminum foil paper and bake on grill grates for 30 minutes per side. Transfer to a rimmed sheet and allow to cool.

Cut the potatoes lengthwise, scoop out the flesh into a bowl. Add butter and 1 cup of cheese. Set aside. Place a small pot over low-medium heat, add cream, then heat for 1 minute. Add the scallions and the barbeque rub and mix well

Add the scallion mixture to the potatoes and cheese in the bowl, combine until it is evenly mixed. Scoop the mixture back into the potato shell and top with cheese.

Bake for 5 minutes or until the cheese melts.

Nutrition:

Calories: 276, Carbs: 28g, Fat: 14.5g, Protein: 3g

Chocolate Pecan Bourbon Pie

Preparation time: 60 minutes
Servings: 6
Method of Preparation: Smoking

Ingredients:

1/4 cup bourbon
1 cup semisweet chocolate chips
1 cup of dark corn syrup
Tbsp of melted unsalted butter
3 large egg (beaten)
1 cup of pecan (chopped)
1 cup of brown sugar
1 pie shell

Directions:

Set the wood pellet smoker-grill to indirect cooking at 4000 F

In a bowl, combine the corn syrup, egg, butter, sugar, and bourbon. Then add the chocolate chips and mix well. Pour the filling into the pie shell.

Place the pie plates on the grid and bake for 45 minutes or until fillings turn brown.

Remove and allow to cool. Refrigerate or serve.

Nutritional value per serving:

Calories: 560, Carbs: 38g, Fat: 23.5g, Protein: 10g

RUBS, SAUCES

Smoked Tomato Cream Sauce

Preparation time: 15 minutes
Cooking time: 1 hour 20 minutes
Servings: 1
Method of Preparation: Smoking

Ingredients:

1 lb. beefsteak tomatoes, fresh and quartered
1-1/2 tbsp olive oil
Black pepper, freshly ground
Salt, kosher
1/2 cup yellow onions, chopped
1 tbsp tomato paste
2 tbsp minced garlic
Pinch cayenne
1/2 cup chicken stock
1/2 cup heavy cream

Directions:

Prepare your smoker using directions from the manufacturer.

Toss tomatoes and 1 tbsp oil in a bowl, mixing, then season with pepper and salt.

Smoke the tomatoes placed on a smoker rack for about 30 minutes. Remove and set aside reserving tomato juices.

Heat 1/2 tbsp oil in a saucepan over high-medium heat.

Add onion and cook for about 3-4 minutes. Add tomato paste and garlic then cook for an additional 1 minute.

Add smoked tomatoes, cayenne, tomato juices, pepper, and salt then cook for about 3-4 minutes. Stir often.

Add chicken stock and boil for about 25-30 minutes under a gentle simmer. Stir often.

Place the mixture in a blender and puree until smooth. Now squeeze the mixture through a sieve, fine-mesh, to discard solids and release the juices,

Transfer the sauce in a saucepan, small, and add the cream.

Simmer for close to 6 minutes over low-medium heat until thickened slightly. Season with pepper and salt.

1.   Serve warm with risotto cakes.

Nutrition:

Calories 50, Total fat 5g, Saturated fat 1g, Total carbs 2g, Net carbs 2g, Protein 0g, Sugar 0g, Fiber 0g, Sodium: 69mg

Smoked Mushroom Sauce

Preparation time: 30 minutes
Cooking time: 1 hours
Servings: 4
Method of Preparation: Smoking

Ingredients:

1-quart chef mix mushrooms
2 tbsp canola oil
1/4 cup julienned shallots
2 tbsp chopped garlic
Salt and pepper to taste
1/4 cup Alfasi Cabernet Sauvignon
1 cup beef stock
2 tbsp margarine

Directions:

Crumple four foil sheets into balls. Puncture multiple places in the foil pan then place mushrooms in the foil pan. Smoke in a pellet grill for about 30 minutes. Remove and cool.

Heat canola oil in a pan, sauté, add shallots and sauté until translucent.

Add mushrooms and cook until supple and rendered down.

Add garlic and season with pepper and salt. Cook until fragrant.

Add beef stock and wine then cook for about 6-8 minutes over low heat. Adjust seasoning.

Add margarine and stir until sauce is thickened and a nice sheen.

Serve and enjoy!

Nutrition:

Calories 300, Total fat 30g, Saturated fat 2g, Total carbs 10g, Net carbs 10g, Protein 4g, Sugar 0g, Fiber 0g, Sodium: 514mg

Smoked Cranberry Sauce

Preparation time: 10 minutes
Cooking time: 1 hours
Servings: 2
Method of Preparation: Grilling

Ingredients:

12 oz bag cranberries

2 chunks ginger, quartered

1 cup apple cider

1 tbsp honey whiskey

5.5 oz fruit juice

1/8 tbsp ground cloves

1/8 tbsp cinnamon

1/2 orange zest

1/2 orange

1 tbsp maple syrup

1 apple, diced and peeled

1/2 cup sugar

1/2 brown sugar

Directions:

Preheat your pellet grill to 375oF.

Place cranberries in a pan then add all other ingredients.

Place the pan on the grill and cook for about 1 hour until cooked through.

Remove ginger pieces and squeeze juices from the orange into tthe sauce.

Serve and enjoy!

Nutrition:

Calories 48, Total fat 0.1g, Saturated fat 0g, Total carbs 12.3g, Net carbs 10g, Protein 0.4g, Sugar 7.5g, Fiber 2.3g, Sodium: 26mg

Smoked Sriracha Sauce

Preparation time: 10 minutes
Cooking time: 1 hours
Servings: 2
Method of Preparation: Smoking

Ingredients:

1 lb. Fresno chiles, stems pulled off and seeds removed

1/2 cup rice vinegar

1/2 cup red wine vinegar

1 carrot, medium and cut into rounds, 1/4 inch

1-1/2 tbsp sugar, dark-brown

4 garlic cloves, peeled

1 tbsp olive oil

1 tbsp kosher salt

1/2 cup water

Directions:

Smoke chiles in a smoker for about 15 minutes.

Bring to boil both vinegars then add carrots, sugar, and garlic. Simmer for about 15 minutes while covered. Cool for 30 minutes.

Place the chiles, olive oil, vinegar-vegetable mixture, salt, and 1/4 cup water into a blender.

Blend for about 1-2 minutes on high. Add remaining water and blend again. You can add another 1/4 cup water if you want your sauce thinner.

Pour the sauce into jars and place in a refrigerator.

Serve.

Nutrition:

Calories 147, Total fat 5.23g, Saturated fat 0.7g, Total carbs 21g, Net carbs 18g, Protein 3g, Sugar 13g, Fiber 3g, Sodium: 671mg

Smoked Soy Sauce

Preparation time: 15 minutes
Cooking time: 1 hours
Servings: 1
Method of Preparation: Smoking

Ingredients:

100ml soy sauce
Bradley flavor briquettes cherry

Directions:

Put soy sauce in a heat-resistant bowl, large-mouth.

Smoke in a smoker at 158-176oF for about 1 hour. Stir a few times.

Remove and cool then put in a bottle. Let sit for one day.

Serve and enjoy!

Nutrition:

Calories 110, Total fat 0g, Saturated fat 0g, Total carbs 25g, Net carbs 25g, Protein 2g, Sugar 25g, Fiber 0g, Sodium: 270mg

Smoked Garlic Sauce

Preparation time: 5 minutes
Cooking time: 30 minutes
Servings: 2
Method of Preparation: Grilling

Ingredients:

3 whole garlic heads
1/2 cup mayonnaise
1/4 cup sour cream
2 tbsp lemon juice
2 tbsp cider vinegar
Salt to taste

Directions:

Cut the garlic heads off then place in a microwave-safe bowl, add 2 tbsp water and cover.

Microwave for about 5-6 minutes on medium.

Heat your grill on medium.

Place the garlic heads in a shallow 'boat' foil and smoke for about 20-25 minutes until soft.

Transfer the garlic heads into a blender. Process for a few minutes until smooth.

Add the remaining ingredients and process until everything is combined.

Enjoy!

Nutrition:

Calories 20, Total fat 0g, Saturated fat 0g, Total carbs 10g, Net carbs 9g, Protein 0g, Sugar 0g, Fiber 1g, Sodium: 0mg

Smoked Cherry BBQ Sauce

Preparation time: 20 minutes
Cooking time: 1 hours
Servings: 2
Method of Preparation: Smoking

Ingredients:

2 lb. dark sweet cherries, pitted
1 large chopped onion
1/2 tbsp red pepper flakes, crushed
1 tbsp kosher salt or to taste
1/2 tbsp ginger, ground
1/2 tbsp black pepper
1/2 tbsp cumin
1/2 tbsp cayenne pepper
1 tbsp onion powder
1 tbsp garlic powder
1 tbsp smoked paprika
2 chopped garlic cloves
1/2 cup pinot noir

2 tbsp yellow mustard

1-1/2 cups ketchup

2 tbsp balsamic vinegar

1/3 cup apple cider vinegar

2 tbsp dark soy sauce

1 tbsp liquid smoke

1/4 cup Worcestershire sauce

1 tbsp hatch chile powder

3 tbsp honey

1 cup brown sugar

3 tbsp molasses

Directions:

Preheat your smoker to 250oF.

Place cherries in a baking dish, medium, and smoke for about 2 hours.

Saute onions and red pepper flakes in a pot, large, with 2 tbsp oil for about 4 minutes until softened.

Add salt and cook for an additional 1 minute.

Add ginger, black pepper, cumin, onion powder, garlic powder, and paprika then drizzle with oil and cook for about 1 minute until fragrant and spices bloom.

Stir in garlic and cook for about 30 seconds.

Pour in pinot noir scraping up for 1 minute for any bits stuck to your pan bottom.

Add yellow mustard, ketchup, balsamic vinegar, apple cider vinegar, dark soy sauce, liquid smoke, and Worcestershire sauce. Stir to combine.

Add cherries and simmer for about 10 minutes.

Add honey, brown sugar, and molasses and stir until combined. Simmer for about 30-45 minutes over low heat until your own liking.

Place everything into a blender and process until a smooth sauce.

Enjoy with favorite veggies or protein. You can refrigerate in jars for up to a month.

Nutrition:

Calories 35, Total fat 0g, Saturated fat 0g, Total carbs 9g, Net carbs 9g, Protein 0g, Sugar 0g, Fiber 0g, Sodium: 0mg

Smoked Garlic White Sauce

Preparation time: 15 minutes
Cooking time: 1 hours
Servings: 2
Method of Preparation: Grilling

Ingredients:

2 cups hickory wood chips, soaked in water for 30 minutes

3 whole garlic heads

1/2 cup mayonnaise

1/3 cup sour cream

1 juiced lemon

2 tbsp apple cider vinegar

Salt to taste

Directions:

Cut garlic heads to expose the inside and place in a container, microwave-safe, with 2 tbsp water. Microwave for about 5-6 minutes on medium.

Preheat your grill. Place garlic heads on a shallow foil "boat" and place it on the grill.

Close the grill and cook for about 20-25 minutes until soft completely. Remove and cool.

Transfer into a blender then add the remaining ingredients. Process until smooth.

Serve immediately or store in a refrigerator for up to 5 days.

Nutrition:

Calories 20, Total fat 0g, Saturated fat 0g, Total carbs 8g, Net carbs 8g, Protein 0g, Sugar 0g, Fiber 0g, Sodium: 45mg

Texas-Style Brisket Rub

Preparation time: 15 minutes
Servings: 1
Method of Preparation: Grilling

Ingredients:
2 tsp Sugar
2 Tbsp Kosher salt
2 tsp Chilli powder
2 Tbsp Black pepper
Tbsp Cayenne pepper
Tbsp Powdered garlic
tsp Grounded cumin
2 Tbsp Powdered onion
1/4 cup paprika, smoked

Directions:
Mix all the ingredients in a small bowl until it is well blended.
Transfer to an airtight jar or container. Store in a cool place.
Nutrition:
Calories: 18, Carbs: 2g, Fat: 1g, Protein: 0.6g

Pork Dry Rub

Preparation time: 15 minutes
Servings: 1 cup
Method of Preparation: Grilling

Ingredients:
Tbsp Kosher salt
2 Tbsp Powered onions
Tbsp Cayenne pepper
1tsp Dried mustard
1/4 cup brown sugar
Tbsp Powdered garlic
Tbsp Powdered chili pepper
1/4 cup smoked paprika
2 Tbsp Black pepper
Directions:

Combine all the ingredients in a small bowl.
Transfer to an airtight jar or container.
Keep stored in a cool, dry place.
Nutrition:
Calories: 16, Carbs: 3g, Fat:0.9g, Protein: 0.8g

Texas Barbeque Rub

Preparation time: 15 minutes
Servings: 1/2 cup
Method of Preparation: Grilling

Ingredients:
1 tsp Sugar
Tbsp Seasoned salt
Tbsp Black pepper
tsp Chilli powder
Tbsp Powdered onions
Tbsp Smoked paprika
1 tsp Sugar
Tbsp Powdered garlic

Directions:
Pour all the ingredients into a small bowl and mix thoroughly.
Keep stored in an airtight jar or container.
Nutrition:
Calories: 22, Carbs: 2g, Fat: 0.2g, Protein: 0.6g

Barbeque Sauce

Preparation time: 15 minutes
Servings: 2 cups
Method of Preparation: Grilling

Ingredients:
1/4 cup of water
1/4 cup red wine vinegar
Tbsp Worcestershire sauce
1 tsp Paprika
1 tsp Salt
Tbsp Dried mustard

1 tsp black pepper
1 cup ketchup
1 cup brown sugar

Directions:

Pour all the ingredients into a food processor, one after the other.

Process until they are evenly mixed.

Transfer sauce to a close lid jar. Store in the refrigerator.

Nutrition:

Calories: 43, Carbs: 10g Fat: 0.3g, Protein: 0.9g

Steak Sauce

Preparation time: 25 minutes
Servings: ½ cup
Method of Preparation: Grilling

Ingredients:

Tbsp Malt vinegar
1/2 tsp Salt
1/2 tsp black pepper
Tbsp Tomato sauce
2 Tbsp brown sugar
1 tsp hot pepper sauce
2 Tbsp Worcestershire sauce
2 Tbsp Raspberry jam.

Directions:

Preheat your grill for indirect cooking at 150°F

Place a saucepan over grates, add all your ingredients, and allow to boil.

Reduce the temperature to Smoke and allow the sauce to simmer for 10 minutes or until sauce is thick.

Nutrition:

Calories: 62.1, Carbs: 15.9g Fat: 0.3g, Protein:0.1g

Bourbon Whiskey Sauce

Preparation time: 45 minutes
Servings: 3cup
Method of Preparation: Grilling

Ingredients:

cups ketchup
1/4 cup Worcestershire sauce
3/4 cup bourbon whiskey
1/3 cup apple cider vinegar
1/2 onions, minced
1/4 cup of tomato paste
cloves of garlic, minced
1/2 tsp Black pepper
1/2 cup brown sugar
1/2 Tbsp Salt
Hot pepper sauce to taste
Tbsp Liquid smoke flavoring

Directions:

Preheat your grill for indirect cooking at 150°F

Place a saucepan over grates, then add the whiskey, garlic, and onions.

Simmer until the onion is translucent. Then add the other ingredients and adjust the temperature to Smoke. Simmer for 20 minutes. For a smooth sauce, sieve.

Nutrition:

Calories: 107, Carbs:16.6g Fat: 1.8g, Protein:0.8g

Chicken Marinade

Preparation time: 35 minutes
Servings: 3 cups
Method of Preparation: Smoking/ Grilling

Ingredients:

halved chicken breast (bone and skin removed)
Tbsp Spicy brown mustard
2/3 cup of soy sauce
tsp Powdered garlic
2 Tbsp Liquid smoke flavoring

2/3 cup extra virgin olive oil
2/3 cup lemon juice
2 tsp Black pepper

Directions:

Mix all the ingredients in a large bowl.

Pour the chicken into the bowl and allow it to marinate for about 3-4hours in the refrigerator. Remove the chicken, then smoke, grill, or roast the chicken.

Nutrition:

Calories: 507, Carbs:46.6g Fat: 41.8g, Protein: 28g

Carne Asada Marinade

Preparation time: 2hours
Servings: 5 cups
Method of Preparation: Grilling

Ingredients:

cloves garlic, chopped
tsp Lemon juice
1/2 cup extra virgin olive oil
1/2 tsp Salt
1/2 tsp Pepper

Directions:

Mix all your ingredients in a bowl.

Pour the beef into the bowl and allow to marinate for 2-3hours before grilling.

Nutrition:

Calories: 465, Carbs: 26g Fat: 15g, Protein: 28g

Grapefruit Juice Marinade

Preparation time: 1hours 10 minutes
Servings: 3 cups
Method of Preparation: Grilling

Ingredients:

1/2 reduced-sodium soy sauce
cups grapefruit juice, unsweetened
1-1/2 lb. Chicken, bone and skin removed
1/4 brown sugar

Directions:

Thoroughly mix all your ingredients in a large bowl.

Add the chicken and allow it to marinate for 2-3 hours before grilling.

Nutrition:

Calories: 489, Carbs: 21.3g Fat: 12g, Protein: 24g

Steak Marinade

Preparation time: 15 minutes
Servings: 2cups
Method of Preparation: Grilling

Ingredients:

Tbsp Worcestershire sauce
Tbsp Red wine vinegar
1/2 cup barbeque sauce
Tbsp soy sauce
1/4 cup steak sauce
1 clove garlic (minced)
1 tsp Mustard
Pepper and salt to taste

Directions:

Pour all the ingredients in a bowl and mix thoroughly.

Use immediately or keep refrigerated.

Nutrition:

Calories: 303, Carbs: 42g Fat: 10g, Protein:2.4g

POULTRY

Herb Roasted Turkey

Preparation time: 15 minutes
Cooking time: 3 hours and 30 minutes
Servings: 12
Method of Preparation: Smoking

Ingredients:
14 pounds turkey, cleaned
2 tablespoons chopped mixed herbs
Pork and poultry rub as needed
1/4 teaspoon ground black pepper
3 tablespoons butter, unsalted, melted
8 tablespoons butter, unsalted, softened
2 cups chicken broth

Directions:
Clean the turkey by removing the giblets, wash it inside out, pat dry with paper towels, then place it on a roasting pan and tuck the turkey wings by tiring with butcher's string.

Switch on the Traeger grill, fill the grill hopper with hickory flavored wood pellets, power the grill on by using the control panel, select 'smoke' on the temperature dial, or set the temperature to 325 degrees F and let it preheat for a minimum of 15 minutes.

Meanwhile, prepared herb butter and for this, take a small bowl, place the softened butter in it, add black pepper and mixed herbs and beat until fluffy.

Place some of the prepared herb butter underneath the skin of turkey by using a handle of a wooden spoon, and massage the skin to distribute butter evenly.

Then rub the exterior of the turkey with melted butter, season with pork and poultry rub, and pour the broth in the roasting pan.

When the grill has preheated, open the lid, place roasting pan containing turkey on the grill grate, shut the grill and smoke for 3 hours and 30 minutes until the internal temperature reaches 165 degrees F and the top has turned golden brown.

When done, transfer turkey to a cutting board, let it rest for 30 minutes, then carve it into slices and serve.

Nutrition:
Calories: 154.6
Fat: 3.1 g
Carbs: 8.4 g
Protein: 28.8 g
Fiber: 0.4 g

Turkey Legs

Preparation time: 24 hours
Cooking time: 5 hours
Servings: 4
Method of Preparation: Grilling

Ingredients:
4 turkey legs
For the Brine:
1/2 cup curing salt
1 tablespoon whole black peppercorns
1 cup BBQ rub
1/2 cup brown sugar
2 bay leaves
2 teaspoons liquid smoke
16 cups of warm water
4 cups ice
8 cups of cold water

Directions:
Prepare the brine and for this, take a large stockpot, place it over high heat, pour warm

water in it, add peppercorn, bay leaves, and liquid smoke, stir in salt, sugar, and BBQ rub and bring it to a boil.

Remove pot from heat, bring it to room temperature, then pour in cold water, add ice cubes and let the brine chill in the refrigerator.

Then add turkey legs in it, submerge them completely, and let soak for 24 hours in the refrigerator.

After 24 hours, remove turkey legs from the brine, rinse well and pat dry with paper towels.

When ready to cook, switch on the Traeger grill, fill the grill hopper with hickory flavored wood pellets, power the grill on by using the control panel, select 'smoke' on the temperature dial, or set the temperature to 250 degrees F and let it preheat for a minimum of 15 minutes.

When the grill has preheated, open the lid, place turkey legs on the grill grate, shut the grill, and smoke for 5 hours until nicely browned and the internal temperature reaches 165 degrees F.

Serve immediately.

Nutrition:
Calories: 416
Fat: 13.3 g
Carbs: 0 g
Protein: 69.8 g
Fiber: 0 g

Turkey Breast

Preparation time: 12 hours
Cooking time: 8 hours
Servings: 6
Method of Preparation: Grilling

Ingredients:
For the Brine:
2 pounds turkey breast, deboned
2 tablespoons ground black pepper
1/4 cup salt
1 cup brown sugar
4 cups cold water
For the BBQ Rub:
2 tablespoons dried onions
2 tablespoons garlic powder
1/4 cup paprika
2 tablespoons ground black pepper
1 tablespoon salt
2 tablespoons brown sugar
2 tablespoons red chili powder
1 tablespoon cayenne pepper
2 tablespoons sugar
2 tablespoons ground cumin

Directions:
Prepare the brine and for this, take a large bowl, add salt, black pepper, and sugar in it, pour in water, and stir until sugar has dissolved.

Place turkey breast in it, submerge it completely and let it soak for a minimum of 12 hours in the refrigerator.

Meanwhile, prepare the BBQ rub and for this, take a small bowl, place all of its ingredients in it and then stir until combined, set aside until required.

Then remove turkey breast from the brine and season well with the prepared BBQ rub.

When ready to cook, switch on the Traeger grill, fill the grill hopper with apple-flavored wood pellets, power the grill on by using the control panel, select 'smoke' on the temperature dial, or set the temperature to 180 degrees F and let it preheat for a minimum of 15 minutes.

When the grill has preheated, open the lid, place turkey breast on the grill grate, shut the grill, change the smoking temperature to 225 degrees F, and smoke for 8 hours until the internal temperature reaches 160 degrees F.

When done, transfer turkey to a cutting board, let it rest for 10 minutes, then cut it into slices and serve.

Nutrition:
Calories: 250
Fat: 5 g
Carbs: 31 g
Protein: 18 g
Fiber: 5 g

Hellfire Chicken Wings

Preparation time: 15 minutes
Cooking time: 40 minutes
Servings: 6
Method of Preparation: Smoking

Ingredients:
3 pounds chicken wings, tips removed
2 tablespoons olive oil
For the Rub:
1 teaspoon onion powder
1 teaspoon salt
1 teaspoon garlic powder
1 tablespoon paprika
1 teaspoon ground black pepper
1 teaspoon celery seed
1 teaspoon cayenne pepper
2 teaspoons brown sugar
For the Sauce:
4 jalapeno peppers, sliced crosswise
8 tablespoons butter, unsalted
1/2 cup hot sauce
1/2 cup cilantro leaves

Directions:
Switch on the Traeger grill, fill the grill hopper with hickory flavored wood pellets, power the grill on by using the control panel, select 'smoke' on the temperature dial, or set the temperature to 350 degrees F and let it preheat for a minimum of 15 minutes.

Prepare the chicken wings and for this, remove tips from the wings, cut each chicken wing through the joint into two pieces, and then place in a large bowl.

Prepare the rub and for this, take a small bowl, place all of its ingredients in it and then stir until combined.

Sprinkle prepared rub on the chicken wings and then toss until well coated.

Meanwhile,

When the grill has preheated, open the lid, place chicken wings on the grill grate, shut the grill and smoke for 40 minutes until golden brown and skin have turned crisp, turning halfway.

Meanwhile, prepare the sauce and for this, take a small saucepan, place it over medium-low heat, add butter in it and when it melts, add jalapeno and cook for 4 minutes.

Then stir in hot sauce and cilantro until mixed and remove the pan from heat.

When done, transfer chicken wings to a dish, top with prepared sauce, toss until coated, and then serve.

Nutrition:
Calories: 250
Fat: 15 g
Carbs: 11 g
Protein: 19 g
Fiber: 1 g

Spicy BBQ Chicken

Preparation time: 8 hours and 10 minutes
Cooking time: 3 hours
Servings: 6
Method of Preparation: Smoking

Ingredients:

1 whole chicken, cleaned
For the Marinade:
1 medium white onion, peeled
6 Thai chilies
5 cloves of garlic, peeled
1 scotch bonnet
3 tablespoons salt
2 tablespoons sugar
2 tablespoons sweet paprika
4 cups grapeseed oil

Directions:

Prepare the marinade, and for this, place all of its ingredients in a food processor and pulse for 2 minutes until smooth.

Smoother whole chicken with the prepared marinade and let it marinate in the refrigerator for a minimum of 8 hours.

When ready to cook, switch on the Traeger grill, fill the grill hopper with apple-flavored wood pellets, power the grill on by using the control panel, select 'smoke' on the temperature dial, or set the temperature to 300 degrees F and let it preheat for a minimum of 15 minutes.

When the grill has preheated, open the lid, place chicken on the grill grate breast-side up, shut the grill and smoke for 3 hours until the internal temperature of chicken reaches 165 degrees F.

When done, transfer chicken to a cutting board, let it rest for 15 minutes, then cut into slices and serve.

Nutrition:

Calories: 100
Fat: 2.8 g
Carbs: 13 g
Protein: 3.5 g
Fiber: 2 g

BBQ Half Chickens

Preparation time: 15 minutes
Cooking time: 75 minutes
Servings: 4
Method of Preparation: Smoking

Ingredients:

3.5-pound whole chicken, cleaned, halved
Summer rub as needed
Apricot BBQ sauce as needed

Directions:

Switch on the Traeger grill, fill the grill hopper with apple-flavored wood pellets, power the grill on by using the control panel, select 'smoke' on the temperature dial, or set the temperature to 375 degrees F and let it preheat for a minimum of 15 minutes.

Meanwhile, cut chicken in half along with backbone and then season with summer rub.

When the grill has preheated, open the lid, place chicken halves on the grill grate skin-side up, shut the grill, change the smoking temperature to 225 degrees F, and smoke for 1 hour and 30 minutes until the internal temperature reaches 160 degrees F.

Then brush chicken generously with apricot sauce and continue grilling for 10 minutes until glazed.

When done, transfer chicken to cutting to a dish, let it rest for 5 minutes, and then serve.

Nutrition:

Calories: 435
Fat: 20 g
Carbs: 20 g
Protein: 42 g
Fiber: 1 g

Teriyaki Wings

Preparation time: 8 hours
Cooking time: 50 minutes
Servings: 8
Method of Preparation: Smoking

Ingredients:

2 ½ pounds large chicken wings
1 tablespoon toasted sesame seeds
For the Marinade:
2 scallions, sliced
2 tablespoons grated ginger
½ teaspoon minced garlic
1/4 cup brown sugar
1/2 cup soy sauce
2 tablespoon rice wine vinegar
2 teaspoons sesame oil
1/4 cup water

Directions:

Prepare the chicken wings and for this, remove tips from the wings, cut each chicken wing through the joint into three pieces, and then place in a large plastic bag.

Prepare the sauce and for this, take a small saucepan, place it over medium-high heat, add all of its ingredients in it, stir until mixed, and bring it to a boil.

Then switch heat to medium level, simmer the sauce for 10 minutes, and when done, cool the sauce completely.

Pour the sauce over chicken wings, seal the bag, turn it upside down to coat chicken wings with the sauce and let it marinate for a minimum of 8 hours in the refrigerator.

When ready to cook, switch on the Traeger grill, fill the grill hopper with maple-flavored wood pellets, power the grill on by using the control panel, select 'smoke' on the temperature dial, or set the temperature to 350 degrees F and let it preheat for a minimum of 15 minutes.

Meanwhile,

When the grill has preheated, open the lid, place chicken wings on the grill grate, shut the grill and smoke for 50 minutes until crispy and meat is no longer pink, turning halfway.

When done, transfer chicken wings to a dish, sprinkle with sesame seeds and then serve.

Nutrition:

Calories: 150
Fat: 7.5 g
Carbs: 6 g
Protein: 12 g
Fiber: 1 g

Korean Chicken Wings

Preparation time: 4 hours
Cooking time: 1 hour
Servings: 6
Method of Preparation: Grilling

Ingredients:

3 pounds of chicken wings
2 tablespoons olive oil
For the Brine:
1 head garlic, halved
1 lemon, halved
1/2 cup sugar
1 cup of sea salt
4 sprigs of thyme
10 peppercorns
16 cups of water
For the Sauce:
2 teaspoons minced garlic
1/2 cup gochujang hot pepper paste
1 tablespoon grated ginger
2 tablespoons of rice wine vinegar
1/3 cup honey

1/4 cup soy sauce

2 tablespoons lime juice

2 tablespoons toasted sesame oil

1/4 cup melted butter

Directions:

Prepare the brine and for this, take a large stockpot, place it over high heat, pour in water, stir in salt and sugar until dissolved, and bring to a boil.

Then remove the pot from heat, add the remaining ingredients for the brine, and bring the brine to room temperature.

Add chicken wings, submerge them completely, cover the pot and let wings soak for a minimum of 4 hours in the refrigerator.

When ready to cook, switch on the Traeger grill, fill the grill hopper with flavored wood pellets, power the grill on by using the control panel, select 'smoke' on the temperature dial, or set the temperature to 375 degrees F and let it preheat for a minimum of 15 minutes.

Meanwhile, remove chicken wings from the brine, pat dry with paper towels, place them in a large bowl, drizzle with oil and toss until well coated.

When the grill has preheated, open the lid, place chicken wings on the grill grate, shut the grill, and smoke for 1 hour until the internal temperature reaches 165 degrees F.

Meanwhile, prepare the sauce and for this, take a medium bowl, place all of the sauce ingredients in it and whisk until smooth.

When done, transfer chicken wings to a dish, top with prepared sauce, toss until coated, and then serve.

Nutrition:

Calories: 137

Fat: 9 g

Carbs: 4 g

Protein: 8 g

Fiber: 1 g

Garlic Parmesan Chicken Wings

Preparation time: 15 minutes

Cooking time: 20 minutes

Servings: 6

Method of Preparation: Grilling

Ingredients:

5 pounds of chicken wings

1/2 cup chicken rub

3 tablespoons chopped parsley

1 cup shredded parmesan cheese

For the Sauce:

5 teaspoons minced garlic

2 tablespoons chicken rub

1 cup butter, unsalted

Directions:

Switch on the Traeger grill, fill the grill hopper with cherry flavored wood pellets, power the grill on by using the control panel, select 'smoke' on the temperature dial, or set the temperature to 450 degrees F and let it preheat for a minimum of 15 minutes.

Meanwhile, take a large bowl, place chicken wings in it, sprinkle with chicken rub and toss until well coated.

When the grill has preheated, open the lid, place chicken wings on the grill grate, shut the grill, and smoke for 10 minutes per side until the internal temperature reaches 165 degrees F.

Meanwhile, prepare the sauce and for this, take a medium saucepan, place it over medium heat, add all the ingredients for the sauce in it and cook for 10 minutes until smooth, set aside until required.

When done, transfer chicken wings to a dish, top with prepared sauce, toss until mixed, garnish with cheese and parsley and then serve.

Nutrition:

Calories: 180

Fat: 1 g

Carbs: 8 g

Protein: 0 g

Fiber: 0 g

Rosemary Orange Chicken

Preparation time: 2 hours

Cooking time: 45 minutes

Servings: 6

Method of Preparation: Smoking

Ingredients:

4 pounds chicken, backbone removed

For the Marinade:

2 teaspoons salt

3 tablespoons chopped rosemary leaves

2 teaspoons Dijon mustard

1 orange, zested

1/4 cup olive oil

¼ cup of orange juice

Directions:

Prepare the chicken and for this, rinse the chicken, pat dry with paper towels and then place in a large baking dish.

Prepare the marinade and for this, take a medium bowl, place all of its ingredients in it and whisk until combined.

Cover chicken with the prepared marinade, cover with a plastic wrap, and then marinate for a minimum of 2 hours in the refrigerator, turning halfway.

When ready to cook, switch on the Traeger grill, fill the grill hopper with flavored wood pellets, power the grill on by using the control panel, select 'smoke' on the temperature dial, or set the temperature to 350 degrees F and let it preheat for a minimum of 5 minutes.

When the grill has preheated, open the lid, place chicken on the grill grate skin-side down, shut the grill and smoke for 45 minutes until well browned, and the internal temperature reaches 165 degrees F.

When done, transfer chicken to a cutting board, let it rest for 10 minutes, cut it into slices, and then serve.

Nutrition:

Calories: 258

Fat: 17.4 g

Carbs: 5.2 g

Protein: 19.3 g

Fiber: 0.3 g

Lemon Chicken Breast

Preparation time: 15 minutes

Cooking time: 30 minutes

Servings: 4

Method of Preparation: Smoking

Ingredients:

6 chicken breasts, skinless and boneless

½ cup oil

1-3 fresh thyme sprigs

1teaspoon ground black pepper

2teaspoon salt

2teaspoons honey

1garlic clove, chopped

1lemon, juiced and zested

Lemon wedges

Directions:

Take a bowl and prepare the marinade by mixing thyme, pepper, salt, honey, garlic, lemon zest, and juice. Mix well until dissolved

Add oil and whisk

Clean breasts and pat them dry, place in a bag alongside marinade and let them sit in the fridge for 4 hours

Preheat your smoker to 400 degrees F

Drain chicken and smoke until the internal temperature reaches 165 degrees, for about 15 minutes

Serve and enjoy!

Nutrition: Calories: 230 Fats: 7g Carbs: 1g Fiber: 2g

Smokey Fried Chicken

Preparation Time: 10 minutes

Cooking time: 3 hours 30 minutes

Servings: 6-8

Method of Preparation: Smoking

Ingredients:

The Meat

2 Whole fryer chickens – (3 – ½ lb.)

Ingredients

Coarse Kosher Salt

Vegetable oil

Black pepper.

Fresh buttermilk.

Hot sauce – 2 tbsp.

Brown sugar – 1 tbsp.

All-purpose flour – 2-1/2 cups.

Garlic powder – 2 tbsp.

Onion powder – 2 tbsp.

Poultry shake – 1 tbsp.

Peanut or grapeseed oil

Directions:

Start the smoker with the lid open, after the fire has been established, then close the lid. Set the temperature at 200F. Preheat it at this temperature for about 15 minutes.

Use cold water to rinse the chicken. To dry it pat the chicken pieces and then place it on a baking sheet.

Use vegetable oil to rub outside the chicken and season it with salt and pepper.

Arrange the chicken on the grill grate. Smoke it for about 2-1/ 2 hours. The internal temperature for indicating that the chicken is done, is about 150F.

Afterward, place the chicken on a baking sheet to cool down.

Start cutting the chicken now. Make about 20 pieces; 4 drumsticks, 4 wings, 4 thighs, and 8 breast quarters. Take two plastic bags and divide the chicken pieces evenly between them.

Take a mixing bowl and whisk the buttermilk with hot sauce and brown sugar. Pour half of this in each bag. Refrigerate these bags for an hour.

Take another bowl and whisk flour, 2 tablespoons each of salt and pepper, garlic powder, onion powder, and poultry seasoning in it.

Heat 2 inches of peanut or grapeseed oil on a stovetop. The temperature should be medium-high at about 375 degrees. The pot for this purpose should be a heavy saucepan.

Now, drain the chicken pieces that were in the bag and put them in the flour mixture.

Fry the chicken in batches. After the color golden brown appears, then it means they done. It should take about 6 minutes for breast pieces and a little longer for others.

Put the chicken pieces on the paper towels to drain, and they are ready to serve.

Nutrition:

Calories: 321

Total Carbohydrate 15.5g 6%

Dietary Fiber: 0.3g 1%

Total Sugars 13.5g
Protein: 42.2g
Vitamin D: 0mcg 0%
Calcium: 25mg 2%
Iron: 4mg 24%
Potassium: 454mg 10%

Maple and Bacon Chicken

Preparation time: 20 minutes
Cooking time: 1 and ½ hours
Servings: 7
Method of Preparation: Smoking

Ingredients:

4 boneless and skinless chicken breasts
Salt as needed
Fresh pepper
12 slices bacon, uncooked
1cup maple syrup
½ cup melted butter
1teaspoon liquid smoke

Directions:

Preheat your smoker to 250 degrees Fahrenheit
Season the chicken with pepper and salt
Wrap the breast with 3 bacon slices and cover the entire surface
Secure the bacon with toothpicks
Take a medium-sized bowl and stir in maple syrup, butter, liquid smoke, and mix well
Reserve 1/3rd of this mixture for later use
Submerge the chicken breast into the butter mix and coat them well
Place a pan in your smoker and transfer the chicken to your smoker
Smoker for 1 to 1 and a ½ hours
Brush the chicken with reserved butter and smoke for 30 minutes more until the internal temperature reaches 165 degrees Fahrenheit
Enjoy!

Nutrition: Calories: 458 Fats: 20g Carbs: 65g Fiber: 1g

Paprika Chicken

Preparation time: 20 minutes
Cooking time: 2 – 4 hours
Servings: 7
Method of Preparation: Smoking

Ingredients:

4-6 chicken breast
4 tablespoons olive oil
2tablespoons smoked paprika
½ tablespoon salt
¼ teaspoon pepper
2teaspoons garlic powder
2teaspoons garlic salt
2teaspoons pepper
1teaspoon cayenne pepper
1teaspoon rosemary

Directions:

Preheat your smoker to 220 degrees Fahrenheit using your favorite wood Pellets
Prepare your chicken breast according to your desired shapes and transfer to a greased baking dish
Take a medium bowl and add spices, stir well
Press the spice mix over chicken and transfer the chicken to smoker
Smoke for 1-1 and a ½ hours
Turn-over and cook for 30 minutes more
Once the internal temperature reaches 165 degrees Fahrenheit
Remove from the smoker and cover with foil
Allow it to rest for 15 minutes
Enjoy!
Nutrition: Calories: 237 Fats: 6.1g Carbs: 14g Fiber: 3g

Sweet Sriracha BBQ Chicken

Preparation time: 30 minutes
Cooking time: 1 and ½-2 hours
Servings: 5
Method of Preparation: Smoking

Ingredients:
1cup sriracha
½ cup butter
½ cup molasses
½ cup ketchup
¼ cup firmly packed brown sugar
1teaspoon salt
1teaspoon fresh ground black pepper
1whole chicken, cut into pieces
½ teaspoon fresh parsley leaves, chopped

Directions:
Preheat your smoker to 250 degrees Fahrenheit using cherry wood
Take a medium saucepan and place it over low heat, stir in butter, sriracha, ketchup, molasses, brown sugar, mustard, pepper and salt and keep stirring until the sugar and salt dissolves
Divide the sauce into two portions
Brush the chicken half with the sauce and reserve the remaining for serving
Make sure to keep the sauce for serving on the side, and keep the other portion for basting
Transfer chicken to your smoker rack and smoke for about 1 and a ½ to 2 hours until the internal temperature reaches 165 degrees Fahrenheit
Sprinkle chicken with parsley and serve with reserved BBQ sauce
Enjoy!
Nutrition: Calories: 148 Fats: 0.6g Carbs: 10g Fiber: 1g

Smoked Chicken Drumsticks

Preparation time: 10 minutes

Cooking time: 2 hours 30 minutes
Servings: 5
Method of Preparation: Smoking

Ingredients:
10 chicken drumsticks
2tsp garlic powder
1tsp salt
1tsp onion powder
1/2 tsp ground black pepper
½ tsp cayenne pepper
1tsp brown sugar
1/3 cup hot sauce
1tsp paprika
½ tsp thyme

Directions:
In a large mixing bowl, combine the garlic powder, sugar, hot sauce, paprika, thyme, cayenne, salt, and ground pepper. Add the drumsticks and toss to combine.
Cover the bowl and refrigerate for 1 hour.
Remove the drumsticks from the marinade and let them sit for about 1 hour until they are at room temperature.
Arrange the drumsticks into a rack.
Start your pellet grill on smoke, leaving the lid open for 5 minutes for the fire to start.
Close the lid and preheat grill to 250°F, using hickory or apple hardwood pellets.
Place the rack on the grill and smoke drumsticks for 2 hours, 30 minutes, or until the drumsticks' internal temperature reaches 180°F.
Remove drumsticks from heat and let them rest for a few minutes.
Serve.
Nutrition: Calories: 167 Total Fat: 5.4 g Saturated Fat: 1.4 g Cholesterol: 81 mg Sodium: 946 mg Total Carbohydrate: 2.6 g Dietary Fiber: 0.5 g Total Sugars: 1.3 g Protein: 25.7 g

Chicken Cordon Bleu

Preparation time: 15 minutes
Cooking time: 40 minutes
Servings: 6
Method of Preparation: Grilling

Ingredients:

6 boneless skinless chicken breasts

6 slices of ham

12 slices swiss cheese

1cup panko breadcrumbs

½ cup all-purpose flour

1tsp ground black pepper or to taste

1tsp salt or to taste

4tbsp grated parmesan cheese

2tbsp melted butter

½ tsp garlic powder

½ tsp thyme

¼ tsp parsley

Directions:

Butterfly the chicken breast with a pairing knife. Place the chicken breast in between 2 plastic wraps and pound with a mallet until the chicken breasts are ¼ inch thick.

Place a plastic wrap on a flat surface. Place one fat chicken breast on it.

Place one slice of swiss cheese on the chicken. Place one slice of ham over the cheese and place another cheese slice over the ham.

Roll the chicken breast tightly. Fold both ends of the roll tightly. Pin both ends of the rolled chicken breast with a toothpick.

Repeat step 3 and 4 for the remaining chicken breasts

In a mixing bowl, combine the all-purpose flour, ½ tsp salt, and ½ tsp pepper. Set aside.

In another mixing bowl, combine breadcrumbs, parmesan, butter, garlic, thyme, parsley, ½ tsp salt, and ½ tsp pepper. Set aside.

Break the eggs into another mixing bowl and whisk. Set aside.

Grease a baking sheet.

Bake one chicken breast roll. Dip into the flour mixture, brush with eggs and dip into breadcrumb mixture. The chicken breast should be coated.

Place it on the baking sheet.

Repeat steps 9 and 10 for the remaining breast rolls.

Preheat your grill to 375°F with the lid closed for 15 minutes.

Place the baking sheet on the grill and cook for about 40 minutes, or until the chicken is golden brown.

Remove the baking sheet from the grill and let the chicken rest for a few minutes.

Slice cordon bleu and serve.

Nutrition: Calories: 560 Total Fat: 27.4 g Saturated Fat: 15.9 g Cholesterol: 156mg Sodium: 1158 mg Total Carbohydrate: 23.2 g Dietary Fiber: 1.1 g Total Sugars: 1.2 g Protein: 54.3 g

Smoked Whole Duck

Preparation time: 15 minutes
Cooking time: 2 hours 30 minutes
Servings: 6
Method of Preparation: Grilling

Ingredients:

5 pounds whole duck (trimmed of any excess fat)

1small onion (quartered)

1apple (wedged)

1orange (quartered)

1tbsp freshly chopped parsley

1tbsp freshly chopped sage

½ tsp onion powder

2tsp smoked paprika

1tsp dried Italian seasoning

1tbsp dried Greek seasoning

1tsp pepper or to taste

1tsp sea salt or to taste

Directions:

Remove giblets and rinse duck, inside and pour, under cold running water.

Pat dry with paper towels.

Use the tip of a sharp knife to cut the duck skin all over. Be careful not to cut through the meat.

Tie the duck legs together with butcher's string.

To make a rub, combine the onion powder, pepper, salt, Italian seasoning, Greek seasoning, and paprika in a mixing bowl.

Insert the orange, onion, and apple to the duck cavity. Stuff the duck with freshly chopped parsley and sage.

Season all sides of the duck generously with rub mixture.

Start your pellet grill on smoke mode, leaving the lip open or until the fire starts.

Close the lid and preheat the grill to 325°F for 10 minutes.

Place the duck on the grill grate.

Roast for 2 to 21/2 hours, or until the duck skin is brown and the internal temperature of the thigh reaches 160°F.

Remove the duck from heat and let it rest for a few minutes.

Cut into sizes and serve.

Nutrition: Calories: 809 Total Fat: 42.9 g Saturated Fat: 15.8 g Cholesterol: 337 mg Sodium: 638 mg Total Carbohydrate: 11.7 g Dietary Fiber: 2.4 g Total Sugars: 7.5 g Protein: 89.6 g

Chicken Fajitas on a Wood Pellet Grill

Preparation time: 0 minutes

Cooking time: 20 minutes

Servings: 10

Method of Preparation: Grilling

Ingredients:

Chicken breast - 2 lb. thin sliced

Red bell pepper - 1 large

Onion - 1 large

Orange bell pepper - 1 large

Seasoning mix

Oil - 2 tbsp

Onion powder - ½ tbsp

Granulated garlic - ½ tbsp

Salt - 1 tbsp

Directions:

Preheat the grill to 450 degrees.

Mix the seasonings and oil.

Add the chicken slices to the mix.

Line a large pan with a non-stick baking sheet.

Let the pan heat for 10 minutes.

Place the chicken, peppers, and other vegetables in the grill.

Grill for 10 minutes or until the chicken is cooked.

Remove it from the grill and serve with warm tortillas and vegetables.

Nutrition: Carbohydrates: 5 g Protein: 29 g Fat: 6 g Sodium: 360 mg Cholesterol: 77 mg

Smoked Cornish Chicken in Wood Pellets

Preparation time: 0 minutes
Cooking time: 1 hour 10 minutes
Servings: 6
Method of Preparation: Smoking

Ingredients:

Cornish hens - 6
Canola or avocado oil - 2-3 tbsp
Spice mix - 6 tbsp

Directions:

Preheat your wood pellet grill to 275 degrees.
Rub the whole hen with oil and the spice mix. Use both of these ingredients liberally.
Place the breast area of the hen on the grill and smoke for 30 minutes.
Flip the hen, so the breast side is facing up. Increase the temperature to 400 degrees.
Cook until the temperature goes down to 165 degrees.
Pull it out and leave it for 10 minutes.
Serve warm with a side dish of your choice.
Nutrition: Carbohydrates: 1 g Protein: 57 g Fat: 50 g Sodium: 165 mg Cholesterol: 337 mg

Wild Turkey Egg Rolls

Preparation time: 0 minutes
Cooking time: 40 minutes
Servings: 4-6
Method of Preparation: Grilling

Ingredients:

Corn - ½ cup
Leftover wild turkey meat - 2 cups
Black beans - ½ cup
Taco seasoning - 3 tbsp
Water ½ cup
Rotel chilies and tomatoes - 1 can
Egg roll wrappers- 12
Cloves of minced garlic- 4
1 chopped Poblano pepper or 2 jalapeno peppers
Chopped white onion - ½ cup

Directions:

Add some olive oil to a fairly large skillet. Heat it over medium heat on a stove.
Add peppers and onions. Sauté the mixture for 2-3 minutes until it turns soft.
Add some garlic and sauté for another 30 seconds. Add the Rotel chilies and beans to the mixture. Keeping mixing the content gently. Reduce the heat and then simmer.
After about 4-5 minutes, pour in the taco seasoning and ⅓ cup of water over the meat. Mix everything and coat the meat thoroughly. If you feel that it is a bit dry, you can add 2 tbsp of water. Keep cooking until everything is heated all the way through.
Remove the content from the heat and box it to store in a refrigerator. Before you stuff the mixture into the egg wrappers, it should be completely cool to avoid breaking the rolls.
Place a spoonful of the cooked mixture in each wrapper and then wrap it securely and tightly. Do the same with all the wrappers.
Preheat the pellet grill and brush it with some oil. Cook the egg rolls for 15 minutes on both sides until the exterior is nice and crispy.
Remove them from the grill and enjoy with your favorite salsa!
Nutrition: Carbohydrates: 26.1 g Protein: 9.2 g Fat: 4.2 g Sodium: 373.4 mg Cholesterol: 19.8 mg

BBQ Chicken

Preparation Time: 5 minutes
Cooking Time: 30 MINUTES
Servings: 8-10
Method of Preparation: Smoking

Ingredients:

16 chicken thighs
For the seasoning:
Brine, as required
All-purpose seasoning
For the sauce:
BBQ sauce, of choice – 1 cup
Mustard – ½ cup
Vinegar – 3 tablespoons
Black pepper – 1 tsp
Hot sauce – 3 tablespoons

Directions:

Heat-up your smoker to 275°F (135°C).

Remove the skin from the chicken thighs along with any excess fat. Transfer the skin to the fridge until ready to use.

Transfer the chicken thighs to a bowl and add sufficient brine to cover. Set to one side for 4 hours.

In a bowl, mix all the sauce ingredients; BBQ sauce, mustard, vinegar, black pepper, and hot sauce.

Take out the chicken from the brine, shaking off any excess liquid and season all over with all-purpose seasoning.

Remove the chicken skin from the fridge and wrap it around the chicken.

Place the wrapped chicken in the smoker.

Approximately 45 minutes into cooking, remove from the smoker, and brush the BBQ sauce on top of the chicken.

Return to the smoker for an additional 15-45 minutes, until the internal temperature reaches 165°F (74°C).

Serve and enjoy!

Nutrition:

Calories: 501
Protein: 44g
Vitamin D: 5mcg 26%
Calcium: 122mg 9%
Iron: 16mg: 90%
Potassium: 625mg

Chicken Tortillas with Tzatziki Sauce

Preparation Time: 15 minutes
Cooking Time: 9 HOURS, 10 MINUTES
Servings: 4-6
Method of Preparation: Grilling

Ingredients:

Skinless, boneless chicken thighs (2-lb, 0.9-kgs)
For the rub:
Whole black peppercorns – 2 tablespoons
Lemon zest, finely grated – 3 tablespoons
Kosher salt – 1 tablespoon
For the marinade:
Juice and zest of 1 lemon
Olive oil – ½ cup
Red wine vinegar – 2 tablespoons
2 garlic cloves, pressed
Oregano, chopped – 3 tablespoons
Dried marjoram – 1 teaspoon
Kosher salt – 2 teaspoons
Ground black pepper – 1 teaspoon
The Tzatziki Dip:
Greek yogurt (12-oz, 340.0-gms)
2 large cucumbers, peeled, seeded, grated, water removed
Freshly squeezed lemon juice – ¼ cup

1 garlic clove – peeled, pressed
Olive oil – 1 tablespoon
Kosher salt – 2 teaspoons
For the tacos:
6 store-bought tortillas, warmed
2 ripe tomatoes, thinly sliced
½ red onion, peeled, thinly sliced
A handful of fresh mint sprigs

Directions:

When you are ready to begin cooking, load your grill with cherry wood pellets, set your grill to 350°F (176°C), and with the lid closed, preheat for between 10-15 minutes.

First, rinse the chicken in cold running water. Using kitchen paper towels pat the chicken dry and transfer to a zip lock bag.

To prepare the rub. In a spice mill, crush the peppercorns. Transfer the crushed peppercorns to a small bowl and stir in the lemon zest and salt. Between clean fingertips, rub the seasoning to break up any clumps.

To make the marinade. In a bowl, whisk 1 tablespoon of the rub with the lemon juice, zest, oil, vinegar, garlic, oregano, marjoram, salt, and pepper. Add the remaining rub to a resealable jar. Pour the marinade over the chicken and marinate overnight.

Add the chicken to the grill and cook until it reaches an internal temperature of 170°F (77°C). Remove the bird from the grill and set aside to cool before cutting into bite-sized pieces.

In the meantime, prepare the dip. Add all tzatziki ingredients to a bowl and stir to combine. Serve chilled.

Arrange the chicken on the tortillas, add a dollop of Tzatziki and garnish with tomatoes, onions, and mint.

Serve and enjoy!

Nutrition:
Calories: 641
Protein: 0.7g
Vitamin D: 0mcg
Calcium: 19mg
Iron: 1mg
Potassium: 223mg

Spicy Chipotle Chicken Kabobs

Preparation time: 5 minutes
Cooking Time: 15 MINUTES
Servings: 10
Method of Preparation: Grilling

Ingredients:
Skinless, boneless chicken thighs (2-lb, 0.9-kgs)
10-12 thick-cut bacon rashers
For the rub:
Chipotle chili powder – 5 teaspoons
Chili powder – 5 teaspoons
Ground cumin – 2½ teaspoons
Paprika – 2½ teaspoons
Onion powder – 2½ teaspoons
Garlic powder – 2½ teaspoons
Salt and black pepper – to taste
For the Kabobs
1 medium red onion
1 medium pineapple
BBQ sauce – 1 cup
Apple butter - ⅔ cup
Chipotle peppers in sauce – 2 peppers + 1 tablespoon sauce

Directions:
Before cooking, soak 10 wooden skewers in cold water for 30-40 minutes.

Preheat grill to 400°F (200°C).

Combine the rub ingredients (chili powder, cumin, paprika, onion powder, garlic powder, salt, and black pepper) in a bowl, mixing to combine.

Cut the chicken into bite-sized pieces.

Add the chicken pieces to a pan and rub all over with the seasoning, ensuring that the chicken is entirely covered.

Slice the bacon into strips of approximately 1-ins (2½-cms).

Cut the onions into quarters then peel into single slices.

Peel the pineapple and chop into bite-sized chunks.

Thread the pineapple, onion, bacon, and chicken onto the 10 skewers.

Add the BBQ sauce, apple butter, chipotle peppers, and adobo sauce to a food blender and process until lump-free and smooth.

With a pastry brush, brush the kabobs with the BBQ sauce mixture and transfer to the grill for approximately 10-15 minutes, flipping halfway through cooking, until a meat thermometer inserted into the center of the chicken registers 165°F (74°C).

Before flipping the kabobs, brush with more BBQ sauce.

Brush any remaining BBQ sauce over the kabobs just before serving.

Enjoy!

Nutrition:
Calories: 501
Protein: 44g
Vitamin D: 5mcg 26%
Calcium: 122mg 9%
Iron: 16mg: 90%
Potassium: 625mg

Louisiana Hot Apple-Smoked Turkey

Preparation Time: 10 minutes
Cooking time: 3 HOURS, 45 MINUTES
Servings: 8-10

Ingredients:
1 whole turkey, rinsed, patted dry (14-lb, 6.3-kgs)
The spice injection:
1 bottle beer, room temperature (12-oz, 230-MLS)
Butter, melted – ½ cup
6 cloves of garlic, peeled
Worcestershire sauce – 2 tablespoons
Creole seasoning – 2 tablespoons
Liquid crab boil – 1 tablespoon
Louisiana hot sauce – 1 tablespoon
Seas salt – 1 tablespoon
Cayenne pepper – ½ teaspoon
For the rub:
Onion powder – ½ teaspoon
Garlic powder – ½ teaspoon
Paprika – 1 teaspoon
Cumin – ¼ teaspoon
Dried thyme – ½ teaspoon
Dried oregano – ¼ teaspoon
Sea salt – ¼ teaspoon
Freshly ground black pepper – ¼ teaspoon
Cayenne pepper – 1/8 teaspoon
Vegetable oil – 1 tablespoon

Directions:
Fire up your grill or smoker to 325°F (165°C). When the temperature is reached, add Applewood pellets.

First, prepare the injection. To a food blender, add allspice injection ingredients and blend until smooth.

Using a meat syringe, inject the spicy mixture into the meat all over. Space the injections approximately 1-ins (5-cms) apart.

Next, prepare the rub. In a bowl, combine all rub ingredients, excluding the oil.

Season the turkey all over and in its cavity with the prepared rub.

Nutrition:

Calories: 321

Total Carbohydrate 15.5g 6%

Dietary Fiber: 0.3g 1%

Total Sugars 13.5g

Protein: 42.2g

Vitamin D: 0mcg 0%

Calcium: 25mg 2%

Iron: 4mg 24%

Potassium: 454mg 10%

Spicy Turkey Cheeseburgers

Preparation Time: 5 minutes

Cooking time: 25 minutes

Method of Preparation: Grilling

Servings: 4

Ingredients:

Ground turkey (1-lb, 0.4-kgs)

1 onion, peeled, chopped – ½ cup

Cilantro, chopped – 2 tablespoons

1 chipotle Chile in adobo sauce

Garlic powder – 1 teaspoon

Onion powder – 1 teaspoon

Salt - pinch

Seasoning rub, of choice – 1 tablespoon

4 slices of Pepper Jack cheese

4 hamburger buns

Directions:

Preheat your grill to 300°F (150°C).

In a mixing bowl, combine the turkey with the onion, cilantro, and chili pepper in adobo sauce, garlic powder, onion powder, salt, and seasoning rub, mix to combine.

Using clean hands, form the mixture into 4 patties shapes.

Transfer the burgers to the grill and cook until the turkey's juices run clear. This will take approximately 6-7 minutes on each side.

A minute or so before you remove the patties from the grill, top with the Pepper Jack cheese and serve in a burger bun.

Nutrition:

Calories: 641

Protein: 0.7g

Vitamin D: 0mcg

Calcium: 19mg

Iron: 1mg

Potassium: 223mg

Whole Maple-Smoked Turkey

Preparation Time: 15 minutes

Cooking time: 5 hours, 35 minutes

Servings: 15-20

Method of Preparation: Grilling

Ingredients:

1 whole turkey (16 –lb., 7.2-kgs)

Olive oil

100% pure maple syrup – 1 cup

Butter – ¼ cup

Seasoning salt

Freshly ground black pepper

Directions:

Load your grill with maple pellets and preheat to 350°F (177°C).

Rub the whole turkey with a light coating of olive oil.

Place the turkey directly on the preheated grill, breast side facing upward and increase the internal temperature of the bird by 100°F (39°C). It is best to use a meat thermometer to do this.

Reduce the grill heat down to 225°F (107°C), until the turkey achieves an internal temperature of 170°F (80°C), this will take between 4-5 hours, depending on the outside temperature and variety of wood pellets.

To make the glaze. In a pan, combine the maple syrup with the butter, salt, and a dash of black pepper.

Brush the glaze all over the bird.

Continue to brush the turkey with the glaze every 60 minutes or so.

When the turkey reaches an internal temperature of 170°F (74°C), remove from the grill. Cover it up with aluminum foil and allow to rest for between 15-30 minutes before serving.

Nutrition:
Calories: 321
Total Carbohydrate 15.5g 6%
Dietary Fiber: 0.3g 1%
Total Sugars 13.5g
Protein: 42.2g
Vitamin D: 0mcg 0%
Calcium: 25mg 2%
Iron: 4mg 24%
Potassium: 454mg 10%

Smoked Whole Chicken

Preparation Time: 10 minutes
Cooking time: 1 hour 55 minutes
Servings: 4-6
Method of Preparation: Smoking with apple-wood pellets

Ingredients:
1 Whole roasting chicken – 3-4 lb.
For the mixture:
4 Garlic cloves.
Red onion – ½ and chopped
½ lemon.

For the Dry Rub:
Brown sugar – 1 cup.
Kosher salt – ½ cup.
Smoked paprika – 4 tbsp.
Coarse black pepper – 2 tbsp.
Cumin – ½ tbsp.
Onion powder – ½ tbsp.
Garlic powder – ½ tbsp.
Cayenne pepper – 1 tsp.
Directions:
Combine all the ingredients for the in order to make the dry rub. We only need a ¼ cup for the recipe. You can keep other of later use.

Preheat the wood pellet smoker to 225 degrees temperature.

Make sure the cavity inside the chicken is clean and remove any remaining residue. Clean the chicken thoroughly and cover it with dry rub.

Stuff the chicken's cavity with red onion, lemon, and garlic.

Tie the legs and wings of the chicken closer to the body. It is done to make sure that they do not overcook.

Put the chicken inside the smoker. Let it smoke for an hour. After an hour, get the temperature high up to 350 degrees. Until the internal temperature reaches 160 degrees, do not take the chicken out. The time it reaches that temperature depends on the size of the bird.

After taking out the chicken, let it rest for 10 minutes before serving it.

Nutrition:
Calories: 501
Protein: 44g
Vitamin D: 5mcg 26%
Calcium: 122mg 9%
Iron: 16mg: 90%
Potassium: 625mg

Smoked Whole Chicken with Carolina Glaze

Preparation Time: 10 minutes
Cooking time: 2 hours
Servings: 4
Method of Preparation: Smoking with apple-wood pellets

Ingredients:
Fryer chicken (halved) – (4-5 lb.)
Salt - 2 tbsp.
Freshly cracked pepper – 2 tbsp.
Glaze
For the Glaze:
Carolina BBQ sauce – 2 cups.
Honey – 2/3 cup.
Dijon mustard – 2 tbsp.
Directions:
First, rinse your chicken thoroughly and pat it dry. Take a cookie sheet and place the chicken pieces on it.
Season it well with salt and pepper. Put the chicken in the refrigerator in an isolated spot. This step should be almost 6 hours before you want to start cooking.
Now preheat the smoker up to 225 degrees.
Take the chicken out of the refrigerator. The color of chicken may be darker, but it is normal after dehydration and salting.
Now, put the chicken on the smoker. Wait until the internal temperature is 150 -155 degrees Fahrenheit. When it reaches that temperature, then put the glaze on the chicken with a brush.
Continue cooking until the temperature reaches 165 degrees then take the chicken out of the smoker. Glaze it once more. Cover the chicken with a foil sheet so that the juices redistribute. Leave it like that for 15 minutes.
Serve and enjoy.
Nutrition:
Calories: 641
Protein: 0.7g
Vitamin D: 0mcg
Calcium: 19mg
Iron: 1mg
Potassium: 223mg

Cajun Smoked Chicken Wings

Preparation Time: 8 minutes
Cooking time: 1 hour 30 minutes
Servings: 6-8
Method of Preparation: Smoking with apple-wood pellets

Ingredients:
Chicken Wings (cut into drumettes and flats) – (3 lb.)
For the Rub:
Kosher Salt – 1/4 tsp.
Baking powder – 1 tbsp.
Paprika – 1 tsp.
Garlic Powder – ½ tsp.
Onion powder – ½ tsp.
Dry thyme – ½ tsp.
Dried oregano – ¼ tsp.
Cumin – ¼ tsp.
Black pepper – ¼ tsp.
Cayenne pepper – 1/8 tsp.
For the Sauce:
Butter – 1/4 cup.
Louisiana style hot sauce – 1/4 cup.
Worcestershire sauce – 1 tbsp.
Directions:
Firstly, for preparing the rub, mix together garlic powder, paprika, onion powder, cumin, oregano. Cayenne, baking powder, thyme, salt, and pepper.

Rinse your chicken wings carefully and pat them with dry towels. Take a large bowl to fit all of the wings. Sprinkle the rub on top of it. Make sure the wings are evenly coated.

Put the wire rack in the baking sheet, which is line with aluminum foil. Arrange wings closely in a single layer. Place it in the refrigerator overnight.

Just keep the lid open until the fire is established in the smoker. Preheat for 10-15 minutes with the lid closed.

Smoke the chicken wings for about 30 minutes. Crank up the temperature after 30 minutes to about 350 degrees F. Let it smoke for about 45 minutes.

Now take out the wings in a bowl and add the sauce so that it coats all of the wings.

Transfer to a platter, and the dish is ready to serve.

Nutrition:
Calories: 501
Protein: 44g
Vitamin D: 5mcg 26%
Calcium: 122mg 9%
Iron: 16mg: 90%
Potassium: 625mg

Smoked Chicken

Preparation Time: 10 minutes
Cooking time: 4 hours
Servings: 6
Method of Preparation: Smoking

Ingredients:
1 gallon of water
½ cup of Kosher salt
1 cup of brown sugar
For the Rub:
Traeger big game rub
1 Lemon, halved

1 tbsp of garlic, minced
3 Garlic cloves, whole
1 Yellow onion, medium, quartered
4-5 Thyme sprigs
3-3 ½ lbs. of a whole chicken
Directions:
Dissolve the brown sugar and kosher salt in a gallon of water. Place the chicken in this brine, soaking it completely. Refrigerate the chicken overnight.

Preheat the smoker to 225^0 F for about 15 minutes with the lid closed.

Take the chicken out from the brine and dry it. Rub the chicken with the Traeger big game rub and minced garlic.

Now, stuff the cavity with garlic, lemon, onion, and thyme. Tie the chicken legs.

Place the chicken on the grill grate directly and smoke it for about 3 hours or until the internal temperature reaches 160^0 F.

Remove the chicken and rest it for about 30 minutes.

Slice and serve!

Nutrition:
Carbohydrate—0 g
Protein:26 g
Fat:16 g

Chicken, Applewood Smoked

Preparation Time: 15 minutes
Cooking time: 5 hours
Servings: 6
Method of Preparation: Smoking

Ingredients:
2 tbsp of chili powder
¼ cup of dark brown sugar, packed
1 tbsp of smoked paprika
1 tbsp of garlic powder

1 tbsp of onion powder

1 tsp of salt

1 tbsp of oregano

4-5 lbs. of a whole chicken

Directions:

Clean the chicken and rinse it with cold water. Dry it with a paper towel.

Cut the chicken at the center. Put it in a glass dish.

Mix all the dry ingredients in a small bowl. Rub the chicken in the dish well.

Wrap the bowl with plastic and put it in the refrigerator for about 12 hours.

Preheat the smoker at 225^0 F. Put the chicken in the smoker with the breast side up and close the lid.

Cook it for about 4-5 hours or until the chicken reaches an internal temperature of 165^0 F.

Remove the chicken and rest it for about 10 minutes.

Slice and serve!

Nutrition:

Carbohydrate:8 g

Protein: 28.9 g

Fat:23 g

Glazed Smoked Chicken

Preparation Time: 10 minutes

Cooking time: 3 hours

Servings: 12-15

Method of Preparation: Smoking

Ingredients:

2 gallons of water

2 tbsp of cayenne pepper, ground

2 tbsp of pickling spices

1 tsp of allspice

2 tsp of garlic powder

2 tsp of black pepper

2 tsp of onion powder

2 tsp of celery salt

½ cup of brown sugar

3 cups of kosher salt

2 tsp of liquid smoke

2 tbsp of maple extract

¼ cup of Cajun seasoning

½ cup of olive oil

For the Mop:

2 cups of water

2 cups of apple cider vinegar

2 tbsp of salt

2 tbsp of black pepper

For the Glaze:

6 tbsp of butter

2 tbsp of honey

8 lbs. of chicken

Directions:

Mix water, allspice, pickling spices, cayenne pepper, black pepper, onion powder, garlic powder, celery salt, brown sugar, and kosher salt in a pot. Bring it to a boil.

Allow the brine to cool.

Now, combine this brine with liquid smoke and maple extract. Set it aside.

Rinse the chicken. Pat it dry.

Add the brine to the chicken. Set it aside for at least 4 hours or a maximum of 12 hours.

Remove the chicken pieces from the brine. Rinse them well with cold water. Pat dry.

Now, coat the chicken pieces with olive oil. Season well with cajun seasoning.

Prepare the mop after that by mixing vinegar, salt, water, and pepper and bring it to a boil. Set it aside.

Preheat the smoker to 230^0 F. Smoke the chicken for about 2 hours. Baste it with the mop at 30-minute intervals.

Now, prepare the glaze. Mix one part of honey and three parts of butter. Prepare as much as required according to how much chicken you are cooking.

When the chicken is almost ready, apply the prepared glaze all over it. Place the chicken pieces on a hot grill and complete the rest of the cooking. The skin needs to be crisp up. This process will take just a few minutes for every side.

Remove the pieces from the grill and serve immediately!

Nutrition Information:

Carbohydrate: 15.9 g

Protein: 56.7 g

Fat: 60.5 g

Chicken Brined with Lemon

Preparation Time: 10 minutes

Cooking time: 3 hours

Servings: 8

Method of Preparation: Grilling

Ingredients:

¾ cup of kosher salt

2 ½ quarts of water

¾ cup of fresh lemon juice

2 tsp of black pepper, freshly ground

2 tbsp of any hot sauce or frank's red hot

2 tsp of poultry seasoning

2 tbsp of paprika ancho spice rub

2 lbs. of chicken, backbones removed, split through breast

1 cup of hardwood chips, soaked and drained for 1 hour

Directions:

Put the lemon juice, salt, water, pepper, hot sauce and poultry seasoning in a saucepan. Bring it to a boil while continuously stirring to dissolve the salt.

Remove and set it aside to cool.

Place two chicken halves in two plastic reseal able bags of a gallon each.

Divide the brine into two parts and pour one part each in each of the bags. Seal and refrigerate the bags for about 8 hours.

After 8 hours, remove the chickens from the bags and pat them dry.

Sprinkle and massage the meat with the paprika-ancho spice rub.

Light a starter chimney with charcoal fire. Put the coals that lit to the grill. Start indirect grilling. Rearrange the coals to the sides of the grill in order to create a big space at the center.

Keep a drip pan in this space and fill it with water. Add the lit coals to the smoker firebox. Spread half of the soaked hardwoods on the coal.

Place the chickens over the pan on the grill with their skin side down.

Cover the chickens and cook them at 250^0 F for an hour or so.

Flip the chicken pieces at intervals to ensure they are crisp.

Now, turn the skin side of chickens up and allow them to cook for about 2 hours more, flipping them at intervals.

Cook until the internal temperature of the birds reaches 165^0 F.

Remove the chickens and rest them for 10 minutes.

Serve!

Nutrition:

Carbohydrate:2.8 g

Protein: 33.6 g

Fat: 9 g

BBQ-Seasoned Chicken Breast

Preparation Time: 10 minutes
Cooking time: 1 hour 30 minutes
Servings: 6
Method of Preparation: Smoking

Ingredients:

2 lbs. of chicken breasts, skinless and boneless

½ cup of chicken brine (recommended but optional)

1 cup of BBQ sauce

⅓ cup of BBQ spice rub

Directions:

Prepare the brine as instructed while dividing the ingredients into half.

Now, place the chicken in the brine bowl. Cover the bowl and refrigerate it for about 2 hours.

Preheat the smoker to 250^0 F. Remove the chicken from the brine. Pat it dry.

Apply the spice rub to the chicken breasts properly.

Place the chicken in the smoker and cook it for about 90 minutes until the internal temperature of the chicken breasts reaches 165^0 F.

Apply the BBQ sauce with a brush on the chicken breasts and smoke them for 10 more minutes.

Remove the chicken breasts from the smoker and rest them for 5 minutes.

Slice and serve!

Nutrition Information:

Carbohydrate:19 g

Protein:32 g

Fat:4 g

Spicy Chicken Thighs

Preparation Time: 10 minutes
Cooking time: 3-4 hours
Servings: 8
Method of Preparation: Smoking

Ingredients:

2 tbsp OF olive oil

6 chicken thighs with the skin on

2 tbsp of chili powder

2 tbsp of paprika

1 tbsp of thyme

2 tbsp of cayenne

1 tbsp of garlic powder

1 tbsp of pepper and salt

Directions:

Preheat the smoker to a temperature of 200 to 220 degrees.

In a bowl, add the dry seasonings and mix them well to form a rub.

Coat the chicken thighs with olive oil well.

Now, sprinkle the dry seasoning mix over the chicken and coat it completely.

Place the chicken thighs and the wood chips in the smoker at the same time.

Smoke the chicken thighs for about 2 hours while constantly rotating to ensure that they cook well.

When the internal temperature of the thighs reaches 165 degrees, it is ready to be serve!

Nutrition Information:

Carbohydrate:3.7 g

Protein:11.7 g

Fat:14 g

MEAT (BEEF, LAMB, RIBS AND PORK)

Grilled Bloody Mary Flank Steak

Preparation time: 8 hours
Cooking time: 15 minutes
Method of Preparation: Grilling
Servings: 4

Ingredients:

1½ pounds (680 g) flank steak
Marinade:
2 cup Traeger Smoked Bloody Mary Mix
½ cup vodka
½ cup vegetable oil
3 clove garlic, minced
1 whole lemon or lime, juiced
1 tablespoon Worcestershire sauce
1 teaspoon celery salt
1 teaspoon coarse ground black pepper
Hot sauce, to taste

Whisk together all the ingredients except the steak in a small bowl until combined.

Place the steak in a resealable plastic bag and pour half the marinade over it. Allow to marinate for at least 6 hours or overnight. Refrigerate the remaining half of the marinade in an airtight container.

When ready to cook, set the Traeger temperature to High and preheat.

Pour the remaining marinade into a small saucepan and let simmer over medium heat until it has reduced by half. Keep warm and set aside.

Drain the steak and discard the marinade. Pat it dry with paper towels.

Arrange the steak directly on the grill and cook each side for 7 to 10 minutes.

Transfer the steak to a cutting board and cool for 3 minutes before thinly slicing on a sharp diagonal. Serve the steak with the warmed marinade on the side.

Smoked Tomahawk Steak

Preparation time: 5 minutes
Cooking time: 1 hour
Method of Preparation: Grilling
Servings: 4

Ingredients:

1 (32 ounces / 907 g) bone-in Tomahawk rib-eye steak, 2 inch thick
Kosher salt, to taste
Meat Church Holy Cow BBQ Rub
3 tablespoons butter

Directions:

Lightly season the steak on all sides with salt. Let sit at room temperature for 1 hour.

When ready to cook, set Traeger temperature to 225ºF (107ºC) and preheat, lid closed for 15 minutes. For optimal flavor, use Super Smoke if available.

Rinse the steak and pat it dry with paper towels. Liberally season both sides of the steak with Meat Church Holy Cow BBQ Rub.

Arrange the steak directly on the grill and cook for about 45 minutes, or until it reaches an internal temperature of 120ºF (49ºC). The cooking time depends on the thickness.

Remove the steak from the grill and rest for 10 minutes lightly tented with aluminum foil.

Meanwhile, put a cast iron skillet on the grill. Increase the grill temperature to 500ºF (260ºC). Put the steak on the dry cast iron griddle and sear for 1 minute. Flip the steak and sear for 1 minute more. Doing this should bring your steak to an internal temperature of no more than 130ºF (54ºC).

Remove the steak and top with a generous amount of butter. Continue to cook for about 5 minutes, or until the internal temperature registers 130ºF (54ºC), for medium-rare.

Let the steak rest for 10 minutes before slicing and serving.

Cocoa-Rubbed Steak for Two

Preparation time: 50 minutes
Cooking time: 50 minutes
Method of Preparation: Grilling
Servings: 4

Ingredients:
2 whole rib-eye roasts, trimmed
1 cup Traeger Coffee Rub
¼ cup cocoa powder

Directions:
Cut the roast into 2½-inch-thick steaks. Reserve 2 steaks and freeze the remaining steaks for later use.

Mix the Traeger Coffee rub and cocoa powder in a bowl. Season the steaks lightly with the rub mixture. Reserve the remaining rub mixture for later use. Allow the steaks to sit at room temperature for 45 minutes.

When ready to cook, set the Traeger to 225ºF (107ºC) and preheat, lid closed for 15 minutes.

Lay the steaks on the hot grill and cook for 40 minutes, flipping the steaks halfway through, or until the desired internal temperature is reached, between 105 to 110ºF (41 to 43ºC).

Remove the steaks from the grill and allow to rest on the counter.

Increase the temperature to High and preheat, lid closed for 15 minutes. For optimal results, set to 500ºF (260ºC) if available.

Return the steaks to the grill and cook for 8 minutes, flipping the steaks halfway through the cooking time, or until it reaches a finished temperature of 130ºF (54ºC), for medium rare. Cool for 5 minutes before serving.

Smoked Rib-Eye Caps

Preparation time: 5 minutes
Cooking time: 45 minutes
Method of Preparation: Smoking
Servings: 4

Ingredients:
1½ pounds (680 g) rib-eye cap, trimmed
2 tablespoons Traeger Beef Rub
2 tablespoons Traeger Coffee Rub

Directions:
Cut the cap into 4 even portions and roll into steaks. Tie with butcher's twine to secure.

Mix both rubs in a small bowl, then lightly season the steaks with the rub mixture.

When ready to cook, set Traeger to 225ºF (107ºC) and preheat, lid closed for 15 minutes. For optimal flavor, use Super Smoke if available.

Lay the steaks directly on the grill and smoke for 30 to 45 minutes, or until the internal temperature reaches 120ºF (49ºC).

Remove the steaks from the grill and set aside to rest.

Increase the grill temperature to 450ºF (232ºC). Return the steaks to the grill and cook each side for 3 to 4 minutes, or until the internal temperature reaches 130ºF (54ºC).

Remove the steaks from the grill. Rest for 5 minutes and serve.

Spiced Tomahawk Steaks

Preparation time: 5 minutes
Cooking time: 1 hour
Method of Preparation: Smoking
Servings: 4

Ingredients:

2 tablespoons ground black pepper

2 tablespoons kosher salt

1 tablespoon paprika

½ tablespoon brown sugar

½ tablespoon onion powder

½ tablespoon garlic powder

1 teaspoon ground mustard

¼ teaspoon cayenne pepper

2 large Tomahawk steaks

Directions:

Stir together all the ingredients except the steaks in a small bowl. Liberally season the steaks with the rub mixture.

When ready to cook, set Traeger temperature to 225ºF (107ºC) and preheat, lid closed for 15 minutes. For optimal flavor, use Super Smoke if available.

Arrange the steaks directly on the grill and smoke until the internal temperature reaches 120ºF (49ºC), 45 minutes to 1 hour.

Remove the steaks from the grill and set aside to rest.

Increase the grill temperature to 450ºF (232ºC). Return the steaks to the grill and cook each side for 7 to 10 minutes, or until the internal temperature registers 130ºF (54ºC).

Remove the steaks from the grill cool for 5 minutes before serving.

Beef Tenderloin with Cherry Tomato Vinaigrette

Preparation time: 10 minutes
Cooking time: 40 minutes
Method of Preparation: Grilling
Servings: 6

Ingredients:

1 whole beef tenderloin

Extra-virgin olive oil, as needed

1 bottle Traeger Prime Rib Rub

Salt and pepper, to taste

Vinaigrette:

6 whole plum tomatoes

2 tablespoons balsamic vinegar

1 teaspoon thyme, minced

Directions:

When ready to cook, set the temperature to 450ºF (232ºC) and preheat, lid closed for 15 minutes.

Tuck the thin end of the tenderloin underneath the roast and secure it with butcher's string. Rub the tenderloin with olive oil and season both sides with Prime Rib Rub or salt and pepper. Put the tenderloin on a rack in a shallow roasting pan.

Place the pan with the tenderloin on the preheated grill and roast for 20 minutes.

Adjust the temperature to 350ºF (177ºC) and roast for an additional 20 minutes until cooked to the desired doneness, 130ºF (54ºC) for medium rare, 140ºF (60ºC) for medium or 150ºF (66ºC) for well done.

Meanwhile, make the vinaigrette by combining the tomatoes, balsamic vinegar, olive oil, and thyme in a food processor. Pulse until smoothly puréed. Season with Prime Rib Rub or salt and pepper to taste.

Remove the tenderloin from the grill and serve with the vinaigrette.

Grilled Beef Short Ribs

Preparation time: 15 minutes
Cooking time: 8 to 10 hours
Method of Preparation: Grilling
Servings: 8

Ingredients:
4 (4-bone) beef short rib racks, membrane removed
½ cup Traeger Beef Rub
1 cup apple juice

Directions:
Season the ribs with Traeger Beef Rub on both sides.

When ready to cook, set Traeger temperature to 225ºF (107ºC) and preheat, lid closed for 15 minutes.

Place the ribs, bone-side down, on the grill and cook for 8 to 10 hours, spritzing or mopping with apple juice every 60 minutes, or until the internal temperature reaches 205ºF (96ºC).

Remove the ribs from the grill and let rest for 5 minutes before slicing and serving.

Smoked Beef Brisket with Mop Sauce

Preparation time: 15 minutes
Cooking time: 12 hours
Method of Preparation: Smoking
Servings: 4

Ingredients:
1 (6 pounds) flat cut brisket, trimmed
Traeger Beef Rub, as needed
Traeger Texas Spicy BBQ Sauce, for serving
Mop Sauce:
2 cup beef broth
2 tablespoons Worcestershire sauce
¼ cup apple cider vinegar, apple cider or apple juice

Directions:
When ready to cook, set Traeger temperature to 180ºF (82ºC) and preheat, lid closed for 15 minutes.

Season the brisket with Traeger Beef Rub on both sides. Whisk all the mop sauce ingredients together in a spray bottle.

Place the brisket, fat-side down, on the grill and smoke for 3 to 4 hours, spraying the brisket with the mop sauce every hour.

Remove the brisket from the grill and increase the temperature to 225ºF (107ºC).

Place the brisket back on the grill and continue to cook for about 6 to 8 hours, spraying occasionally with the mop sauce, or until an instant-read thermometer inserted in the thickest part of the meat registers 204ºF (96ºC).

Wrap the brisket with foil and allow to rest for 30 minutes. Slice the brisket across the grain and serve alongside the BBQ Sauce.

Steak Skewers with Cherry BBQ Sauce

Preparation time: 20 minutes
Cooking time: 25 minutes
Servings: 4
Method of Preparation: Grilling

Ingredients:
2 tablespoons butter
1 medium onion, chopped
2 clove garlic, minced
2 cups fresh or frozen dark sweet cherries, pitted and coarsely chopped
1 cup ketchup
¼ cup cider vinegar

⅔ cup brown sugar

1 tablespoon Worcestershire sauce

½ teaspoon pepper

2 teaspoons ground mustard

1½ pounds (680 g) flank steak, cut into about 16 slices

Olive oil, as needed

Traeger Prime Rib Rub, to taste

Chopped scallions, for serving

Directions:

Melt the butter in a large saucepan over medium heat. Add the onion and sauté for 2 minutes until softened. Add the garlic and cook for 1 minute more.

Add the cherries, ketchup, vinegar, brown sugar, Worcestershire sauce, pepper, and mustard and stir well. Cook, uncovered, over medium-low heat for 20 minutes, stirring occasionally, or until the cherries are softened and the sauce has thickened.

Carefully stab each slice of steak through the center, lengthwise, with a Traeger skewer. Using a meat pounder, smash each steak skewer until about ½ inch thick.

Drizzle the beef skewers with olive oil and season with Prime Rib Rub on both sides.

When ready to cook, set the temperature to High and preheat, lid closed for 10 to 15 minutes.

Arrange the steak skewers on the grill and cook each side for about 1 to 2 minutes.

Remove the steak skewers from the grill and let rest for 5 to 10 minutes. Use a spoon to mash the cherries in the sauce. Brush the steak with the cherry barbecue sauce and serve sprinkled with the chopped scallions.

Seared Strip Steak with Butter

Preparation time: 15 minutes

Cooking time: 1 hour 10 minutes

Servings: 4

Method of Preparation: Smoking

Ingredients:

4 (1½ inch thick) New York strip steaks

Traeger Beef Rub, as needed

4 tablespoons butter, melted

Directions:

When ready to cook, set Traeger temperature to 225ºF (107ºC) and preheat, lid closed for 15 minutes. For optimal flavor, use Super Smoke if available.

Season the steaks with Traeger Beef Rub.

Arrange the steaks directly on the grill and smoke for 60 minutes, or until they reach an internal temperature of 105 to 110ºF (41 to 43ºC).

Remove the steaks from the grill and set aside to rest.

Increase the grill temperature to 500ºF (260ºC) and preheat, lid closed for 15 minutes.

Place the steaks back on the grill and sear for 4 minutes. Flip the steaks and spread 1 tablespoon of melted butter onto each steak. Continue to sear for 4 minutes more, or until cooked to the desired temperature, 130ºF (54ºC) to 135ºF (57ºC) for medium-rare.

Remove the steaks from the grill and cool for 5 minutes before serving.

Seared Rib-Eye Steaks

Preparation time: 5 minutes

Cooking time: 50 minutes

Servings: 2

Method of Preparation: Grilling

Ingredients:

2 (1½ inch thick) rib-eye steaks

Meat Church Gourmet Garlic and Herb Seasoning

Meat Church Holy Cow BBQ Rub

2 tablespoons butter

Directions:

When ready to cook, set Traeger temperature to 225°F (107°C) and preheat, lid closed for 15 minutes. For optimal flavor, use Super Smoke if available.

Season the steaks on both sides with the seasoning and rub.

Arrange the steaks on the grill and cook for 30 to 45 minutes, or until an instant-read thermometer inserted in the thickest part of the meat registers 120°F (49°C).

Remove the steaks from the grill and set aside to cool.

Increase the grill temperature to 500°F (260°C) and return the steaks to the grill and sear for 3 minutes.

Remove the steaks from the grill and top with the butter. Lightly tent the steaks with foil to melt the butter. Cool for 5 minutes before slicing and slicing.

Garlic-Mustard Roasted Prime Rib

Preparation time: 15 minutes

Cooking time: 4 hours

Servings: 6

Method of Preparation: Grilling

Ingredients:

1 (8 to 10 pounds / 3.6 to 4.5 kg) 4-bone prime rib roast, trimmed

4 clove garlic, mashed to a paste

3 tablespoons Dijon mustard

2 tablespoons Worcestershire sauce

2 teaspoons dried rosemary

2 teaspoons dried thyme

Coarse salt and freshly ground black pepper, to taste

Prepared horseradish, for serving (optional)

Directions:

Tie the prime rib roast between the bones with butcher's twine.

Stir together the garlic, mustard, Worcestershire sauce, rosemary, and thyme in a small bowl until well incorporated.

Slather the outside of the prime rib roast with the garlic mixture and generously season both sides with salt and black pepper. Place the prime rib roast in the refrigerator, uncovered, for up to 8 hours.

When ready to cook, set Traeger temperature to 250°F (121°C) and preheat, lid closed for 15 minutes.

Arrange the prime rib, fat-side up, on the grill and roast for 3½ to 4 hours, or until the internal temperature of the meat (the tip of the temperature probe should be in the center of the meat) registers 120°F (49°C) for rare, 130°F (54°C) for medium rare.

Transfer the prime rib to a cutting board and loosely tent with foil. Let rest for 30 minutes.

When ready, remove the twine. Using a sharp knife, remove the rack of bone following the curvature of the meat. Carve the meat across the grain into ½-inch-thick slices. Serve the meat alongside the horseradish, if desired.

Grilled Lamb and Apricot Kabobs

Preparation time: 15 minutes
Cooking time: 8 to 10 minutes
Servings: 4
Method of Preparation: Grilling

Ingredients:

½ cup olive oil
½ cup lemon juice
2 tablespoons minced fresh mint
1 tablespoon lemon zest
½ tablespoon finely chopped cilantro
½ tablespoon salt
2 teaspoons black pepper
1 teaspoon cumin
3 pounds (1.4 kg) boneless leg of lamb, cut into 2-inch cubes
15 whole dried apricots
2 whole red onions, cut into ⅛-inch thick

Directions:

In a medium bowl, stir together the olive oil, lemon juice, mint, lemon zest, cilantro, salt, pepper and cumin. Add the lamb shoulder to the bowl and toss to coat. Set in the refrigerator and marinate overnight.

Remove the lamb from the marinade and thread lamb, apricots, and red onion alternatively until the skewer is full.

When ready to cook, set Traeger temperature to 400ºF (204ºC) and preheat, lid closed for 15 minutes.

Lay the skewers on the grill grate and cook for 8 to 10 minutes, or until the onions are lightly browned and the lamb is cooked to the desired temperature.

Remove the skewers from the grill and serve immediately.

Spicy Braised Lamb Shoulder

Preparation time: 10 minutes
Cooking time: 5 hours 2 minutes
Servings: 4
Method of Preparation: Grilling

Ingredients:

2 ounces (57 g) guajillo peppers, deseeded
2 tablespoons plus ½ cup water, divided
3 cloves garlic
2 tablespoons olive oil
1 tablespoon lime juice
1 tablespoon smoked paprika
1 tablespoon fresh oregano
1 tablespoon salt
¼ tablespoon ground coriander seeds
¼ tablespoon ground cumin seeds
¼ tablespoon ground pumpkin seeds
3 pounds (1.4 kg) lamb shoulders

Directions:

In a microwave-safe bowl, cover the guajillo chilies with water and microwave on high for 2 minutes. Let cool slightly, then transfer the soft chilies and 2 tablespoons of the water to a blender. Add the remaining ingredients, except for the lamb shoulders, to the blender. Pulse until smooth.

Arrange the lamb in a roast pan and rub ½ cup of the sauce all over the meat. Let marinate at room temperature for at least 2 hours and up to 12 hours.

When ready to cook, set Traeger temperature to 325ºF (163ºC) and preheat, lid closed for 15 minutes.

Add ½ cup of the water to the roast pan and cover the pan loosely with foil. Cook the lamb for 2½ hours, adding water to the pan a few times.

Remove the foil and cook for another 2½ hours, or until the lamb is browned and tender, occasionally spooning the juices on top.

Remove from the grill and let cool for 20 minutes before shredding. Spoon the remaining liquid in the bottom of the pan over the lamb.

Serve immediately.

Grilled Lamb Leg

Preparation time: 10 minutes
Cooking time: 30 to 40 minutes
Servings: 8
Method of Preparation: Grilling

Ingredients:

5 pounds (2.3 kg) leg of lamb, butterflied and boneless
1 whole onion, sliced into rings
Marinade:
1 whole lemon, juiced and rinds reserved
4 cloves garlic, minced
1 cup olive oil
¼ cup red wine vinegar
2½ teaspoons minced rosemary
1 teaspoon thyme
1 teaspoon salt
1 teaspoon ground black pepper

Directions:

In a mixing bowl, whisk together all the ingredients for the marinade.

Remove any netting from the lamb and place into a large resealable plastic bag. Pour the marinade into the bag and add the onion. Massage the bag to distribute the marinade and herbs. Refrigerate for several hours or overnight.

Remove the lamb from the marinade and pat dry with paper towels. Discard the marinade.

When ready to cook, set the Traeger to High and preheat, lid closed for 15 minutes.

Arrange the lamb on the grill grate, fat-side down. Grill for 30 to 40 minutes per side, or until the internal temperature reaches 135ºF (57ºC) for medium-rare.

Let the lamb leg cool for 5 minutes before slicing. Serve warm.

Roasted Breaded Rack of Lamb

Preparation time: 10 minutes
Cooking time: 20 minutes
Servings: 4
Method of Preparation: Grilling

Ingredients:

1 rack of lamb, frenched (about 1½ pounds / 680 g)
½ cup yellow mustard
1 tablespoon salt
1 teaspoon ground black pepper
1 cup panko breadcrumbs
1 tablespoon minced Italian parsley
1 teaspoon minced rosemary
1 teaspoon minced sage

Directions:

Rub the rack of lamb with the mustard and season with salt and pepper.

In a shallow baking dish, combine the remaining ingredients. Dredge the lamb in the bread crumb mixture.

When ready to cook, set Traeger temperature to 500ºF (260ºC) and preheat, lid closed for 15 minutes.

Place the rack of lamb on the grill grate, bone-side down, and cook for 20 minutes, or until the internal temperature reaches 120ºF (49ºC).

Remove from the grill and let rest for 5 to 10 minutes before slicing. Serve warm.

Garlicky Grilled Rack of Lamb

Preparation time: 5 minutes
Cooking time: 30 minutes
Servings: 4
Method of Preparation: Grilling

Ingredients:
8 cloves garlic
1 bunch fresh thyme
1 tablespoon kosher salt
2 teaspoons extra-virgin olive oil
1 teaspoon sherry vinegar
2 pounds (907 g) rack of lamb

Directions:
In a blender, combine all the ingredients, except for the rack of lamb. Pulse until smooth. Rub the paste all over the rack of lamb.

When ready to cook, set Traeger temperature to 450ºF (232ºC) and preheat, lid closed for 15 minutes.

Lay the rack of lamb, fat-side down, on the grill and cook for 20 minutes. Turn over so the fat side is up and cook for an additional 10 minutes. A thermometer inserted in the center of the lamb should register 160ºF (71ºC).

Let cool for 10 minutes before slicing into chops. Serve warm.

Grilled Stuffed Turkey Breast

Preparation time: 10 minutes
Cooking time: 52 minutes
Servings: 6
Method of Preparation: Grilling

Ingredients:
5 pounds (2.3 kg) turkey breasts, cooked
5 slices bacon, cut into small pieces
¾ cup fresh mushrooms
1 bunch scallion, chopped
⅛ cup white wine
3 tablespoons panko breadcrumbs
Salt, to taste
Black pepper, to taste

Directions:
When ready to cook, set Traeger temperature to 375ºF (191ºC) and preheat, lid closed for 15 minutes.

Slice the turkey breast horizontally, making sure not to slice all the way through. Lay the breast open flat.

In a skillet over medium heat, cook the bacon for 5 minutes, or until crispy. Remove the bacon and set aside. Sauté the mushrooms in the bacon grease for 5 minutes, or until browned. Add the scallions and cook for an additional 2 minutes. Pour in the wine and cook down until no wine remains. Stir in the breadcrumbs and bacon and season with salt and pepper.

Set the filling in the refrigerator to cool for 15 to 20 minutes.

Once chilled, spread the filling over the turkey breast, pressing lightly to make sure it adheres. Roll the turkey breast tightly and tie with cooking twine at about 1-inch intervals. Tuck the ends of the turkey breast under and tie with twine lengthwise.

Season the outside of the turkey breast with salt and pepper. Place on the grill and cook for 40 minutes, or until an instant-read thermometer inserted in the thickest part of the meat registers 165ºF (74ºC).

Remove the turkey from the grill and let cool for 10 minutes before slicing. Serve warm.

BBQ St. Louis-Style Ribs

Preparation time: 5 minutes
Cooking time: 6 hours 10 minutes
Servings: 4
Method of Preparation: Grilling

Ingredients:

2 racks of St. Louis-style ribs
¼ cup Traeger Pork & Poultry Rub
1 cup apple juice
1 bottle Traeger Sweet & Heat BBQ Sauce

Directions:

Trim the ribs and peel off the membrane from the back of the ribs. Brush the Traeger Pork & Poultry Rub all over the ribs. Let marinate for 20 minutes and up to 4 hours if refrigerated.

When ready to cook, set Traeger temperature to 225ºF (107ºC) and preheat, lid closed for 15 minutes.

Place the ribs, bone-side down, on the grill grate. Pour the apple juice in a spray bottle and spritz the ribs evenly. Smoke for 3 hours.

Remove the ribs from the grill and wrap in aluminum foil. Leave an opening at one end, pour in the remaining apple juice into the foil and wrap tightly.

Place the ribs back on the grill, meat-side down. Smoke for an additional 3 hours.

After 1 hour, start checking the internal temperature of the ribs. The ribs are done when the internal temperature reaches 203ºF (95ºC).

When done, remove from the foil and brush the Traeger Sweet & Heat BBQ Sauce all over the ribs.

Return to the grill and cook for an additional 10 minutes to set the sauce.

After sauce has set, take the ribs off the grill and let rest for 10 minutes.

Slice the ribs in between the bones and serve warm.

Balsamic Smoked Pork Chops

Preparation time: 10 minutes
Cooking time: 65 to 70 minutes
Servings: 4
Method of Preparation: Grilling

Ingredients:

4 (8-ounce / 227-g) bone-in pork rib chops
Traeger Pork & Poultry Rub, as needed
Olive oil, as needed
Glaze:
½ cup balsamic vinegar
¼ cup brown sugar
2 sprigs rosemary, finely chopped
Ginger ale beer, as needed

Directions:

When ready to cook, set Traeger temperature to 180ºF (82ºC) and preheat, lid closed for 15 minutes.

Brush the pork chops all over with the Traeger Pork & Poultry Rub, gently pressing the seasoning into the meat.

Place the pork chops on the grill grate and smoke for 30 minutes.

Meanwhile, make the glaze: Place all the ingredients in a saucepan over medium-low heat. Cook for about 15 to 20 minutes, or until it thickens to the point that it can coat the back of a spoon but still be pourable. Keep the glaze warm while the pork chops finish smoking.

Remove the pork chops and set the Traeger to High and preheat, lid closed for 10 to 15 minutes. Lightly drizzle the chops with olive oil and return to the grill grate.

Cook the chops for 20 minutes, or until an instant-read thermometer inserted in the thickest part of the meat registers at least 145ºF (63ºC). Let the pork chops cool for 10 minutes and baste with the glaze.

Remove from the grill and let rest for 10 minutes before cutting. Serve warm.

Juicy BBQ Ribs

Preparation time: 10 minutes
Cooking time: 2 hours 20 minutes
Servings: 6
Method of Preparation: Grilling

Ingredients:

4 rack baby back ribs
½ cup white grape juice
½ cup apple juice
Honey, as needed
Traeger BBQ Sauce, as needed
Rub:
⅔ cup brown sugar
½ cup paprika
⅓ cup garlic powder
2 tablespoons chili powder
2 tablespoons onion powder
1 tablespoon freshly ground white pepper
1 tablespoon cayenne pepper
1 tablespoon ground black pepper
1½ teaspoons ground cumin
1½ teaspoons dried oregano

Directions:

In a bowl, stir together all the ingredients for the rub. Season the ribs with the rub on both sides.

When ready to cook, set Traeger temperature to 275ºF (135ºC) and preheat, lid closed for 15 minutes.

Place the seasoned ribs on the grill and cook for 45 minutes.

Meanwhile, combine the grape and apple juices in a small bowl and set aside.

Remove the ribs from the grill and place them, bone-side down, on a large disposable foil pan. Pour the juice mixture over the ribs.

Drizzle with the honey. Wrap up the ribs completely with the foil and seal the edges. Return the ribs to the grill and cook for 1 hour. Remove the ribs from the foil and place directly on the grill grate. Set the temperature to 350ºF (177ºC) and cook for 30 additional minutes.

Rub the ribs with the Traeger BBQ Sauce and cook for an additional 5 minutes to set the sauce. Transfer the ribs to a cutting board. Slice into single serving-size pieces and serve.

Traeger Smoked Queso

Preparation time: 10 minutes
Cooking time: 1 hour
Servings: 8
Method of Preparation: Smoking

Ingredients:

1 pound (454 g) hot pork sausage
1 pound (454 g) smoked Gouda cheese
1 (2-pound / 907-g) block Velveeta cheese
1 (10-ounce / 284-g) can RO*TEL Fire Roasted Diced Tomatoes & Green Chilies
1 (10-ounce / 284-g) can RO*TEL Original Diced Tomatoes & Green Chilies
1 (10-ounce / 284-g) can cream of mushroom soup
4 tablespoons Traeger Coffee Rub
½ cup chopped cilantro

Directions:

In a skillet over medium heat, cook the pork sausage for 15 minutes, breaking into small chunks. Remove the sausage from the skillet. Drain the sausage and discard the grease.

When ready to cook, set Traeger temperature to 350ºF (177ºC) and preheat, lid closed for 15 minutes.

Cut the smoked Gouda into 1-inch cubes and cut the block of Velveeta into 5 to 6 large pieces.

Place the cheeses in an oven safe dish. Add the canned tomatoes and chilies with the liquid. Pour in the cream of mushroom soup. Add the cooked sausage and Traeger Coffee Rub.

Place the dish on the grill and smoke the queso for 45 minutes, stirring 3 to 4 times.

After 40 minutes, add most of the cilantro to the dish and continue smoking for 5 minutes.

Top with the remaining cilantro and serve hot.

BBQ Honey Pork Belly

Preparation time: 5 minutes
Cooking time: 4 hours
Servings: 8
Method of Preparation: Grilling

Ingredients:
1 skinless pork belly, cut into 1-inch cubes (about 5 to 7 pounds / 2.3 to 3.2 kg)
Meat Church Honey Hog, as needed
1 cup apple juice, for spritzing
1½ cups Traeger Apricot BBQ Sauce
½ cup clover honey

Directions:
When ready to cook, set Traeger temperature to 275ºF (135ºC) and preheat, lid closed for 15 minutes.

In a large bowl, toss together the pork belly cubes and Meat Church Honey Hog until well coated. Let sit for at least 15 minutes.

Place the pork belly cubes, fat-side down, on the grill. Cook for 3 hours, spritzing with apple juice every 45 minutes or whenever it starts to look dry.

Remove the pork when the internal temperature of the meat reaches 195ºF (91ºC) on a meat thermometer.

Transfer the cubes to a half-size aluminum pan. Season with more Meat Church Honey Hog.

Cover the cubes with the Traeger Apricot BBQ Sauce. Drizzle clover honey over the top. Toss the cubes thoroughly until completely coated.

Place the pan back to the grill and cook uncovered for 1 more hour, or until all liquid has reduced and caramelized.

Let cool for 15 minutes before serving. Serve warm.

Spicy Smoked StLouis Ribs

Preparation time: 10 minutes
Cooking time: 4 hours
Servings: 4
Method of Preparation: Smoking

Ingredients:
2 rack St. Louis-style ribs
2 cups apple juice
Rub:
¼ cup brown sugar
1 tablespoon onion powder
1 tablespoon cumin
1 tablespoon smoked paprika
1 tablespoon garlic salt
½ tablespoon red pepper flakes
1 teaspoon ground coriander

Directions:
When ready to cook, set Traeger temperature to 250ºF (121ºC) and preheat, lid closed for 15 minutes.

In a small bowl, whisk together all the ingredients for the rub. Season the ribs generously on all sides with the rub.

Place the seasoned ribs on the grill and smoke for 2 hours.

Remove from the grill and wrap the ribs in a double layer of foil. Pour the apple juice over the ribs into the foil pack. Place the ribs back to the grill and cook for 2 more hours.

Remove the ribs from grill and let rest for 10 minutes. Serve warm.

Chile Verde Braised Pork Shoulder

Preparation time: 20 minutes
Cooking time: 2 hours
Servings: 6
Method of Preparation: Grilling

Ingredients:

1 pork shoulder, bone removed and cut into 1½-inch cubes (about 2 to 3 pounds / 0.9 to 1.4 kg)
1 tablespoon all-purpose flour
Salt, to taste
Black pepper, to taste
1-pound (454 g) tomatillos, husked and washed
1 medium yellow onion, peeled and cut into 1-inch chunks
2 jalapeños
4 cloves garlic
4 tablespoons olive oil, divided
2 cans green chiles
2 cups chicken stock
1 tablespoon cumin
1 tablespoon dried oregano
¼ cup chopped cilantro
½ lime, juiced

Directions:

In a medium bowl, toss the pork shoulder with the flour, salt and pepper until well coated.

When ready to cook, set Traeger temperature to 500ºF (260ºC) and preheat, lid closed for 15 minutes.

Place a large cast iron skillet directly on the bottom rack of the grill and let preheat for 20 minutes.

Place the tomatillos, onion, jalapeños and garlic on a parchment-lined sheet tray. Drizzle with 2 tablespoons of the olive oil and season with salt and pepper. Stir to coat.

Pour the remaining 2 tablespoons of the olive oil in the cast iron skillet and add the pork shoulder. Spread the meat out evenly.

Place the sheet tray on the top rack. Close the lid and cook for 20 minutes, undisturbed. The pork should be evenly browned on the bottom and the veggies should be tender and lightly browned.

Remove the vegetables from the grill and transfer to a blender. Pulse until smooth. Pour the puréed vegetables into the skillet with the pork along with the green chiles, chicken stock, cumin and oregano.

Close the lid and reduce the temperature to 325ºF (163ºC). Cook for 60 to 90 minutes, or until the liquid has reduced and the pork is fork tender.

Remove from the grill. Top with the chopped cilantro and drizzle with the lime juice. Serve immediately.

Traeger Grilled Pork Chops

Preparation time: 5 minutes
Cooking time: 30 minutes
Servings: 2
Method of Preparation: Grilling

Ingredients:

2 (1½-inch thick) pork chops
¼ cup red wine

¼ cup olive oil

3 tablespoons chopped fresh rosemary

Traeger Blackened Saskatchewan Rub, as needed

Salt, to taste

Directions:

In a large bowl, stir together all the ingredients, except for the pork chops. Add the pork chops to the bowl and let marinate in the refrigerator for 2 hours.

When ready to cook, set Traeger temperature to 500ºF (260ºC) and preheat, lid closed for 15 minutes.

Place the marinated chops directly on the grill grate and cook for 30 minutes, or until an instant-read thermometer inserted in the thickest part of the meat registers 140ºF (60ºC).

Remove from the grill and let cool for 5 minutes before serving.

Butter-Sugar Glazed BBQ Pork Ribs

Preparation time: 5 minutes

Cooking time: 4 hours 50 minutes

Servings: 6

Method of Preparation: Grilling

Ingredients:

2 rack St. Louis-style ribs, membrane removed

1 cup Traeger Pork & Poultry Rub

4 tablespoons agave, divided

4 tablespoons butter, divided

2 tablespoons brown sugar, divided

1 bottle Traeger Sweet & Heat BBQ Sauce

Directions:

When ready to cook, set Traeger temperature to 225ºF (107ºC) and preheat, lid closed for 15 minutes.

Brush the ribs all over with the Traeger Pork & Poultry Rub. Let marinate for 15 to 20 minutes. Place the ribs, bone-side down, on the grill and cook for 3 hours.

Meanwhile, prepare the brown sugar wrap. Spread 2 tablespoons of the agave, 2 tablespoons of the butter and 1 tablespoon of the brown sugar on top of a double layer of aluminum foil. Repeat for the second foil.

After 3 hours, place one rack of ribs, meat-side down, in the prepared foil and wrap. Repeat with the second rack.

Increase the temperature of the grill to 250ºF (121ºC) and place the wrapped ribs, meat-side down, on the grill. Cook for another 1½ hours, or until an instant-read thermometer inserted in the meat registers 205ºF (96ºC).

Remove the ribs from the grill and discard the foil. Return the unwrapped ribs to the grill and cook for 10 more minutes.

Remove from the grill and rub with the Traeger Sweet & Heat BBQ Sauce. Return the ribs to the grill and cook for another 10 minutes.

Let cool for 10 minutes before slicing. Serve warm.

Traeger Braised BBQ Ribs

Preparation time: 5 minutes

Cooking time: 5 hours 10 minutes

Method of Preparation: Grilling

Ingredients:

2 rack St. Louis-style ribs, patted dry and membrane removed

¼ cup Traeger Big Game Rub

1 cup apple juice

Traeger BBQ Sauce, as needed

Directions:

Brush the ribs all over with the Traeger Big Game Rub. Let marinate for 20 minutes and up to 4 hours if refrigerated.

When ready to cook, set Traeger temperature to 225ºF (107ºC) and preheat, lid closed for 15 minutes.

Arrange the ribs, bone-side down, on the grill and cook for 5 hours.

After 1 hour, put the apple juice in a spray bottle and spritz the ribs. Spritz every 45 minutes thereafter.

After 4½ hours, check the internal temperature of ribs. The ribs are done when the internal temperature reaches 200ºF (93ºC). If not, check back in another 30 minutes.

When done, brush the ribs all over with the Traeger BBQ Sauce. Cook for 10 more minutes to set the sauce.

Remove the ribs from the grill and let rest for 10 minutes. Slice the ribs in between the bones and serve warm.

Apricot BBQ Smoked Pork Tenderloin

Preparation time: 5 minutes
Cooking time: 48 minutes
Servings: 4
Method of Preparation: Smoking

Ingredients:
2 pounds (907 g) pork tenderloin, trimmed
3 ounces (85 g) Traeger Big Game Rub
1 cup Traeger Apricot BBQ Sauce

Directions:
Brush the pork tenderloin all over with the Traeger Big Game Rub and let marinate for 30 minutes.

When ready to cook, set Traeger temperature to 180ºF (82ºC) and preheat, lid closed for 15 minutes.

Arrange the pork tenderloin on the grill grate and smoke for 45 minutes.

Remove the pork from the grill. Set Traeger temperature to High and preheat, lid closed for 15 minutes.

Place the pork back to the grill grate and grill each side of the pork tenderloin for 90 seconds, or until an instant-read thermometer inserted in the thickest part of the meat registers 145ºF (63ºC).

Brush the pork with the Traeger Apricot BBQ Sauce. Transfer to a plate and let cool for 20 minutes before serving.

Brown Sugar Baked Pork Belly

Preparation time: 5 minutes
Cooking time: 2o to 30 minutes
Servings: 2
Method of Preparation: Grilling

Ingredients:
½ cup brown sugar
1 tablespoon ground fennel
2 teaspoons kosher salt
1 teaspoon ground black pepper
1-pound (454 g) pork belly, diced

Directions:
Fold a piece of aluminum foil in half and crimp the edges so there is a rim. Using a fork, poke holes in the bottom of the foil.

When ready to cook, set Traeger temperature to 350ºF (177ºC) and preheat, lid closed for 15 minutes.

In a large bowl, stir together all the ingredients, except for the pork belly.

Add the diced pork belly to the bowl and toss until well coated. Transfer the pork pieces to the foil.

Place the foil on the grill and bake for 20 to 30 minutes, or until the pork belly is crispy, glazed and bubbly.

Let rest for 5 minutes before serving.

Fajita Favorite Pork Shoulder

Preparation time: 15 mins
Cooking time: 10 hours
Servings: 20
Method of Preparation: Grilling

Ingredients:
For Brine:
4 C. hot water
1 C. kosher salt
¼ C. brown sugar
2 tbsp. black peppercorn
12 C. cold water
8 C. apple cider
¼ C. apple cider vinegar
¼ C. Worcestershire sauce
For Pork:
8½ pounds pork shoulder roast, trimmed
¼-½ C. pork rub

Directions:
For brine: in a large container, add the hot water, salt, brown sugar and peppercorn and stir until completely dissolved.

Add the cold water, apple cider, vinegar and Worcestershire sauce and mix until well combined.

With a sharp knife, score the pork on both sides and place in the brine.

Cover the container and refrigerate for 24 hours. Remove the pork from container and discard the brine.

Rinse the pork shoulder under running cold water thoroughly.

With paper towels, pat dry the pork shoulder completely.

Rub the pork shoulder with pork rub generously. Place the pork shoulder onto a baking sheet and refrigerate for 2 hours or up to overnight.

Set the temperature of Traeger Grill to 150-160 degrees F and preheat with closed lid for 15 mins.

Place the pork shoulder onto the grill and cook for about 4 hours.

Now, set the temperature of Traeger Grill to 250 degrees F and cook for about 4-6 hours.

Remove the pork shoulder from grill and place onto a baking sheet for about 40-60 mins.

With two forks, shred the meat and serve.

Nutrition:
Calories: 626
Carbohydrates: 15g
Protein: 45g
Fat: 41.4g
Sugar: 13.5g
Sodium: 5890mg
Fiber: 0.3g

Simplest Pork Belly

Preparation time: 10 mins
Cooking time: 8 hours
Servings: 12
Method of Preparation: Grilling

Ingredients:
1 (5-lb.) pork belly, skin removed
Kosher salt and coarsely ground black pepper, to taste

Directions:
Set the temperature of Traeger Grill to 225 degrees F and preheat with closed lid for 15 mins, using charcoal.

Rub the pork belly with salt and black pepper generously.

Arrange the pork belly onto the grill and cook for about 6-8 hours,

Remove the pork belly from grill and place onto a cutting board for about 10-15 mins before slicing.

With a sharp knife, cut the pork belly into desired-sized slices and serve.

Nutrition:

Calories: 534

Carbohydrates: 0g

Protein: 28.9g

Fat: 46.7g

Sugar: 0g

Sodium: 790mg

Fiber: 0g

Beautiful Christmas Ham

Preparation time: 15 mins

Cooking time: 1 hour 20 mins

Servings: 16

Method of Preparation: Grilling

Ingredients:

1 C. honey

¼ C. dark corn syrup

1 (7-lb.) ready-to-eat ham

¼ C. whole cloves

½ C. butter, softened

Directions:

Set the temperature of Traeger Grill to 325 degrees F and preheat with closed lid for 15 mins, using charcoal.

In a small pan, add honey and corn syrup and cook until heated slightly, stirring continuously.

Remove the pan of glaze from heat and set aside.

With a sharp knife, score the ham in a cross pattern.

Insert whole cloves at the crossings.

Coat the ham with butter evenly.

Arrange ham in foil-lined roasting pan and top with ¾ of glaze evenly.

Place the pan onto the grill and cook for about 1¼ hours, coating with remain glaze after every 10-15 mins.

Remove the ham from grill and place onto a cutting board for about 20-25 mins before serving.

With a sharp knife, cut the ham into desired-sized slices and serve.

Nutrition:

Calories: 457

Carbohydrates: 29.7g

Protein: 33.2g

Fat: 23.1g

Sugar: 18.7g

Sodium: 2633mg

Fiber: 3.2g

Backyard Cookout Sausages

Preparation time: 15 mins

Cooking time: 23 mins

Servings: 6

Method of Preparation: Grilling

Ingredients:

½ C. apricot jam

1 tbsp. Dijon mustard

12 breakfast sausage links

Directions:

Set the temperature of Traeger Grill to 350 degrees F and preheat with closed lid for 15 mins.

In a small pan, add jam and mustard over medium-low heat and cook until warmed.

Reduce the heat to low to keep the glaze warm.

Arrange the sausage links onto grill and cook for about 10-15 mins, flipping twice.

Coat the sausage links with jam glaze evenly and cook for about 2-3 mins.

Remove the sausage links from grill and serve alongside the remaining glaze.

Nutrition:

Calories: 575

Carbohydrates: 17.3g

Protein: 29.5g

Fat: 42.7g

Sugar: 11.6g

Sodium: 1164mg

Fiber: 0.2g

Elegant Lamb Chops

Preparation time: 15 mins

Cooking time: 30 mins

Servings: 4

Method of Preparation: Grilling

Ingredients:

4 lamb shoulder chops

4 C. buttermilk

1 C. cold water

¼ C. kosher salt

2 tbsp. olive oil

1 tbsp. Texas-style rub

Directions:

In a large bowl, add buttermilk, water and salt and stir until salt is dissolved.

Add chops and coat with mixture evenly.

Refrigerate for at least 4 hours.

Remove the chops from bowl and rinse under cold running water.

Coat the chops with olive oil and then sprinkle with rub evenly.

Set the temperature of Traeger Grill to 240 degrees F and preheat with closed lid for 15 mins, using charcoal.

Arrange the chops onto grill and cook for about 25-30 mins or until desired doneness.

Meanwhile, preheat the broiler of oven. Grease a broiler pan.

Remove the chops from grill and place onto the prepared broiler pan.

Transfer the broiler pan into the oven and broil for about 3-5 mins or until browned.

Remove the chops from oven and serve hot.

Nutrition:

Calories: 414

Carbohydrates: 11.7g

Protein: 5.6g

Fat: 22.7g

Sugar: 11.7g

Sodium: 7000mg

Fiber: 0g

Easy-to-Prepare Lamb Chops

Preparation time: 10 mins

Cooking time: 12 mins

Servings: 6

Method of Preparation: Grilling

Ingredients:

6 (6-oz.) lamb chops

3 tbsp. olive oil

Salt and freshly ground black pepper, to taste

Directions:

Set the temperature of Traeger Grill to 450 degrees F and preheat with closed lid for 15 mins.

Coat the lamb chops with oil and then, season with salt and black pepper evenly.

Arrange the chops onto the grill and cook for about 4-6 mins per side.

Remove the chops from grill and serve hot.

Nutrition:

Calories: 376

Carbohydrates: 0g

Protein: 47.8g

Fat: 19.5g

Sugar: 0g

Sodium: 156mg

Fiber: 0g

Foolproof Lamb Chops

Preparation time: 15 mins

Cooking time: 17 mins

Servings: 4

Method of Preparation: Grilling

Ingredients:

½ C. extra-virgin olive oil, divided

¼ C. onion, chopped roughly

2 garlic cloves, chopped roughly

2 tbsp. balsamic vinegar

2 tbsp. soy sauce

1 tsp. Worcestershire sauce

1 tbsp. fresh rosemary, chopped

2 tsp. Dijon mustard

Freshly ground black pepper, to taste

4 (5-oz.) lamb chops

Salt, to taste

Directions:

In a small pan, heat 1 tbsp. of olive oil over medium heat and sauté the onion and garlic for about 4-5 mins.

Remove from the heat and transfer into a blender.

In the blender, add the vinegar, soy sauce, Worcestershire sauce, rosemary, mustard and black pepper and pulse until well combined.

While the motor is running, slowly add the remaining oil and pulse until smooth.

Transfer the sauce into a bowl and set aside.

Set the temperature of Traeger Grill to 500 degrees F and preheat with closed lid for 15 mins.

Coat the lamb chops with remaining oil and then, season with salt and black pepper evenly.

Arrange the chops onto the grill and cook for about 4-6 mins per side.

Remove the chops from grill and serve hot alongside the sauce.

Nutrition:

Calories: 496

Carbohydrates: 2.8g

Protein: 40.6g

Fat: 35.8g

Sugar: 0.8g

Sodium: 641mg

Fiber: 0.7g

Deliciously Spicy Rack of Lamb

Preparation time: 15 mins

Cooking time: 3 hours

Servings: 6

Method of Preparation: Grilling

Ingredients:

2 tbsp. paprika

½ tbsp. coriander seeds

1 tsp. cumin seeds

1 tsp. ground allspice

1 tsp. lemon peel powder

Salt and freshly ground black pepper, to taste

2 (1½-lb.) rack of lamb ribs, trimmed

Directions:

Set the temperature of Traeger Grill to 225 degrees F and preheat with closed lid for 15 mins.

In a coffee grinder, add all the ingredients except rib racks and grind into a powder.

Coat the rib racks with spice mixture generously.

Arrange the rib racks onto the grill and cook for about 3 hours.

Remove the rib racks from grill and place onto a cutting board for about 10-15 mins before slicing.

With a sharp knife, cut the rib racks into equal-sized individual ribs and serve.

Aromatic Herbed Rack of Lamb

Preparation time: 15 mins
Cooking time: 2 hours
Servings: 3
Method of Preparation: Grilling

Ingredients:
2 tbsp. fresh sage
2 tbsp. fresh rosemary
2 tbsp. fresh thyme
2 garlic cloves, peeled
1 tbsp. honey
Salt and freshly ground black pepper, to taste
¼ C. olive oil
1 (1½-lb.) rack of lamb, trimmed

Directions:
In a food processor, add all the ingredients except for oil and rack of lamb rack and pulse until well combined.
While motor is running, slowly add oil and pulse until a smooth paste is formed.
Coat the rib rack with paste generously and refrigerate for about 2 hours.
Set the temperature of Traeger Grill to 225 degrees F and preheat with closed lid for 15 mins.
Arrange the rack of lamb onto the grill and cook for about 2 hours.
Remove the rack of lamb from grill and place onto a cutting board for about 10-15 mins before slicing.

With a sharp knife, cut the rack into individual ribs and serve.

Holiday Dinner Leg of Lamb

Preparation time: 15 mins
Cooking time: 5 hours
Servings: 8
Method of Preparation: Grilling

Ingredients:
½ C. olive oil
½ C. red wine vinegar
½ C. dry white wine
1 tbsp. garlic, minced
1 tsp. dried marjoram, crushed
1 tsp. dried rosemary, crushed
Salt and freshly ground black pepper, to taste
1 (5-lb.) leg of lamb

Directions:
In a bowl, add all the ingredients except for leg of lamb and mix until well combined.
In a large resealable bag, add marinade and leg of lamb.
Seal the bag and shake to coat completely.
Refrigerate for about 4-6 hours, flipping occasionally.
Set the temperature of Traeger Grill to 225 degrees F and preheat with closed lid for 15 mins.
Place the leg of lamb onto the grill and cook for about 4-5 hours.

Remove the leg of lamb from grill and place onto a cutting board for about 20 mins before slicing.

With a sharp knife, cut the leg of lamb into desired-sized slices and serve.

Nutrition:

Calories: 653

Carbohydrates: 1g

Protein: 79.7g

Fat: 33.4g

Sugar: 0.2g

Sodium: 237mg

Fiber: 0.1g

Fancy Gathering's Lamb Shoulder

Preparation time: 15 mins
Cooking time: 2½ hours
Servings: 8
Method of Preparation: Grilling

Ingredients:

1 (5-lb.) bone-in lamb shoulder, trimmed

2 tbsp. olive oil

1 tbsp. fresh lemon juice

1 tbsp. fresh ginger, peeled

4-6 garlic cloves, peeled

½ tbsp. ground cumin

½ tbsp. paprika

½ tbsp. ground turmeric

½ tbsp. ground allspice

Salt and freshly ground black pepper, to taste

Directions:

With a sharp knife, score the skin of the lamb shoulder into a diamond pattern.

In a food processor, add the remaining ingredients and pulse until smooth.

Coat the lamb shoulder with pureed mixture generously.

Arrange the lamb shoulder into a large baking dish and refrigerate, covered overnight.

Remove the baking dish of shoulder from refrigerator and set aside at room temperature for at least 1 hour before cooking.

Set the temperature of Traeger Grill to 225 degrees F and preheat with closed lid for 15 mins. Place the lamb shoulder onto the grill and cook for about 2½ hours.

Remove the lamb shoulder from grill and place onto a cutting board for about 20 mins before slicing.

With a sharp knife, cut the lamb shoulder into desired-sized slices and serve.

Nutrition:

Calories: 41

Carbohydrates: 2g

Protein: 58.1g

Fat: 18.8g

Sugar: 0.1g

Sodium: 222mg

Fiber: 0.5g

Spicy & Tangy Lamb Shoulder

Preparation time: 15 mins
Cooking time: 5¾ hours
Servings: 6
Method of Preparation: Grilling

Ingredients:

1 (5-lb.) bone-in lamb shoulder, trimmed

3-4 tbsp. Moroccan seasoning

2 tbsp. olive oil

1 C. water

¼ C. apple cider vinegar

Directions:

Set the temperature of Traeger Grill to 275 degrees F and preheat with closed lid for 15 mins, using charcoal.

Coat the lamb shoulder with oil evenly and then rub with Moroccan seasoning generously.

Place the lamb shoulder onto the grill and cook for about 45 mins.

In a food-safe spray bottle, mix together vinegar and water.

Spray the lamb shoulder with vinegar mixture evenly.

Cook for about 4-5 hours, spraying with vinegar mixture after every 20 mins.

Remove the lamb shoulder from grill and place onto a cutting board for about 20 mins before slicing.

With a sharp knife, cut the lamb shoulder in desired sized slices and serve.

Nutrition:

Calories: 563

Carbohydrates: 3.1g

Protein: 77.4g

Fat: 25.2g

Sugar: 1.4g

Sodium: 1192mg

Fiber: 0g

Wine Braised Lamb Shank

Preparation time: 15 mins

Cooking time: 10 hours

Servings: 2

Method of Preparation: Grilling

Ingredients:

2 (1¼-lb.) lamb shanks

1-2 C. water

¼ C. brown sugar

1/3 C. rice wine

1/3 C. soy sauce

1 tbsp. dark sesame oil

4 (1½x½-inch) orange zest strips

2 (3-inch long) cinnamon sticks

1½ tsp. Chinese five-spice powder

Directions:

Set the temperature of Traeger Grill to 225-250 degrees F and preheat with closed lid for 15 mins. , using charcoal and soaked apple wood chips.

With a sharp knife, pierce each lamb shank at many places.

In a bowl, add remaining all ingredients and mix until sugar is dissolved.

In a large foil pan, place the lamb shanks and top with sugar mixture evenly.

Place the foil pan onto the grill and cook for about 8-10 hours, flipping after every 30 mins. (If required, add enough water to keep the liquid ½-inch over).

Remove from the grill and serve hot.

Nutrition:

Calories: 1200

Carbohydrates: 39.7g

Protein: 161.9g

Fat: 48.4

Sugar: 29g

Sodium: 2000mg

Fiber: 0.3g

Cheesy Lamb Burgers

Preparation time: 15 mins

Cooking time: 20 mins

Servings: 4

Method of Preparation: Grilling

Ingredients:

2 lb. ground lamb

1 C. Parmigiano-Reggiano cheese, grated

Salt and freshly ground black pepper, to taste

Directions:

Set the temperature of Traeger Grill to 425 degrees F and preheat with closed lid for 15 mins.

In a bowl, add all ingredients and mix well.

Make 4 (¾-inch thick) patties from mixture.

With your thumbs, make a shallow but wide depression in each patty.

Arrange the patties onto the grill, depression-side down and cook for about 8 mins.

Flip and cook for about 8-10 mins.

Serve immediately.

Nutrition:

Calories: 502

Carbohydrates: 0g

Protein: 71.7g

Fat: 22.6g

Sugar: 0g

Sodium: 331mg

Fiber: 0g

Grilled Lamb Burgers

Preparation time: 10 minutes

Cooking time: 15 minutes

Servings: 5

Method of Preparation: Grilling

Ingredients:

1 1/4 pounds of ground lamb.

1 egg.

1 teaspoon of dried oregano.

1 teaspoon of dry sherry.

1 teaspoon of white wine vinegar.

4 minced cloves of garlic.

Red pepper

1/2 cup of chopped green onions.

1 tablespoon of chopped mint.

2 tablespoons of chopped cilantro.

2 tablespoons of dry breadcrumbs.

1/8 teaspoon of salt to taste.

1/4 teaspoon of ground black pepper to taste.

5 hamburger buns.

Directions:

Preheat a Wood Pellet Smoker or Grill to 350-450 degrees F then grease it grates. Using a large mixing bowl, add in all the ingredients on the list aside from the buns then mix properly to combine with clean hands. Make about five patties out of the mixture then set aside.

Place the lamb patties on the preheated grill and cook for about seven to nine minutes turning only once until an inserted thermometer reads 160 degrees F. Serve the lamb burgers on the hamburger, add your favorite toppings and enjoy.

Nutrition:

Calories: 376

Fat: 18.5 g

Carbohydrates: 25.4 g

Protein: 25.5 g

Fiber: 1.6 g

Traeger Stuffed Burgers

Preparation time: 20 minutes

Cooking time: 15 minutes

Servings: 6

Method of Preparation: Grilling

Ingredients:

3 lb. ground beef

1/2 tbsp onion powder

1/4 tbsp garlic powder

1 tbsp salt

1/2 tbsp pepper

1-1/2 cups Colby jack cheese, shredded

Johnny's seasoning salt

6 slices Colby Jack cheese

Directions:

Preheat your Traeger to 3750F.

Mix beef, onion powder, garlic powder, salt, and pepper until well combined. Make 12 patties.

Place cheese on the burger patty and cover with another patty then seal the edges.

Season with salt, then place the patties on the grill. Cook the patties on the grill grate for 8 minutes, flip the patties and cook for additional 5 minutes.

Place a slice of cheese on each patty and grill with the lid closed to melt the cheese.

Remove the patties from the Traeger and let rest for 10 minutes. Serve and enjoy with a toasted bun.

Nutrition:

Calories 463, Total fat 29g, Saturated fat 18g, Total carbs 1g, Net carbs 1g Protein 67g, Sugars 2g, Fiber 0g, Sodium 590mg

Grilled Lamb Sandwiches

Preparation time: 5 minutes
Cooking time: 50 minutes
Servings: 6
Method of Preparation: Grilling

Ingredients:

1 (4 pounds) boneless lamb.
1 cup of raspberry vinegar.
2 tablespoons of olive oil.
1 tablespoon of chopped fresh thyme.
2 pressed garlic cloves.
1/4 teaspoon of salt to taste.
1/4 teaspoon of ground pepper.
Sliced bread.

Directions:

Using a large mixing bowl, add in the raspberry vinegar, oil, and thyme then mix properly to combine. Add in the lamb, toss to combine then let it sit in the refrigerator for about eight hours or overnight. Next, discard the marinade the season the lamb with salt and pepper to taste. Preheat a Wood Pellet Smoker and grill t0 400-500 degrees F, add in the seasoned lamb and grill for about thirty to forty minutes until it attains a temperature of 150 degrees F. Once cooked, let the lamb cool for a few minutes, slice as desired then serve on the bread with your favorite topping.

Nutrition:

Calories: 407

Fat: 23 g

Carbohydrates: 26 g

Protein: 72 g

Fiber: 2.3 g

Lamb Chops

Preparation time: 10 minutes
Cooking time: 12 minutes
Servings: 6
Method of Preparation: Grilling

Ingredients:

6 (6-ounce) lamb chops
3 tablespoons olive oil
Ground black pepper

Directions:

Preheat the pallet grill to 450 degrees F.

Coat the lamb chops with oil and then, season with salt and black pepper evenly.

Arrange the chops in pallet grill grate and cook for about 4-6 minutes per side.

Nutrition:

Calories: 376

Fat: 19.5 g

Carbohydrates: 0 g

Protein: 47.8 g

Fiber: 0 g

Lamb Ribs Rack

Preparation time: 10 minutes
Cooking time: 2 hours
Servings: 2
Method of Preparation: Grilling

Ingredients:
2 tablespoons fresh sage
2 tablespoons fresh rosemary
2 tablespoons fresh thyme
2 peeled garlic cloves
1 tablespoon honey
Black pepper
¼ cup olive oil
1 (1½-pound) trimmed rack lamb ribs

Directions:
Combine all ingredients. While motor is running, slowly add oil and pulse till a smooth paste is formed. Coat the rib rack with paste generously and refrigerate for about 2 hours. Preheat the pallet grill to 225 degrees F. Arrange the rib rack in pallet grill and cook for about 2 hours.
Remove the rib rack from pallet grill and transfer onto a cutting board for about 10-15 minutes before slicing. With a sharp knife, cut the rib rack into equal sized individual ribs and serve.

Nutrition:
Calories: 826
Fat: 44.1 g
Carbohydrates: 5.4 g
Protein: 96.3 g
Fiber: 1 g

Lamb Shank

Preparation time: 10 minutes
Cooking time: 4 hours
Servings: 6
Method of Preparation: Grilling

Ingredients:
8-ounce red wine
2-ounce whiskey
2 tablespoons minced fresh rosemary
1 tablespoon minced garlic
Black pepper
6 (1¼-pound) lamb shanks

Directions:
In a bowl, add all ingredients except lamb shank and mix till well combined.
In a large resealable bag, add marinade and lamb shank.
Seal the bag and shake to coat completely.
Refrigerate for about 24 hours.
Preheat the pallet grill to 225 degrees F.
Arrange the leg of lamb in pallet grill and cook for about 4 hours.

Nutrition:
Calories: 1507
Fat: 62 g
Carbohydrates: 68.7 g
Protein:163.3 g
Fiber: 6 g

Leg of a Lamb

Preparation time: 10 minutes
Cooking time: 2 hours and 30 minutes
Servings: 10
Method of Preparation: Grilling

Ingredients:
1 (8-ounce) package softened cream cheese
¼ cup cooked and crumbled bacon
1 seeded and chopped jalapeño pepper
1 tablespoon crushed dried rosemary
2 teaspoons garlic powder
1 teaspoon onion powder
1 teaspoon paprika
1 teaspoon cayenne pepper

Salt, to taste

1 (4-5-pound) butterflied leg of lamb

2-3 tablespoons olive oil

Directions:

For filling in a bowl, add all ingredients and mix till well combined.

For spice mixture in another small bowl, mix all ingredients together.

Place the leg of lamb onto a smooth surface. Sprinkle the inside of leg with some spice mixture.

Place filling mixture over the inside surface evenly. Roll the leg of lamb tightly and with a butcher's twine, tie the roll to secure the filling

Coat the outer side of roll with olive oil evenly and then sprinkle with spice mixture.

Preheat the pallet grill to 225-240 degrees F.

Arrange the leg of lamb in pallet grill and cook for about 2-2½ hours. Remove the leg of lamb from pallet grill and transfer onto a cutting board. With a piece of foil, cover leg loosely and transfer onto a cutting board for about 20-25 minutes before slicing.

With a sharp knife, cut the leg of lamb in desired sized slices and serve.

Nutrition:

Calories: 715

Fat: 38.9 g

Carbohydrates: 2.2 g

Protein: 84.6 g

Fiber: 0.1 g

Lamb Breast

Preparation time: 10 minutes

Cooking time: 2 hours and 40 minutes

Servings: 2

Method of Preparation: Grilling

Ingredients:

1 (2-pound) trimmed bone-in lamb breast

½ cup white vinegar

¼ cup yellow mustard

½ cup BBQ rub

Directions:

Preheat the pallet grill to 225 degrees F.

Rinse the lamb breast with vinegar evenly.

Coat lamb breast with mustard and the, season with BBQ rub evenly.

Arrange lamb breast in pallet grill and cook for about 2-2½ hours.

Remove the lamb breast from the pallet grill and transfer onto a cutting board for about 10 minutes before slicing.

With a sharp knife, cut the lamb breast in desired sized slices and serve.

Nutrition:

Calories: 877

Fat: 34.5 g

Carbohydrates: 2.2 g

Protein: 128.7 g

Smoked Lamb Shoulder Chops

Preparation time: 4 hours

Cooking time: 25-30 minutes

Servings: 4

Method of Preparation: Grilling

Ingredients:

4 lamb shoulder chops

4 cups buttermilk

1 cup cold water

¼ cup kosher salt

2 tablespoons olive oil

1 tablespoon Texas style rub

Directions:

In a large bowl, add buttermilk, water and salt and stir till salt is dissolved.

Add chops and coat with mixture evenly.

Refrigerate for at least 4 hours. Remove the chops from bowl and rinse under cold water. Coat the chops with olive oil and then sprinkle with rub evenly. Preheat the pallet grill to 240 degrees F. Arrange the chops in pallet grill grate and cook for about 25-30 minute or till desired doneness. Meanwhile preheat the broiler of oven. Cook the chops under broiler till browned.

Nutrition:
Calories: 328
Fat: 18.2 g
Carbohydrates:11.7 g
Protein: 30.1 g
Fiber: 0 g

Lamb Skewers

Preparation time: 5 minutes
Cooking time: 8-12 minutes
Servings: 6
Method of Preparation: Smoking

Ingredients:
One lemon, juiced
Two crushed garlic cloves
Two chopped red onions
One t. chopped thyme
Pepper
Salt
One t. oregano
1/3 c. oil
½ t. cumin
Two pounds cubed lamb leg

Directions:
Refrigerate the chunked lamb.
The remaining ingredients should be mixed together. Add in the meat. Refrigerate overnight. Pat the meat dry and thread onto some metal or wooden skewers. Wooden skewers should be soaked in water.

Add wood pellets to your smoker and follow your cooker's startup procedure. Preheat your smoker, with your lid closed, until it reaches 450. Grill, covered, for 4-6 minutes on each side. Serve.

Nutrition:
Calories: 201
Fat: 9 g
Carbohydrates: 3 g
Protein: 24 g
Fiber: 1 g

Brown Sugar Lamb Chops

Preparation time: 2 hours
Cooking time: 10-15 minutes
Servings: 4
Method of Preparation: Smoking

Ingredients:
Pepper
One t. garlic powder
Salt
Two t. tarragon
One t. cinnamon
¼ c. brown sugar
4 lamb chops
Two t. ginger

Directions:
Combine the salt, garlic powder, pepper, cinnamon, tarragon, ginger, and sugar. Coat the lamb chops in the mixture and chill for two hours. Add wood pellets to your smoker and follow your cooker's startup procedure. Preheat your smoker, with your lid closed, until it reaches 450. Place the chops on the grill, cover, and smoke for 10-15 minutes per side. Serve.

Nutrition:
Calories: 210
Fat: 11 g
Carbohydrates: 3 g
Protein: 25 g
Fiber: 1 g

Bacon-Wrapped Sausages in Brown Sugar

Preparation Time: 20 minutes
Cooking time: 30 minutes
Servings: 8
Method of Preparation: Grilling

Ingredients:
1-pound bacon strips, halved
14 ounces cocktail sausages
½-cup brown sugar
Directions:
Place bacon strips on clean working space, roll them by using a rolling pin, and then wrap a sausage with a bacon strip, securing with a toothpick.

Place wrapped sausage in a casserole dish, repeat with the other sausages, place them into the casserole dish in a single layer, cover with sugar and then let them sit for 30 minutes in the refrigerator.

When ready to cook, switch on the Traeger grill, fill the grill hopper with apple-flavored wood pellets, power the grill on by using the control panel, select 'smoke' on the temperature dial, or set the temperature to 350 degrees F and let it preheat for a minimum of 15 minutes.

Meanwhile, remove the casserole dish from the refrigerator and then arrange sausage on a cookie sheet lined with parchment paper.

When the grill has preheated, open the lid, place cookie sheet on the grill grate, shut the grill and smoke for 30 minutes.

When done, transfer sausages to a dish and then serve.

Nutrition:
Calories: 270 Cal
Fat: 27 g
Carbs: 18 g
Protein: 9 g
Fiber: 2 g

Sweet and Hot BBQ Ribs

Preparation Time: 10 minutes
Cooking time: 5 hours and 10 minutes
Servings: 4
Method of Preparation: Grilling

Ingredients:
2 racks of pork ribs, bone-in, membrane removed
6 ounces pork and poultry rub
8 ounces apple juice
16 ounces sweet and heat BBQ sauce
Directions:
Sprinkle pork and poultry rub on all sides of pork ribs until evenly coated, rub well and marinate for a minimum of 30 minutes.

When ready to cook, switch on the Traeger grill, fill the grill hopper with pecan flavored wood pellets, power the grill on by using the control panel, select 'smoke' on the temperature dial, or set the temperature to 225 degrees F and let it preheat for a minimum of 15 minutes.

When the grill has preheated, open the lid, place pork ribs on the grill grate bone-side down, shut the grill and smoke for 1 hour, spraying with 10 ounces of apple juice frequently.

Then wrap ribs in aluminum foil, pour in remaining 6 ounces of apple juice, and wrap tightly.

Return wrapped ribs onto the grill grate meat-side down; shut the grill and smoke for 3 to 4 hours until internal temperature reaches 203 degrees F.

Remove wrapped ribs from the grill, uncover it and then brush well with the sauce.

Return pork ribs onto the grill grate and then grill for 10 minutes until glazed.

When done, transfer ribs to a cutting board, let rest for 10 minutes, then cut it into slices and serve.

Nutrition:
Calories: 250.8 Cal
Fat: 16.3 g
Carbs: 6.5 g
Protein: 18.2 g
Fiber: 0.2 g

Lemon Pepper Pork Tenderloin

Preparation Time: 20 minutes
Cooking time: 20 minutes
Servings: 6
Method of Preparation: Grilling

Ingredients:
2 pounds pork tenderloin, fat trimmed
For the Marinade:
½ teaspoon minced garlic
2 lemons, zested
1 teaspoon minced parsley
1/2 teaspoon salt
1/4 teaspoon ground black pepper
1-teaspoon lemon juice
2 tablespoons olive oil
Directions:
Prepare the marinade and for this, take a small bowl, place all of its ingredients in it and whisk until combined.

Take a large plastic bag, pour marinade in it, add pork tenderloin, seal the bag, turn it upside down to coat the pork and let it marinate for a minimum of 2 hours in the refrigerator.

When ready to cook, switch on the Traeger grill, fill the grill hopper with apple-flavored wood pellets, power the grill on by using the control panel, select 'smoke' on the temperature dial, or set the temperature to 375 degrees F and let it preheat for a minimum of 15 minutes.

When the grill has preheated, open the lid, place pork tenderloin on the grill grate, shut the grill and smoke for 20 minutes until internal temperature reaches 145 degrees F, turning pork halfway.

When done, transfer pork to a cutting board, let it rest for 10 minutes, then cut it into slices and serve.

Nutrition:
Calories: 288.5 Cal
Fat: 16.6 g
Carbs: 6.2 g
Protein: 26.4 g
Fiber: 1.2 g

Chinese BBQ Pork

Preparation Time: 10 minutes
Cooking time: 2 hours
Servings: 8
Method of Preparation: Grilling

Ingredients:
2 pork tenderloins, silver skin removed
For the Marinade:
½ teaspoon minced garlic
1 1/2 tablespoon brown sugar
1-teaspoon Chinese five-spice
1/4 cup honey
1-tablespoon Asian sesame oil
1/4 cup hoisin sauce
2 teaspoons red food coloring
1-tablespoon oyster sauce, optional
3 tablespoons soy sauce
For the Five-Spice Sauce:
1/4 teaspoon Chinese five-spice
3 tablespoons brown sugar

1-teaspoon yellow mustard

1/4 cup ketchup

Directions:

Prepare the marinade and for this, take a small bowl, place all of its ingredients in it and whisk until combined.

Take a large plastic bag, pour marinade in it, add pork tenderloin, seal the bag, turn it upside down to coat the pork and let it marinate for a minimum of 8 hours in the refrigerator.

Switch on the Traeger grill, fill the grill hopper with maple-flavored wood pellets, power the grill on by using the control panel, select 'smoke' on the temperature dial, or set the temperature to 225 degrees F and let it preheat for a minimum of 5 minutes.

Meanwhile, remove pork from the marinade, transfer marinade into a small saucepan, place it over medium-high heat and cook for 3 minutes, and then set aside until cooled.

When the grill has preheated, open the lid, place pork on the grill grate, shut the grill and smoke for 2 hours, basting with the marinade halfway.

Meanwhile, prepare the five-spice sauce and for this, take a small saucepan, place it over low heat, add all of its ingredients, stir until well combined and sugar has dissolved and cooked for 5 minutes until hot and thickened, set aside until required.

When done, transfer pork to a dish, let rest for 15 minutes, and meanwhile, change the smoking temperature of the grill to 450 degrees F and let it preheat for a minimum of 10 minutes.

Then return pork to the grill grate and cook for 3 minutes per side until slightly charred.

Transfer pork to a dish, let rest for 5 minutes, and then serve with prepared five-spice sauce.

Nutrition:

Calories: 280 Cal

Fat: 8 g

Carbs: 12 g

Protein: 40 g

Fiber: 0 g

Smoked Sausages

Preparation Time: 15 minutes
Cooking time: 3 hours
Method of Preparation: Smoking
Servings: 4

Ingredients:

3 pounds ground pork

1-tablespoon onion powder

1-tablespoon garlic powder

1-teaspoon curing salt

4-teaspoon black pepper

1/2 tablespoon salt

1/2 tablespoon ground mustard

Hog casings, soaked

1/2 cup ice water

Directions:

Switch on the Traeger grill, fill the grill hopper with flavored wood pellets, power the grill on by using the control panel, select 'smoke' on the temperature dial, or set the temperature to 225 degrees F and let it preheat for a minimum of 15 minutes.

Meanwhile, take a medium bowl, place all the ingredients in it except for water and hog casings, and stir until well mixed.

Pour in water, stir until incorporated, place the mixture in a sausage stuffer, then stuff the hog casings and tie the link to the desired length.

When the grill has preheated, open the lid, place the sausage links on the grill grate, shut the grill, and smoke for 2 to 3 hours until the internal temperature reaches 155 degrees F.

When done, transfer sausages to a dish; let them rest for 5 minutes, then slice and serve.

Nutrition:

Calories: 230 Cal

Fat: 22 g

Carbs: 2 g

Protein: 14 g

Fiber: 0 g

BBQ Baby Back Ribs

Preparation Time: 15 minutes

Cooking time: 6 hours

Servings: 8

Method of Preparation: Grilling

Ingredients:

2 racks of baby back pork ribs, membrane removed

Pork and poultry rub as needed

1/2 cup brown sugar

1/3 cup honey, warmed

1/3 cup yellow mustard

1-tablespoon Worcestershire sauce

1-cup BBQ sauce

1/2 cup apple juice, divided

Directions:

Switch on the Traeger grill, fill the grill hopper with hickory flavored wood pellets, power the grill on by using the control panel, select 'smoke' on the temperature dial, or set the temperature to 180 degrees F and let it preheat for a minimum of 15 minutes.

Meanwhile, take a small bowl, place mustard, and Worcestershire sauce in it, pour in ¼-cup apple juice and whisk until combined and smooth paste comes together.

Brush this paste on all sides of ribs and then season with pork and poultry rub until coated.

When the grill has preheated, open the lid, place ribs on the grill grate meat-side up, shut the grill and smoke for 3 hours.

After 3 hours, transfer ribs to a rimmed baking dish, let rest for 15 minutes, and meanwhile, change the smoking temperature of the grill to 225 degrees F and let it preheat for a minimum of 10 minutes.

Then return pork into the rimmed baking sheet to the grill grate and cook for 3 minutes per side until slightly charred.

When done, remove the baking sheet from the grill and work on one rib at a time, sprinkle half of the sugar over the rib, drizzle with half of the honey and half of the remaining apple juice, cover with aluminum foil to seal completely.

Repeat with the remaining ribs, return foiled ribs on the grill grate, shut with lid, and then smoke for 2 hours.

After 2 hours, uncover the grill, brush them with BBQ sauce generously, arrange them on the grill grate and grill for 1 hour until glazed.

When done, transfer ribs to a cutting board, let it rest for 15 minutes, slice into pieces and then serve.

Nutrition:

Calories: 334 Cal

Fat: 22.5 g

Carbs: 6.5 g

Protein: 24 g

Fiber: 0.1 g

FISH & SEAFOOD

Juicy Smoked Salmon

Preparation time: 6 hours
Cooking time: 50 minutes
Servings: 5
Method of Preparation: Smoking

Ingredients:
½ cup of sugar
2 tablespoon salt
2 tablespoons crushed red pepper flakes
½ cup fresh mint leaves, chopped
¼ cup brandy
1 (4 pounds) salmon, bones removed
2 cups alder wood pellets, soaked in water

Directions:
Take a medium-sized bowl and add brown sugar, crushed red pepper flakes, mint leaves, salt, and brandy until a paste forms
Rub the paste all over your salmon and wrap the salmon with a plastic wrap
Allow them to chill overnight
Preheat your smoker to 220 degrees Fahrenheit and add wood Pellets
Transfer the salmon to the smoker rack and cook smoke for 45 minutes
Once the salmon has turned red-brown and the flesh flakes off easily, take it out and serve!

Nutrition:
Calories: 370
Fats: 28g
Carbs: 1g
Fiber: 0g

Peppercorn Tuna Steaks

Preparation time: 8 hours
Cooking time: 10 minutes

Servings: 3
Method of Preparation: Smoking

Ingredients:
¼ cup of salt
2 pounds yellowfin tuna
¼ cup Dijon mustard
Freshly ground black pepper
2 tablespoons peppercorn

Directions:
Take a large-sized container and dissolve salt in warm water (enough water to cover fish)
Transfer tuna to the brine and cover, refrigerate for 8 hours
Preheat your smoker to 250 degrees Fahrenheit with your preferred wood
Remove tuna from bring and pat it dry
Transfer to grill pan and spread Dijon mustard all over
Season with pepper and sprinkle peppercorn on top
Transfer tuna to smoker and smoker for 1 hour
Enjoy!

Nutrition:
Calories: 707
Fats: 57g
Carbs: 10g
Fiber: 2g

Stuffed Shrimp Tilapia

Preparation time: 20 minutes
Cooking time: 45 minutes
Servings: 5
Method of Preparation: Smoking

Ingredients:
5 ounces fresh, farmed tilapia fillets

2 tablespoons extra virgin olive oil

1 and ½ teaspoons smoked paprika

1 and ½ teaspoons Old Bay seasoning

Shrimp stuffing

1-pound shrimp, cooked and deveined

1 tablespoon salted butter

1 cup red onion, diced

1 cup Italian breadcrumbs

½ cup mayonnaise

1 large egg, beaten

2 teaspoons fresh parsley, chopped

1 and ½ teaspoons salt and pepper

Directions:

Take a food processor and add shrimp, chop them up

Take a skillet and place it over medium-high heat, add butter and allow it to melt

Sauté the onions for 3 minutes

Add chopped shrimp with cooled Sautéed onion alongside remaining ingredients listed under stuffing ingredients and transfer to a bowl

Cover the mixture and allow it to refrigerate for 60 minutes

Rub both sides of the fillet with olive oil

Spoon 1/3 cup of the stuffing to the fillet

Flatten out the stuffing onto the bottom half of the fillet and fold the Tilapia in half

Secure with 2 toothpicks

Dust each fillet with smoked paprika and Old Bay seasoning

Preheat your smoker to 400 degrees Fahrenheit

Add your preferred wood Pellets and transfer the fillets to a non-stick grill tray

Transfer to your smoker and smoker for 30-45 minutes until the internal temperature reaches 145 degrees Fahrenheit

Allow the fish to rest for 5 minutes and enjoy!

Nutrition:

Calories: 620

Fats: 50g

Carbs: 6g

Fiber: 1g

Togarashi Smoked Salmon

Preparation time: 16 hours

Cooking time: 20 hours 15 minutes

Servings: 10

Method of Preparation: Grilling

Ingredients:

Salmon filet - 2 large

Togarashi for seasoning

For Brine:

Brown sugar - 1 cup

Water - 4 cups

Kosher salt - ⅓ cup

Directions:

Remove all the thorns from the fish filet.

Mix all the brine ingredients until the brown sugar is dissolved completely.

Put the mix in a big bowl and add the filet to it.

Leave the bowl to refrigerate for 16 hours.

After 16 hours, remove the salmon from this mix. Wash and dry it.

Place the salmon in the refrigerator for another 2-4 hours. (This step is important. DO NOT SKIP IT.)

Season your salmon filet with Togarashi.

Start the wood pellet grill with the 'smoke' option and place the salmon on it.

Smoke for 4 hours.

Make sure the temperature does not go above 180 degrees or below 130 degrees.

Remove from the grill and serve it warm with a side dish of your choice.

Nutrition:

Carbohydrates: 19 g

Protein: 10 g
Fat: 6 g
Sodium: 3772 mg
Cholesterol: 29 mg

BBQ Oysters

Preparation time: 1-2 hours
Cooking time: 16 minutes
Servings: 4-6
Method of Preparation: Grilling

Ingredients:
Shucked oysters - 12
Unsalted butter - 1 lb.
Chopped green onions - 1 bunch
Honey Hog BBQ Rub or Meat Church "The Gospel" - 1 tbsp
Minced green onions - ½ bunch
Seasoned breadcrumbs - ½ cup
Cloves of minced garlic - 2
Shredded pepper jack cheese - 8 oz
Traeger Heat and Sweet BBQ sauce

Directions:
Preheat the pellet grill for about 10-15 minutes with the lid closed.

To make the compound butter, wait for the butter to soften. Then combine the butter, onions, BBQ rub, and garlic thoroughly.

Lay the butter evenly on plastic wrap or parchment paper. Roll it up in a log shape and tie the ends with butcher's twine. Place these in the freezer to solidify for an hour. This butter can be used on any kind of grilled meat to enhance its flavor. Any other high-quality butter can also replace this compound butter.

Shuck the oysters, keeping the juice in the shell. Sprinkle all the oysters with breadcrumbs and place them directly on the grill. Allow them to cook for 5 minutes. You will know they are cooked when the oysters begin to curl slightly at the edges.

Once they are cooked, put a spoonful of the compound butter on the oysters. Once the butter melts, you can add a little bit of pepper jack cheese to add more flavor to them.

The oysters must not be on the grill for longer than 6 minutes, or you risk overcooking them. Put a generous squirt of the BBQ sauce on all the oysters. Also, add a few chopped onions.

Allow them to cool for a few minutes and enjoy the taste of the sea!

Nutrition:
Carbohydrates: 2.5 g
Protein: 4.7 g
Fat: 1.1 g
Sodium: 53 mg
Cholesterol: 25 mg

Grilled Shrimp

Preparation time: 0 minutes
Cooking time: 15 minutes
Servings: 4
Method of Preparation: Grilling

Ingredients:
Jumbo shrimp peeled and cleaned - 1 lb.
Oil - 2 tbsp
Salt - ½ tbsp
Skewers - 4-5
Pepper - ⅛ tbsp
Garlic salt - ½ tbsp

Directions:
Preheat the wood pellet grill to 375 degrees.
Mix all the ingredients in a small bowl.
After washing and drying the shrimp, mix it well with the oil and seasonings.
Add skewers to the shrimp and set the bowl of shrimp aside.

Open the skewers and flip them.

Cook for 4 more minutes. Remove when the shrimp is opaque and pink.

Nutrition:

Carbohydrates: 1.3 g

Protein: 19 g

Fat: 1.4 g

Sodium: 805 mg

Cholesterol: 179 mg

Teriyaki Smoked Shrimp

Preparation time: 0 minutes

Cooking time: 20 minutes

Servings: 6

Method of Preparation: Smoking

Ingredients:

Uncooked shrimp - 1 lb.

Onion powder - ½ tbsp

Garlic powder - ½ tbsp

Teriyaki sauce - 4 tbsp

Mayo - 4 tbsp

Minced green onion - 2 tbsp

Salt - ½ tbsp

Directions:

Remove the shells from the shrimp and wash thoroughly.

Preheat the wood pellet grill to 450 degrees.

Season with garlic powder, onion powder, and salt.

Cook the shrimp for 5-6 minutes on each side.

Once cooked, remove the shrimp from the grill and garnish it with spring onion, teriyaki sauce, and mayo.

Nutrition:

Carbohydrates: 2 g

Protein: 16 g

Sodium: 1241 mg

Cholesterol: 190 mg

Jerk Shrimp

Preparation time: 15 minutes

Cooking time: 6

Servings: 12

Method of Preparation: Smoking

Ingredients:

2 pounds shrimp, peeled, deveined

3 tablespoons olive oil

1 teaspoon garlic powder

1 teaspoon of sea salt

1/4 teaspoon ground cayenne

1 tablespoon brown sugar

1/8 teaspoon smoked paprika

1 tablespoon smoked paprika

1/4 teaspoon ground thyme

1 lime, zested

Directions:

Switch on the Traeger grill, fill the grill hopper with flavored wood pellets, power the grill on by using the control panel, select 'smoke' on the temperature dial, or set the temperature to 450 degrees F and let it preheat for a minimum of 5 minutes.

Meanwhile, prepare the spice mix and for this, take a small bowl, place all of its ingredients in it and stir until mixed.

Take a large bowl, place shrimps in it, sprinkle with prepared spice mix, drizzle with oil, and toss it until well coated.

When the grill has preheated, open the lid, place shrimps on the grill grate, shut the grill and smoke for 3 minutes per side until firm and thoroughly cooked.

When done, transfer shrimps to a dish and then serve.

Nutrition:

Calories: 131

Fat: 4.3 g

Carbs: 0 g

Protein: 22 g

Fiber: 0 g

Lobster Tails

Preparation time: 10 minutes
Cooking time: 35 minutes
Servings: 4
Method of Preparation: Smoking

Ingredients:

2 lobster tails, each about 10 ounces
For the Sauce:
2 tablespoons chopped parsley
1/4 teaspoon garlic salt
1 teaspoon paprika
1/4 teaspoon ground black pepper
1/4 teaspoon old bay seasoning
8 tablespoons butter, unsalted
2 tablespoons lemon juice

Directions:

Switch on the Traeger grill, fill the grill hopper with flavored wood pellets, power the grill on by using the control panel, select 'smoke' on the temperature dial, or set the temperature to 450 degrees F and let it preheat for a minimum of 15 minutes.

Meanwhile, prepare the sauce and for this, take a small saucepan, place it over medium-low heat, add butter in it and when it melts, add the remaining ingredients for the sauce and stir until combined, set aside until required.

Prepare the lobster and for this, cut the shell from the middle to the tail by using kitchen shears and then take the meat from the shell, keeping it attached at the base of the crab tail.

Then, butterfly the crab meat by making a slit down the middle, place lobster tails on a baking sheet, pour 1 tablespoon of sauce over each lobster tail, and reserve the remaining sauce.

When the grill has preheated, open the lid, place crab tails on the grill grate, shut the grill and smoke for 30 minutes until opaque.

When done, transfer lobster tails to a dish and then serve with the remaining sauce.

Nutrition:

Calories: 290
Fat: 22 g
Carbs: 1 g
Protein: 20 g

Lemon Garlic Scallops

Preparation time: 10 minutes
Cooking time: 5 minutes
Servings: 6
Method of Preparation: Smoking

Ingredients:

1 dozen scallops
2 tablespoons chopped parsley
Salt as needed
1 tablespoon olive oil
1 tablespoon butter, unsalted
1 teaspoon lemon zest
For the Garlic Butter:
½ teaspoon minced garlic
1 lemon, juiced
4 tablespoons butter, unsalted, melted

Directions:

Switch on the Traeger grill, fill the grill hopper with alder flavored wood pellets, power the grill on by using the control panel, select 'smoke' on the temperature dial, or set the temperature 400 degrees F and let it preheat for a minimum of 15 minutes.

Meanwhile, remove frill from scallops, pat dry with paper towels, and season with salt and black pepper.

When the grill has preheated, open the lid, place a skillet on the grill grate, add butter and oil, and when the butter melts, place seasoned scallops on it and then cook for 2 minutes until seared.

Meanwhile, prepare the garlic butter for this, take a small bowl, place all of its ingredients in it, and whisk until combined.

Flip the scallops, top with some of the prepared garlic butter, and cook for another minute.

When done, transfer scallops to a dish, top with remaining garlic butter, sprinkle with parsley and lemon zest and then serve.

Nutrition:

Calories: 184

Fat: 10 g

Carbs: 1 g

Protein: 22 g

Fiber: 0.2 g

Halibut in Parchment

Preparation time: 15 minutes

Cooking time: 15 minutes

Servings: 4

Method of Preparation: Smoking

Ingredients:

16 asparagus spears, trimmed, sliced into 1/2-inch pieces

2 ears of corn kernels

4 ounces halibut fillets, pin bones removed

2 lemons, cut into 12 slices

Salt as needed

Ground black pepper as needed

2 tablespoons olive oil

2 tablespoons chopped parsley

Directions:

Switch on the Traeger grill, fill the grill hopper with flavored wood pellets, power the grill on by using the control panel, select 'smoke' on the temperature dial, or set the temperature to 450 degrees F and let it preheat for a minimum of 5 minutes.

Meanwhile, cut out 18-inch long parchment paper, place a fillet in the center of each parchment, season with salt and black pepper, and then drizzle with oil.

Cover each fillet with three lemon slices, overlapping slightly, sprinkle one-fourth of asparagus and corn on each fillet, season with some salt and black pepper, and seal the fillets and vegetables tightly to prevent steam from escaping the packet.

When the grill has preheated, open the lid, place fillet packets on the grill grate, shut the grill and smoke for 15 minutes until packets have turned slightly brown and puffed up.

When done, transfer packets to a dish, let them stand for 5 minutes, then cut 'X' in the center of each packet, carefully uncover the fillets an vegetables, sprinkle with parsley, and then serve.

Nutrition:

Calories: 186.6

Fat: 2.8 g

Carbs: 14.2 g

Protein: 25.7 g

Fiber: 4.1 g

Wine Infused Salmon

Servings: 4

Cooking time: 5 hours

Preparation time: 15 mins

Method of Preparation: Grilling

Ingredients:

2 C. low-sodium soy sauce

1 C. dry white wine

1 C. water

½ tsp. Tabasco sauce

1/3 C. sugar

¼ C. salt

½ tsp. garlic powder

½ tsp. onion powder
Freshly ground black pepper, to taste
4 (6-oz.) salmon fillets

Directions:

In a large bowl, add all ingredients except salmon and stir until sugar is dissolved.

Add salmon fillets and coat with brine well.

Refrigerate, covered overnight.

Remove salmon from bowl and rinse under cold running water.

With paper towels, pat dry the salmon fillets.

Arrange a wire rack in a sheet pan.

Place the salmon fillets onto wire rack, skin side down and set aside to cool for about 1 hour.

Set the temperature of Traeger Grill to 165 degrees F and preheat with closed lid for 15 mins, using charcoal.

Place the salmon fillets onto the grill, skin side down and cook for about 3-5 hours or until desired doneness.

Remove the salmon fillets from grill and serve hot.

Nutrition:

Calories: 377

Carbohydrates: 26.3g

Protein: 41.1g

Fat: 10.5g

Sugar: 25.1g

Sodium: 14000mg

Fiber: 0g

Citrus Salmon

Servings: 6
Cooking time: 30 mins
Preparation time: 15 mins
Method of Preparation: Grilling

Ingredients:
2 (1-lb.) salmon fillets

Salt and freshly ground black pepper, to taste
1 tbsp. seafood seasoning
2 lemons, sliced
2 limes, sliced

Directions:

Set the temperature of Traeger Grill to 225 degrees F and preheat with closed lid for 15 mins.

Season the salmon fillets with salt, black pepper and seafood seasoning evenly.

Place the salmon fillets onto the grill and top each with lemon and lime slices evenly.

Cook for about 30 mins.

Remove the salmon fillets from grill and serve hot.

Nutrition:

Calories: 327

Carbohydrates: 1g

Protein: 36.1g

Fat: 19.8g

Sugar: 0.2g

Sodium: 237mg

Fiber: 0.3g

Omega- Rich Salmon

Servings: 6
Cooking time: 20 mins
Preparation time: 15 mins
Method of Preparation: Grilling

Ingredients:
6 (6-oz.) skinless salmon fillets
1/3 C. olive oil
¼ C. spice rub
¼ C. honey
2 tbsp. Sriracha
2 tbsp. fresh lime juice

Directions:

Set the temperature of Traeger Grill to 300 degrees F and preheat with closed lid for 15 mins.

Coat salmon fillets with olive oil and season with rub evenly.

In a small bowl, mix together remaining ingredients.

Arrange salmon fillets onto the grill, flat-side up and cook for about 7-10 mins per side, coating with honey mixture once halfway through.

Serve hot alongside remaining honey mixture.

Nutrition:

Calories: 384

Carbohydrates: 15.7g

Protein: 33g

Fat: 21.7g

Sugar: 11.6g

Sodium: 621mg

Fiber: 0g

Enticing Mahi-Mahi

Servings: 4

Cooking time: 10 mins

Preparation time: 10 mins

Method of Preparation: Grilling

Ingredients:

4 (6-oz.) mahi-mahi fillets

2 tbsp. olive oil

Salt and freshly ground black pepper, to taste

Directions:

Set the temperature of Traeger Grill to 350 degrees F and preheat with closed lid for 15 mins.

Coat fish fillets with olive oil and season with salt and black pepper evenly.

Place the fish fillets onto the grill and cook for about 5 mins per side.

Remove the fish fillets from grill and serve hot.

Nutrition:

Calories: 195

Carbohydrates: 0g

Protein: 31.6g

Fat: 7g

Sugar: 0g

Sodium: 182mg

Fiber: 0g

Super-Tasty Trout

Servings: 8

Cooking time: 5 hours

Preparation time: 15 mins

Method of Preparation: Grilling

Ingredients:

1 (7-lb.) whole lake trout, butterflied

½ C. kosher salt

½ C. fresh rosemary, chopped

2 tsp. lemon zest, grated finely

Directions:

Rub the trout with salt generously and then, sprinkle with rosemary and lemon zest.

Arrange the trout in a large baking dish and refrigerate for about 7-8 hours.

Remove the trout from baking dish and rinse under cold running water to remove the salt.

With paper towels, pat dry the trout completely.

Arrange a wire rack in a sheet pan.

Place the trout onto the wire rack, skin side down and refrigerate for about 24 hours.

Set the temperature of Traeger Grill to 180 degrees F and preheat with closed lid for 15 mins, using charcoal.

Place the trout onto the grill and cook for about 2-4 hours or until desired doneness.

Remove the trout from grill and place onto a cutting board for about 5 mins before serving.

Nutrition:

Calories: 633

Carbohydrates: 2.4g

Protein: 85.2g

Fat: 31.8g

Sugar: 0g

Sodium: 5000mg

Fiber: 1.6g

No-Fuss Tuna Burgers

Servings: 6
Cooking time: 15 mins
Preparation time: 15 mins
Method of Preparation: Grilling

Ingredients:
2 lb. tuna steak
1 green bell pepper, seeded and chopped
1 white onion, chopped
2 eggs
1 tsp. soy sauce
1 tbsp. blackened Saskatchewan rub
Salt and freshly ground black pepper, to taste

Directions:
Set the temperature of Traeger Grill to 500 degrees F and preheat with closed lid for 15 mins.
In a bowl, add all the ingredients and mix until well combined.
With greased hands, make patties from mixture. Place the patties onto the grill close to the edges and cook for about 10-15 mins, flipping once halfway through.
Serve hot.

Nutrition:
Calories: 313
Carbohydrates: 3.4g
Protein: 47.5g
Fat: 11g
Sugar: 1.9g
Sodium: 174mg
Fiber: 0.7g

Lively Flavored Shrimp

Servings: 6
Cooking time: 30 mins
Preparation time: 15 mins
Method of Preparation: Grilling

Ingredients:
8 oz. salted butter, melted
¼ C. Worcestershire sauce
¼ C. fresh parsley, chopped
1 lemon, quartered
2 lb. jumbo shrimp, peeled and deveined
3 tbsp. BBQ rub

Directions:
In a metal baking pan, add all ingredients except for shrimp and BBQ rub and mix well.
Season the shrimp with BBQ rub evenly.
Add the shrimp in the pan with butter mixture and coat well.
Set aside for about 20-30 mins.
Set the temperature of Traeger Grill to 250 degrees F and preheat with closed lid for 15 mins.
Place the pan onto the grill and cook for about 25-30 mins.
Remove the pan from grill and serve hot.

Nutrition:
Calories: 462
Carbohydrates: 4.7g
Protein: 34.9g
Fat: 33.3g
Sugar: 2.1g
Sodium: 485mg
Fiber: 0.2g

Flavor-Bursting Prawn Skewers

Servings: 5
Cooking time: 8 mins
Preparation time: 15 mins
Method of Preparation: Grilling

Ingredients:
¼ C. fresh parsley leaves, minced
1 tbsp. garlic, crushed
2½ tbsp. olive oil
2 tbsp. Thai chili sauce

1 tbsp. fresh lime juice

1½ pounds prawns, peeled and deveined

Directions:

In a large bowl, add all ingredients except for prawns and mix well.

In a resealable plastic bag, add marinade and prawns.

Seal the bag and shake to coat well

Refrigerate for about 20-30 mins.

Set the temperature of Traeger Grill to 450 degrees F and preheat with closed lid for 15 mins.

Remove the prawns from marinade and thread onto metal skewers.

Arrange the skewers onto the grill and cook for about 4 mins per side.

Remove the skewers from grill and serve hot.

Nutrition:

Calories: 234

Carbohydrates: 4.9g

Protein: 31.2g

Fat: 9.3g

Sugar: 1.7g

Sodium: 562mg

Fiber: 0.1g

Yummy Buttery Clams

Servings: 6

Cooking time: 8 mins

Preparation time: 15 mins

Method of Preparation: Grilling

Ingredients:

24 littleneck clams

½ C. cold butter, chopped

2 tbsp. fresh parsley, minced

3 garlic cloves, minced

1 tsp. fresh lemon juice

Directions:

Set the temperature of Traeger Grill to 450 degrees F and preheat with closed lid for 15 mins.

Scrub the clams under cold running water.

In a large casserole dish, mix together remaining ingredients.

Place the casserole dish onto the grill.

Now, arrange the clams directly onto the grill and cook for about 5-8 mins or until they are opened. (Discard any that fail to open).

With tongs, carefully transfer the opened clams into the casserole dish and remove from grill.

Serve immediately.

Nutrition:

Calories: 306

Carbohydrates: 6.4g

Protein: 29.3g

Fat: 7.6g

Sugar: 0.1g

Sodium: 237mg

Fiber: 0.1g

Crazy Delicious Lobster Tails

Servings: 4

Cooking time: 25 mins

Preparation time: 15 mins

Method of Preparation: Grilling

Ingredients:

½ C. butter, melted

2 garlic cloves, minced

2 tsp. fresh lemon juice

Salt and freshly ground black pepper, to taste

4 (8-oz.) lobster tails

Directions:

Set the temperature of Traeger Grill to 450 degrees F and preheat with closed lid for 15 mins.

In a metal pan, add all ingredients except for lobster tails and mix well.

Place the pan onto the grill and cook for about 10 mins.

Meanwhile, cut down the top of the shell and expose lobster meat.

Remove pan of butter mixture from grill.

Coat the lobster meat with butter mixture.

Place the lobster tails onto the grill and cook for about 15 mins, coating with butter mixture once halfway through.

Remove from grill and serve hot.

Nutrition:

Calories: 409

Carbohydrates: 0.6g

Protein: 43.5g

Fat: 24.9g

Sugar: 0.1g

Sodium: 1305mg

Fiber: 0g

Baked Steelhead

Preparation Time: 15 minutes

Cooking time: 20 minutes

Servings: 4 - 6

Method of Preparation: Grilling

Ingredients:

1 Lemon

2 Garlic cloves, minced

½ Shallot, minced

3 tablespoon Butter, unsalted

Saskatchewan seasoning, blackened

Italian Dressing

1 Steelhead, (a fillet)

Directions:

Preheat the grill to 350F with closed lid.

In an iron pan place the butter. Place the pan in the grill while preheating so that the butter melts.

Coat the fillet with Italian dressing. Rub with Saskatchewan rub. Make sure the layer is thin.

Mince the garlic and shallot. Remove the pan from the grill and add the garlic and shallots.

Spread the mixture on the fillet. Slice the lemon into slices. Place the slice on the butter mix.

Place the fish on the grate. Cook 20 - 30 minutes.

Nutrition:

Calories: 230

Protein: 28g

Fiber: 0g

Carbohydrates 2g

Fat: 14g

Whole Vermillion Snapper

Preparation Time: 15 minutes

Cooking time: 25 minutes

Servings: 6

Method of Preparation: Grilling

Ingredients:

2 Rosemary springs

4 Garlic cloves, chopped (peeled)

1 Lemon, thinly sliced

Black pepper

Sea Salt

1 Vermillion Snapper, gutted and scaled

Directions:

Preheat the grill to high with closed lid.

Stuff the fish with garlic. Sprinkle with rosemary, black pepper, sea salt and stuff with lemon slices.

Grill for 25 minutes.

Nutrition:

Calories: 240

Protein: 43g

Carbohydrates: 0g

Fat: 3g

Fiber: 0g

Grilled Clams with Garlic Butter

Preparation Time: 10 minutes

Cooking time: 8 minutes

Servings: 6 - 8

Method of Preparation: Grilling

Ingredients:

1 Lemon, cut wedges

1 - 2 teaspoon Anise - flavored Liqueur

2 tablespoon Parsley, minced

2 - 3 Garlic cloves, minced

8 tablespoon butter, chunks

24 of Littleneck Clams

Directions:

Clean the clams with cold water. Discard those who are with broken shells or don't close.

Preheat the grill to 450F with closed lid.

In a casserole dish squeeze juice from 2 wedges, and add parsley, garlic, butter, and liqueur. Arrange the littleneck clams on the grate. Grill 8 minutes, until open. Discard those that won't open.

Transfer the clams in the baking dish.

Serve in a shallow dish with lemon wedges. Enjoy!

Nutrition:

Calories: 273

Protein: 4g

Carbohydrates: 0.5g

Fiber: 0g

Fat: 10g

Simple but Delicious Fish Recipe

Preparation Time: 45 minutes

Cooking time: 10 minutes

Servings: 4 - 6

Method of Preparation: Grilling

Ingredients:

4 lbs. fish cut it into pieces (portion size)

1 tablespoon minced Garlic

1/3 cup of Olive oil

1 cup of Soy Sauce

Basil, chopped

2 Lemons, the juice

Directions:

Preheat the grill to 350F with closed lid.

Combine the ingredients in a bowl. Stir to combine. Marinade the fish for 45 minutes.

Grill the fish until it reaches 145F internal temperature.

Serve with your favorite side dish and enjoy!

Nutrition:

Calories: 153

Protein: 25g

Carbohydrates: 1g

Fiber: 0.3g

Fat: 4g

Crab Legs on the Grill

Preparation Time: 15 minutes

Cooking time: 30 minutes

Servings: 4 - 6

Method of Preparation: Grilling

Ingredients:

1 cup melted Butter

3 lb. Halved Crab Legs

2 tablespoon Lemon juice, fresh

1 tablespoon Old Bay

2 Garlic cloves, minced

For garnish, chopped parsley

For serving: Lemon wedges

Directions:

Place the crab legs in a roasting pan.

In a bowl combine the lemon juice, butter, and garlic. Mix. Pour over the legs. Coat well. Sprinkle with old bay.

Preheat the grill to 350F with closed lid.

Place the roasting pan on the grill and cook 20 - 30 minutes busting two times with the sauce in the pan.

Place the legs on a plate. Divide the crab sauce among 4 bowls for dipping.

Nutrition:

Calories: 170

Proteins: 20g

Carbohydrates: 0

Fiber: 0g

Fat: 8g

Seared Tuna Steaks

Preparation Time: 5 minutes

Cooking time: 5 minutes

Servings: 2 - 4

Method of Preparation: Grilling

Ingredients:

3 -inch Tuna

Black pepper

Sea Salt

Olive oil

Sriracha

Soy Sauce

Directions:

Baste the tuna steaks with oil and sprinkle with black pepper and salt.

Preheat the grill to high with closed lid.

Grill the tuna for 2 ½ minutes per side.

Remove from the grill. Let it rest for 5 minutes.

Cut into thin pieces and serve with Sriracha and Soy Sauce. Enjoy.

Nutrition:

Calories: 120

Proteins: 34g

Carbohydrates: 0g

Fiber: 0g

Fat: 1.5g

Roasted Shrimp Mix

Preparation Time: 30 minutes

Cooking time: 1h 30 minutes

Servings: 8 - 12

Method of Preparation: Grilling

Ingredients:

3 lb. Shrimp (large), with tails, divided

2 lb. Kielbasa Smoked Sausage

6 corns cut into 3 pieces

2 lb. Potatoes, red

Old Bay

Directions:

Preheat the grill to 275F with closed lid.

First, cook the sausage on the grill. Cook for 1 hour.

Increase the temperature to high. Season the corn and potatoes with Old Bay. Now roast until they become tender.

Season the shrimp with the Old Bay and cook on the grill for 20 minutes.

In a bowl combine the cooked ingredients. Toss. Adjust seasoning with Old Bay and serve. Enjoy!

Nutrition:

Calories: 530

Proteins: 20g

Carbohydrates: 32g

Fat: 35g

Fiber: 1g

VEGETABLES, SIDES AND MEATLESS DISHES

Roasted Parmesan Cheese Broccoli

Preparation time: 5 min
Cooking time: 45 min
Servings: 3 to 4
Method of Preparation: Grilling

Ingredients:

3 cups broccoli, stems trimmed

1 tbsp lemon juice

1 tbsp olive oil

2 garlic cloves, minced

1/2 tsp kosher salt

1/2 tsp ground black pepper

1 tsp lemon zest

1/8 cup parmesan cheese, grated

Directions:

Preheat pellet grill to 375°F.

Place broccoli in a resealable bag. Add lemon juice, olive oil, garlic cloves, salt, and pepper. Seal the bag and toss to combine. Let the mixture marinate for 30 minutes.

Pour broccoli into a grill basket. Place basket on grill grates to roast. Grill broccoli for 14-18 minutes, flipping broccoli halfway through. Grill until tender yet a little crispy on the outside.

Remove broccoli from grill and place on a serving dish—zest with lemon and top with grated parmesan cheese. Serve immediately and enjoy!

Nutrition:

Calories: 82.6

Fat: 4.6 g

Cholesterol: 1.8 mg

Carbohydrate: 8.1 g

Fiber: 4.6 g

Sugar: 0

Protein: 5.5

Cajun Style Grilled Corn

Preparation time: 5 min
Cooking time: 25 min
Servings: 4
Method of Preparation: Grilling

Ingredients:

4 ears corn, with husks

1 tsp dried oregano

1 tsp paprika

1 tsp garlic powder

1 tsp onion powder

1/2 tsp kosher salt

1/2 tsp ground black pepper

1/4 tsp dried thyme

1/4 tsp cayenne pepper

2 tsp butter, melted

Directions:

Preheat pellet grill to 375°F.

Peel husks back but do not remove. Scrub and remove silks.

Mix oregano, paprika, garlic powder, onion powder, salt, pepper, thyme, and cayenne in a small bowl.

Brush melted butter over corn.

Rub seasoning mixture over each ear of corn. Pull husks up and place corn on grill grates. Grill for about 12-15 minutes, turning occasionally.

Remove from grill and allow to cool for about 5 minutes. Remove husks, then serve and enjoy!

Nutrition:
Calories: 278
Fat: 17.4 g
Cholesterol: 40.7 mg
Carbohydrate: 30.6 g
Fiber: 4.5 g
Sugar: 4.6 g
Protein: 5.4 g

Grilled Cherry Tomato Skewers

Preparation time: 10 min
Cooking time: 50 min
Servings: 4
Method of Preparation: Grilling

Ingredients:
24 cherry tomatoes
1/4 cup olive oil
3 tbsp balsamic vinegar
4 garlic cloves, minced
1 tbsp fresh thyme, finely chopped
1 tsp kosher salt
1 tsp ground black pepper
2 tbsp chives, finely chopped

Directions:
Preheat pellet grill to 425°F.
In a medium-sized bowl, mix olive oil, balsamic vinegar, garlic, and thyme. Add tomatoes and toss to coat.
Let tomatoes sit in the marinade at room temperature for about 30 minutes.
Remove tomatoes from marinade and thread 4 tomatoes per skewer.
Season both sides of each skewer with kosher salt and ground pepper.
Place on grill grate and grill for about 3 minutes on each side, or until each side is slightly charred.

Remove from grill and allow to rest for about 5 minutes. Garnish with chives, then serve and enjoy!

Nutrition:
Calories: 228
Fat: 10 g
Cholesterol: 70 mg
Carbohydrate: 7 g
Fiber: 2 g
Sugar: 3 g
Protein: 27 g

Roasted Vegetable Medley

Preparation time: 20 min
Cooking time: 50 min
Servings: 4 to 6
Method of Preparation: Grilling

Ingredients:
2 medium potatoes, cut to 1-inch wedges
2 red bell peppers, cut into 1-inch cubes
1 small butternut squash, peeled and cubed to 1-inch cube
1 red onion, cut to 1-inch cubes
1 cup broccoli, trimmed
2 tbsp olive oil
1 tbsp balsamic vinegar
1 tbsp fresh rosemary, minced
1 tbsp fresh thyme, minced
1 tsp kosher salt
1 tsp ground black pepper

Directions:
Preheat pellet grill to 425°F.
In a large bowl, combine potatoes, peppers, squash, and onion.
In a small bowl, whisk together olive oil, balsamic vinegar, rosemary, thyme, salt, and pepper.
Pour marinade over vegetables and toss to coat.
Allow resting for about 15 minutes.

Place marinated vegetables into a grill basket, and place a grill basket on the grill grate. Cook for about 30-40 minutes, occasionally tossing in the grill basket.

Remove veggies from grill and transfer to a serving dish. Allow to cool for 5 minutes, then serve and enjoy!

Nutrition:

Calories: 158.6

Fat: 7.4 g

Cholesterol: 0

Carbohydrate: 22 g

Fiber: 7.2 g

Sugar: 3.1 g

Protein: 5.2 g

Smokey Roasted Cauliflower

Preparation time: 10 min

Cooking time: 1 hour 20 min

Servings: 4 to 6

Method of Preparation: Smoking

Ingredients:

1 head cauliflower

1 cup parmesan cheese

Spice ingredients:

1 tbsp olive oil

2 cloves garlic, chopped

1 tsp kosher salt

1 tsp smoked paprika

Directions:

Preheat pellet grill to 180°F. If applicable, set smoke setting to high.

Cut cauliflower into bite-size flowerets and place in a grill basket. Place basket on the grill grate and smoke for an hour.

Mix spice ingredients in a small bowl while the cauliflower is smoking. Remove cauliflower from the grill after an hour and let cool.

Change grill temperature to 425°F. After the cauliflower has cooled, put cauliflower in a resealable bag, and pour marinade in the bag. Toss to combine in the bag.

Place cauliflower back in a grill basket and return to grill. Roast in the grill basket for 10-12 minutes or until the outsides begin to get crispy and golden brown.

Remove from grill and transfer to a serving dish. Sprinkle parmesan cheese over the cauliflower and rest for a few minutes so the cheese can melt. Serve and enjoy!

Nutrition:

Calories: 70

Fat: 35 g

Cholesterol: 0

Carbohydrate: 7 g

Fiber: 3 g

Sugar: 3 g

Protein: 3 g

Smoked Deviled Eggs

Preparation time: 15 min

Cooking time: 50 min

Servings: 4 to 6

Method of Preparation: Smoking

Ingredients:

6 large eggs

1 slice bacon

1/4 cup mayonnaise

1 tsp Dijon mustard

1 tsp apple cider vinegar

1/4 tsp paprika

Pinch of kosher salt

1 tbsp chives, chopped

Directions:

Preheat pellet grill to 180°F and turn smoke setting on, if applicable.

Bring a pot of water to a boil. Add eggs and hard boil eggs for about 12 minutes.

Remove eggs from pot and place them into an ice-water bath. Once eggs have cooled completely, peel them and slice in half lengthwise.

Place sliced eggs on grill, yolk side up. Smoke for 30 to 45 minutes, depending on how much smoky flavor you want.

While eggs smoke, cook bacon until it's crispy.

Remove eggs from the grill and allow to cool on a plate.

Remove the yolks and place all of them in a small bowl. Place the egg whites on a plate.

Mash yolks with a fork and add mayonnaise, mustard, apple cider vinegar, paprika, and salt. Stir until combined.

Spoon a scoop of yolk mixture back into each egg white.

1. Sprinkle paprika, chives, and crispy bacon bits to garnish. Serve and enjoy!

Nutrition:
Calories: 140
Fat: 12 g
Cholesterol: 190 mg
Carbohydrate: 1 g
Fiber: 0
Sugar: 0
Protein: 6 g

Crispy Maple Bacon Brussels Sprouts

Preparation time: 15 min
Cooking time: 1 hour
Servings: 6
Method of Preparation: Grilling

Ingredients:
1 lb. brussels sprouts, trimmed and quartered
6 slices thick-cut bacon

3 tbsp maple syrup
1 tsp olive oil
1/2 tsp kosher salt
1/2 tsp ground black pepper

Directions:
Preheat pellet grill to 425°F.

Cut bacon into 1/2-inch-thick slices.

Place brussels sprouts in a single layer in the cast iron skillet. Drizzle with olive oil and maple syrup, then toss to coat. Sprinkle bacon slices on top then season with kosher salt and black pepper.

Place skillet in the pellet grill and roast for about 40 to 45 minutes, or until the brussels sprouts are caramelized and brown.

Remove skillet from grill and allow brussels sprouts to cool for about 5 to 10 minutes. Serve and enjoy!

Nutrition:
Calories: 175.3
Fat: 12.1 g
Cholesterol: 6.6 mg
Carbohydrate: 13.6 g
Fiber: 2.9 g
Sugar: 7.6 g
Protein: 4.8 g

Sweet Jalapeño Cornbread

Preparation time: 20 min
Cooking time: 50 min
Servings: 12
Method of Preparation: Grilling

Ingredients:
2/3 cup margarine, softened
2/3 cup white sugar
2 cups cornmeal
1 1/3 cups all-purpose flour
4 tsp baking powder
1 tsp kosher salt

3 eggs

1 2/3 cups milk

1 cup jalapeños, deseeded and chopped

Butter, to line baking dish

Directions:

Preheat pellet grill to 400°F.

Beat margarine and sugar together in a medium-sized bowl until smooth.

In another bowl, combine cornmeal, flour, baking powder, and salt.

In a third bowl, combine and whisk eggs and milk.

Pour 1/3 of the milk mixture and 1/3 of the flour mixture into the margarine mixture at a time, whisking just until mixed after each pour.

Once thoroughly combined, stir in chopped jalapeño.

Lightly butter the bottom of the baking dish. Pour cornbread mixture evenly into the baking dish.

Place dish on grill grates and close the lid. Cook for about 23-25 minutes, or until thoroughly cooked. The way to test is by inserting a toothpick into the center of the cornbread - it should come out clean once removed.

Remove dish from the grill and allow to rest for 10 minutes before slicing and serving.

Nutrition:

Calories: 160

Fat: 6 g

Cholesterol: 15 mg

Carbohydrate: 25 g

Fiber: 10 g

Sugar: 0.5 g

Protein: 3 g

Grilled Broccoli

Preparation time: 15 minutes

Cooking time: 3 Minutes

Servings: 1-2

Method of Preparation: Grilling

Ingredients:

2 cups of broccoli, fresh

1 tablespoon of canola oil

1 teaspoon of lemon pepper

Directions:

Place the grill

grate inside the unit and close the hood.

Preheat the grill by turning at high for 10 minutes.

Meanwhile, mix broccoli with lemon pepper and canola oil.

Toss well to coat the ingredients thoroughly.

Place it on a grill grade once add food appears.

Lock the unit and cook for 3 minutes at medium.

Take out and serve.

Nutrition:

Calories: 96

Total Fat: 7.3g

Saturated Fat: 0.5g

Cholesterol: 0mg

Sodium: 30mg

Total Carbohydrate: 6.7g

Dietary Fiber 2.7g

Total Sugars: 1.6g

Protein: 2.7g

Smoked Healthy Cabbage

Preparation time: 10 minutes

Cooking time: 2 hours

Servings: 5

Method of Preparation: Smoking

Ingredients:

1 head cabbage, cored

4 tablespoons butter

2 tablespoons rendered bacon fat

1 chicken bouillon cube

1 teaspoon fresh ground black pepper

1 garlic clove, minced

Directions:

Preheat your smoker to 240 degrees Fahrenheit using your preferred wood

Fill the hole of your cored cabbage with butter, bouillon cube, bacon fat, pepper and garlic

Wrap the cabbage in foil about two-thirds of the way up

Make sure to leave the top open

Transfer to your smoker rack and smoke for 2 hours

Unwrap and enjoy!

Nutrition:

Calories: 231

Fats: 10g

Carbs: 26g

Fiber: 1g

Garlic and Rosemary Potato Wedges

Preparation time: 15 minutes

Cooking time: 1 hour 30 minutes

Servings: 4

Method of Preparation: Smoking

Ingredients:

4-6 large russet potatoes, cut into wedges

¼ cup olive oil

2 garlic cloves, minced

2 tablespoons rosemary leaves, chopped

2 teaspoon salt

1 teaspoon fresh ground black pepper

1 teaspoon sugar

1 teaspoon onion powder

Directions:

Preheat your smoker to 250 degrees Fahrenheit using maple wood

Take a large bowl and add potatoes and olive oil

Toss well

Take another small bowl and stir garlic, salt, rosemary, pepper, sugar, onion powder

Sprinkle the mix on all sides of the potato wedge

Transfer the seasoned wedge to your smoker rack and smoke for 1 and a ½ hours

Serve and enjoy!

Nutrition:

Calories: 291

Fats: 10g

Carbs: 46g

Fiber: 2g

Smoked Tomato and Mozzarella Dip

Preparation time: 5 minutes

Cooking time: 1 hour

Servings: 4

Method of Preparation: Smoking

Ingredients:

8 ounces smoked mozzarella cheese, shredded

8 ounces Colby cheese, shredded

½ cup parmesan cheese, grated

1 cup sour cream

1 cup sun-dried tomatoes

1 and ½ teaspoon salt

1 teaspoon fresh ground pepper

1 teaspoon dried basil

1 teaspoon dried oregano

1 teaspoon red pepper flakes

1 garlic clove, minced

½ teaspoon onion powder

French toast, serving

Directions:
Preheat your smoker to 275 degrees Fahrenheit using your preferred wood
Take a large bowl and stir in the cheeses, tomatoes, pepper, salt, basil, oregano, red pepper flakes, garlic, onion powder and mix well
Transfer the mix to a small metal pan and transfer to a smoker
Smoke for 1 hour
Serve with toasted French bread
Enjoy!
Nutrition:
Calories: 174
Fats: 11g
Carbs: 15g
Fiber: 2g

Feisty Roasted Cauliflower

Preparation time: 15 minutes
Cooking time: 10 minutes
Servings: 4
Method of Preparation: Smoking

Ingredients:
1 cauliflower head, cut into florets
1 tablespoon oil
1 cup parmesan, grated
2 garlic cloves, crushed
½ teaspoon pepper
½ teaspoon salt
¼ teaspoon paprika

Directions:
Preheat your Smoker to 180 degrees F
Transfer florets to smoker and smoke for 1 hour
Take a bowl and add all ingredients except cheese
Once smoking is done, remove florets
Increase temperature to 450 degrees F, brush florets with the brush and transfer to grill
Smoke for 10 minutes more

Sprinkle cheese on top and let them sit (Lid closed) until cheese melts
Serve and enjoy!
Nutrition:
Calories: 45
Fats: 2g
Carbs: 7g
Fiber: 1g

Green Beans with Bacon

Preparation time: 10 minutes
Cooking time: 20 minutes
Servings: 6
Method of Preparation: Smoking

Ingredients:
4 strips of bacon, chopped
1 1/2-pound green beans, ends trimmed
1 teaspoon minced garlic
1 teaspoon salt
4 tablespoons olive oil

Directions:
Switch on the Traeger grill, fill the grill hopper with flavored wood pellets, power the grill on by using the control panel, select 'smoke' on the temperature dial, or set the temperature to 450 degrees F and let it preheat for a minimum of 15 minutes.
Meanwhile, take a sheet tray, place all the ingredients in it and toss until mixed.
When the grill has preheated, open the lid, place prepared sheet tray on the grill grate, shut the grill and smoke for 20 minutes until lightly browned and cooked.
When done, transfer green beans to a dish and then serve.
Nutrition:
Calories: 93
Fat: 4.6 g
Carbs: 8.2 g
Protein: 5.9 g
Fiber: 2.9 g

Vegetable Sandwich

Preparation time: 30 minutes

Cooking time: 45 minutes

Servings: 4

Method of Preparation: Smoking

Ingredients:

For the Smoked Hummus:

1 1/2 cups cooked chickpeas

1 tablespoon minced garlic

1 teaspoon salt

4 tablespoons lemon juice

2 tablespoon olive oil

1/3 cup tahini

For the Vegetables:

2 large portobello mushrooms

1 small eggplant, destemmed, sliced into strips

1 teaspoon salt

1 small zucchini, trimmed, sliced into strips

½ teaspoon ground black pepper

1 small yellow squash, peeled, sliced into strips

¼ cup olive oil

For the Cheese:

1 lemon, juiced

½ teaspoon minced garlic

¼ teaspoon ground black pepper

¼ teaspoon salt

1/2 cup ricotta cheese

To Assemble:

1 bunch basil, leaves chopped

2 heirloom tomatoes, sliced

4 ciabatta buns, halved

Directions:

Switch on the Traeger grill, fill the grill hopper with pecan flavored wood pellets, power the grill on by using the control panel, select 'smoke' on the temperature dial, or set the temperature to 180 degrees F and let it preheat for a minimum of 15 minutes.

Meanwhile, prepare the hummus, and for this, take a sheet tray and spread chickpeas on it.

When the grill has preheated, open the lid, place sheet tray on the grill grate, shut the grill and smoke for 20 minutes.

When done, transfer chickpeas to a food processor, add the remaining ingredients for the hummus in it and pulse for 2 minutes until smooth, set aside until required.

Change the smoking temperature to 500 degrees F, shut with lid, and let it preheat for 10 minutes.

Meanwhile, prepare vegetables and for this, take a large bowl, place all the vegetables in it, add salt and black pepper, drizzle with oil and lemon juice and toss until coated.

Place vegetables on the grill grate, shut with lid, and then smoke for eggplant, zucchini, and squash for 15 minutes and mushrooms for 25 minutes.

Meanwhile, prepare the cheese and for this, take a small bowl, place all of its ingredients in it and stir until well combined.

Assemble the sandwich for this, cut buns in half lengthwise, spread prepared hummus on one side, spread cheese on the other side, then stuff with grilled vegetables and top with tomatoes and basil.

Serve straight away.

Nutrition:

Calories: 560

Fat: 40 g

Carbs: 45 g

Protein: 8.3 g

Fiber: 6.8 g

Cauliflower with Parmesan and Butter

Preparation time: 15 minutes
Cooking time: 45 minutes
Servings: 4
Method of Preparation: Smoking

Ingredients:
One medium head of cauliflower
1 teaspoon minced garlic
1 teaspoon salt
½ teaspoon ground black pepper
1/4 cup olive oil
1/2 cup melted butter, unsalted
1/2 tablespoon chopped parsley
1/4 cup shredded parmesan cheese

Directions:
Switch on the Traeger grill, fill the grill hopper with flavored wood pellets, power the grill on by using the control panel, select 'smoke' on the temperature dial, or set the temperature to 450 degrees F and let it preheat for a minimum of 15 minutes.

Meanwhile, brush the cauliflower head with oil, season with salt and black pepper and then place in a skillet pan.

When the grill has preheated, open the lid, place prepared skillet pan on the grill grate, shut the grill and smoke for 45 minutes until golden brown and the center has turned tender.

Meanwhile, take a small bowl, place melted butter in it, and then stir in garlic, parsley, and cheese until combined.

Baste cheese mixture frequently in the last 20 minutes of cooking and, when done, remove the pan from heat and garnish cauliflower with parsley.

Cut it into slices and then serve.

Nutrition:
Calories: 128
Fat: 7.6 g
Carbs: 10.8 g
Protein: 7.4 g
Fiber: 5 g

Roasted Butternut Squash

Cooking time: 30 minutes
Servings: 4
Method of Preparation: Grilling

Ingredients:
2-pound butternut squash
3 tablespoon extra-virgin olive oil
Traeger Veggie Rub, as needed

Directions:
Fire the Traeger Grill to 3500F. Use desired wood pellets when cooking. Close the lid and preheat for 15 minutes.
Slice the butternut squash into ½ inch thick and remove the seeds. Season with oil and veggie rub.
Place the seasoned squash in a baking tray.
Grill for 30 minutes.

Nutrition:
Calories: 131
Protein: 1.9g
Carbs: 23.6g
Fat: 4.7g Sugar: 0g

Roasted Sheet Pan Vegetables

Servings: 6
Cooking time: 20 minutes
Method of Preparation: Grilling

Ingredients:
1 small purple cauliflower, cut into florets
1 small yellow cauliflower, cut into florets
4 cups butternut squash

2 cups mushroom, fresh

3 tablespoons extra virgin olive oil

2 teaspoons salt

2 teaspoons black pepper

Directions:

Fire the Traeger Grill to 3500F. Use desired wood pellets when cooking. Close the lid and preheat for 15 minutes.

Place the vegetables in a baking tray and season with olive oil, salt, and pepper. Toss to coat all vegetables.

Place in the grill and cook for 20 minutes. Make sure to shake the tray halfway through the cooking time for even cooking.

Nutrition:

Calories: 101

Protein: 3.8g

Carbs: 16.9g

Fat: 3.5g Sugar: 4.4g

Smoked Hummus

Servings: 6

Cooking time: 20 minutes

Method of Preparation: grilling

Ingredients:

1 ½ cups chickpeas, rinsed and drained

¼ cup tahini

1 tablespoon garlic, minced

2 tablespoons extra virgin olive oil

1 teaspoon salt

4 tablespoons lemon juice

Directions:

Fire the Traeger Grill to 3500F. Use desired wood pellets when cooking. Close the lid and preheat for 15 minutes.

Spread the chickpeas on a sheet tray and place on the grill grate. Smoke for 20 minutes.

Let the chickpeas cool at room temperature.

Place smoked chickpeas in a blender or food processor. Add in the rest of the ingredients. Pulse until smooth.

Serve with roasted vegetables if desired.

Nutrition:

Calories: 271

Protein: 12.1g

Carbs: 34.8g

Fat: 10.4g Sugar: 5.7g

Baked Cheesy Corn Pudding

Servings: 6

Cooking time: 30 minutes

Method of Preparation: grilling

Ingredients:

3 cloves of garlic, chopped

3 tablespoons butter

3 cups whole corn kernels

8 ounces cream cheese

1 cup cheddar cheese

1 cup parmesan cheese

1 tablespoon salt

½ tablespoon black pepper

½ cup dry breadcrumbs

1 cup mozzarella cheese, grated

1 tablespoon thyme, minced

Directions:

Fire the Traeger Grill to 3500F. Use desired wood pellets when cooking. Close the lid and preheat for 15 minutes.

In a large saucepan, sauté the garlic and butter for 2 minutes until fragrant. Add the corn, cheddar cheese, parmesan cheese, salt, and pepper. Heat until the corn is melted then pour into a baking dish.

In a small bowl, combine the breadcrumbs, mozzarella cheese, and thyme.

Spread the cheese and bread crumb mixture on top of the corn mixture.

Place the baking dish on the grill grate and cook for 25 minutes.

Allow to rest before removing from the mold.

Nutrition:

Calories: 523

Protein: 29.4g

Carbs: 34g

Fat: 31.2g Sugar: 10.8g

Grilled Corn on The Cob with Parmesan and Garlic

Servings: 6

Cooking time: 30 minutes

Method of Preparation: Grilling

Ingredients:

4 tablespoons butter, melted

2 cloves of garlic, minced

Salt and pepper to taste

8 corns, unhusked

½ cup parmesan cheese, grated

1 tablespoon parsley chopped

Directions:

Fire the Traeger Grill to 4500F. Use desired wood pellets when cooking. Close the lid and preheat for 15 minutes.

Place butter, garlic, salt, and pepper in a bowl and mix until well combined.

Peel the corn husk but do not detach the husk from the corn. Remove the silk. Brush the corn with the garlic butter mixture and close the husks. Place the corn on the grill grate and cook for 30 minutes turning the corn every 5 minutes for even cooking.

Nutrition:

Calories: 272

Protein: 8.8g

Carbs: 38.5g

Fat: 12.3g Sugar: 6.6g

Grilled Asparagus with Wild Mushrooms

Servings: 4

Cooking time: 10 minutes

Method of Preparation: Grilling

Ingredients:

2 bunches fresh asparagus, trimmed

4 cups wild mushrooms, sliced

1 large shallots, sliced into rings

Extra virgin oil as needed

2 tablespoons butter, melted

Directions:

Fire the Traeger Grill to 5000F. Use desired wood pellets when cooking. Close the lid and preheat for 15 minutes.

Place the asparagus, mushrooms, and shallots on a baking tray. Drizzle with oil and butter and season with salt and pepper to taste.

Place on a baking tray and cook for 10 minutes. Make sure to give the asparagus a good stir halfway through the cooking time for even browning.

Nutrition:

Calories: 218

Protein: 15.2g

Carbs: 26.6 g

Fat: 10g Sugar: 12.9g

Smoked -Bean Salad

Servings: 6
Cooking time: 20 minutes
Method of Preparation: Smoking

Ingredients:

1 can Great Northern Beans, rinsed and drained
1 can Red Kidney Beans, rinsed and drained
1pound fresh green beans, trimmed
2 tablespoons olive oil
Salt and pepper to taste
1 shallot, sliced thinly
2 tablespoons red wine vinegar
1 teaspoon Dijon mustard

Directions:

Fire the Traeger Grill to 5000F. Use desired wood pellets when cooking. Close the lid and preheat for 15 minutes.

Place the beans in a sheet tray and drizzle with olive oil. Season with salt and pepper to taste.

Place in the grill and cook for 20 minutes. Make sure to shake the tray for even cooking.

Once cooked, remove the beans and place in a bowl. Allow to cool first.

Add the shallots and the rest of the ingredients. Season with more salt and pepper if desired. Toss to coat the beans with the seasoning.

Nutrition:

Calories: 179
Protein: 8.2 g
Carbs: 23.5g
Fat: 6.5g Sugar: 2.2g

Grilled Artichokes

Servings: 6
Cooking time: 15 minutes
Method of Preparation: Grilling

Ingredients:

3 large artichokes, blanched and halved
3 + 3 tablespoons olive oil
Salt and pepper to taste
1 cup mayonnaise
1 cup yogurt
2 tablespoons parsley, chopped
2 tablespoons capers
Lemon juice to taste

Directions:

Fire the Traeger Grill to 5000F. Use desired wood pellets when cooking. Close the lid and preheat for 15 minutes.

Brush the artichokes with 3 tablespoons of olive oil. Season with salt and pepper to taste.

Place on the grill grate and cook for 15 minutes. Allow to cool before slicing.

Once cooled, slice the artichokes and place in a bowl.

In another bowl, mix together the mayonnaise, yogurt, parsley, capers, and lemon juice. Season with salt and pepper to taste. Mix until well-combined.

Pour sauce over the artichokes.

Toss to coat.

Nutrition:

Calories: 257
Protein: 6.7g
Carbs: 13.2 g
Fat: 20.9g Sugar: 3.7g

Grilled Scallions

Servings: 6
Cooking time: 20 minutes
Method of Preparation: Grilling

Ingredients:

10 whole scallions, chopped
¼ cup olive oil
Salt and pepper to taste

2 tablespoons rice vinegar

1 whole jalapeno, sliced into rings

Directions:

Fire the Traeger Grill to 5000F. Use desired wood pellets when cooking. Close the lid and preheat for 15 minutes.

Place on a bowl all ingredients and toss to coat. Transfer to a parchment-lined baking tray.

Place on the grill grate and cook for 20 minutes or until the scallions char.

Nutrition:

Calories: 135

Protein: 2.2 g

Carbs: 9.7 g

Fat: 10.1g Sugar: 4.6g

Butter Braised Green Beans

Servings: 6

Cooking time: 20 minutes

Method of Preparation: Grilling

Ingredients:

24 ounces Green Beans, trimmed

8 tablespoons butter, melted

Salt and pepper to taste

Directions:

Fire the Traeger Grill to 5000F. Use desired wood pellets when cooking. Close the lid and preheat for 15 minutes.

Place all ingredients in a bowl and toss to coat the beans with the seasoning.

Place the seasoned beans in a sheet tray.

Cook in the grill for 20 minutes.

Nutrition:

Calories: 164

Protein: 1.6g

Carbs: 5.6 g

Fat: 15.8g Sugar: 1.3g

Smoked Baked Kale Chips

Servings: 4

Cooking time: 30 minutes

Method of Preparation: Grilling

Ingredients:

2 bunches kale, stems removed

Olive oil as needed

Salt and pepper to taste

Directions:

Fire the Traeger Grill to 3500F. Use desired wood pellets when cooking. Close the lid and preheat for 15 minutes.

Place all ingredients in a bowl and toss to coat the kale with oil.

Place on a baking tray and spread the leaves evenly on all surface.

Place in the grill and cook for 30 minutes or until the kale leaves become crispy.

Nutrition:

Calories: 206

Protein: 9.9g

Carbs: 21g

Fat: 12g Sugar: 0g

Smoked Pickles

Servings: 6

Cooking time: 15 minutes

Method of Preparation: Grilling

Ingredients:

1-quart water

¼ cup sugar

½ quart white vinegar

½ cup salt

½ teaspoon peppercorns

1 ½ teaspoons celery seeds

1 ½ teaspoons coriander seeds

1 teaspoon mustard seeds

8 cloves of garlic, minced

1 bunch dill weed

12 small cucumbers

Directions:

Place the water, sugar, vinegar, salt, and peppercorns in a saucepan. Bring to a boil over medium flame.

Transfer to a bowl and allow to cool. Add in the rest of the ingredients.

Allow the cucumber to soak in the brine for at least 3 days.

When ready to cook, fire the Traeger Grill to 5000F. Use desired wood pellets when cooking. Close the lid and preheat for 15 minutes.

Pat dry the cucumber with paper towel and place on the grill grate. Smoke for 15 minutes.

Nutrition:

Calories: 67

Protein: 2.4g

Carbs: 12.9g

Fat: 1.1g Sugar:8.5 g

Grilled Zucchini Squash

Servings: 6

Cooking time: 10 minutes

Method of Preparation: Grilling

Ingredients:

3 medium zucchinis, sliced into ¼ inch thick lengthwise

2 tablespoons olive oil

1 tablespoon sherry vinegar

2 thyme leaves, pulled

Salt and pepper to taste

Directions:

Fire the Traeger Grill to 3500F. Use desired wood pellets when cooking. Close the lid and preheat for 15 minutes.

Place zucchini in a bowl and all ingredients. Gently massage the zucchini slices to coat with the seasoning.

Place the zucchini on the grill grate and cook for 5 minutes on each side.

Nutrition:

Calories: 44

Protein: 0.3 g

Carbs: 0.9 g

Fat: 4g Sugar: 0.1g

Smoked Balsamic Potatoes and Carrots

Servings: 6

Cooking time: 10 minutes

Method of Preparation: Smoking

Ingredients:

2 large carrots, peeled and chopped roughly

2 large Yukon Gold potatoes, peeled and wedged

5 tablespoons olive oil

5 tablespoons balsamic vinegar

Salt and pepper to taste

Directions:

Fire the Traeger Grill to 4000F. Use desired wood pellets when cooking. Close the lid and preheat for 15 minutes.

Place all ingredients in a bowl and toss to coat the vegetables with the seasoning.

Place on a baking tray lined with foil.

Place on the grill grate and close the lid. Cook for 30 minutes.

Nutrition:

Calories: 219

Protein: 2.9g

Carbs: 27g

Fat: 11.4g Sugar:4.5 g

Grilled Potato Salad

Preparation time: 15 minutes
Cooking time: 10 minutes
Servings: 8
Method of Preparation: Grilling

Ingredients:

1 ½ pound fingerling potatoes, halved lengthwise
1 small jalapeno, sliced
10 scallions
2 teaspoons salt
2 tablespoons rice vinegar
2 teaspoons lemon juice
2/3 cup olive oil, divided

Directions:

Switch on the Traeger grill, fill the grill hopper with pecan flavored wood pellets, power the grill on by using the control panel, select 'smoke' on the temperature dial, or set the temperature to 450 degrees F and let it preheat for a minimum of 5 minutes.

Meanwhile, prepare scallions, and for this, brush them with some oil.

When the grill has preheated, open the lid, place scallions on the grill grate, shut the grill and smoke for 3 minutes until lightly charred.

Then transfer scallions to a cutting board, let them cool for 5 minutes, then cut into slices and set aside until required.

Brush potatoes with some oil, season with some salt and black pepper, place potatoes on the grill grate, shut the grill and smoke for 5 minutes until thoroughly cooked.

Then take a large bowl, pour in remaining oil, add salt, lemon juice, and vinegar and stir until combined.

Add grilled scallion and potatoes, toss until well mixed, taste to adjust seasoning and then serve.

Nutrition:

Calories: 223.7
Fat: 12 g
Carbs: 27 g
Protein: 1.9 g
Fiber: 3.3 g

Grilled Zucchini

Preparation time: 5 minutes
Cooking time: 10 minutes
Servings: 6
Method of Preparation: Smoking

Ingredients:

4 medium zucchinis
2 tablespoons olive oil
1 tablespoon sherry vinegar
2 sprigs of thyme, leaves chopped
½ teaspoon salt
1/3 teaspoon ground black pepper

Directions:

Switch on the Traeger grill, fill the grill hopper with oak flavored wood pellets, power the grill on by using the control panel, select 'smoke' on the temperature dial, or set the temperature to 350 degrees F and let it preheat for a minimum of 5 minutes.

Meanwhile, cut the ends of each zucchini, cut each in half and then into thirds and place in a plastic bag.

Add the remaining ingredients, seal the bag, and shake well to coat zucchini pieces.

When the grill has preheated, open the lid, place zucchini on the grill grate, shut the grill and smoke for 4 minutes per side.

When done, transfer zucchini to a dish, garnish with more thyme and then serve.

Nutrition:

Calories: 74
Fat: 5.4 g
Carbs: 6.1 g
Protein: 2.6 g
Fiber: 2.3 g

Grilled Sugar Snap Peas

Preparation time: 15 minutes
Cooking time: 10 minutes
Servings: 4
Method of Preparation: Smoking

Ingredients:
2-pound sugar snap peas, ends trimmed
½ teaspoon garlic powder
1 teaspoon salt
2/3 teaspoon ground black pepper
2 tablespoons olive oil

Directions:
Switch on the Traeger grill, fill the grill hopper with apple-flavored wood pellets, power the grill on by using the control panel, select 'smoke' on the temperature dial, or set the temperature to 450 degrees F and let it preheat for a minimum of 15 minutes.

Meanwhile, take a medium bowl, place peas in it, add garlic powder and oil, season with salt and black pepper, toss until mixed and then spread on the sheet pan.

When the grill has preheated, open the lid, place the prepared sheet pan on the grill grate, shut the grill and smoke for 10 minutes until slightly charred.

Serve straight away.

Nutrition:
Calories: 91
Fat: 5 g
Carbs: 9 g
Protein: 4 g
Fiber: 3 g

Grilled Carrots and Asparagus

Preparation time: 10 minutes
Cooking time: 30 minutes
Servings: 6
Method of Preparation: Smoking

Ingredients:
1-pound whole carrots, with tops
1 bunch of asparagus, ends trimmed
Sea salt as needed
1 teaspoon lemon zest
2 tablespoons honey
2 tablespoons olive oil

Directions:
Switch on the Traeger grill, fill the grill hopper with flavored wood pellets, power the grill on by using the control panel, select 'smoke' on the temperature dial, or set the temperature to 450 degrees F and let it preheat for a minimum of 15 minutes.

Meanwhile, take a medium dish, place asparagus in it, season with sea salt, drizzle with oil and toss until mixed.

Take a medium bowl, place carrots in it, drizzle with honey, sprinkle with sea salt and toss until combined.

When the grill has preheated, open the lid, place asparagus and carrots on the grill grate, shut the grill and smoke for 30 minutes.

When done, transfer vegetables to a dish, sprinkle with lemon zest, and then serve.

Nutrition:
Calories: 79.8
Fat: 4.8 g
Carbs: 8.6 g
Protein: 2.6 g
Fiber: 3.5 g

Kale Chips

Preparation time: 10 minutes
Cooking time: 20 minutes
Servings: 6
Method of Preparation: Smoking

Ingredients:

2 bunches of kale, stems removed
½ teaspoon of sea salt
4 tablespoons olive oil

Directions:

Switch on the Traeger grill, fill the grill hopper with apple-flavored wood pellets, power the grill on by using the control panel, select 'smoke' on the temperature dial, or set the temperature to 250 degrees F and let it preheat for a minimum of 15 minutes.

Meanwhile, rinse the kale leaves, pat dry, spread the kale on a sheet tray, drizzle with oil, season with salt and toss until well coated.

When the grill has preheated, open the lid, place sheet tray on the grill grate, shut the grill and smoke for 20 minutes until crisp.

Serve straight away.

Nutrition:

Calories: 110
Fat: 5 g
Carbs: 15.8 g
Protein: 5.3 g
Fiber: 5.6 g

Roasted Root Vegetables

Preparation time: 15 minutes
Cooking time: 45 minutes
Servings: 6
Method of Preparation: Smoking

Ingredients:

1 large red onion, peeled
1 bunch of red beets, trimmed, peeled
1 large yam, peeled
1 bunch of golden beets, trimmed, peeled
1 large parsnips, peeled
1 butternut squash, peeled
1 large carrot, peeled
6 garlic cloves, peeled
3 tablespoons thyme leaves
Salt as needed
1 cinnamon stick
Ground black pepper as needed
3 tablespoons olive oil
2 tablespoons honey

Directions:

Switch on the Traeger grill, fill the grill hopper with hickory flavored wood pellets, power the grill on by using the control panel, select 'smoke' on the temperature dial, or set the temperature to 450 degrees F and let it preheat for a minimum of 15 minutes.

Meanwhile, cut all the vegetables into ½-inch pieces, place them in a large bowl, add garlic, thyme, and cinnamon, drizzle with oil and toss until mixed.

Take a large cookie sheet, line it with foil, spread with vegetables, and then season with salt and black pepper.

When the grill has preheated, open the lid, place prepared cookie sheet on the grill grate, shut the grill and smoke for 45 minutes until tender.

When done, transfer vegetables to a dish, drizzle with honey, and then serve.

Nutrition:

Calories: 164
Fat: 4 g
Carbs: 31.7 g
Protein: 2.7 g
Fiber: 6.4 g

Vegetable Skewers

Preparation time: 10 minutes
Cooking time: 20 minutes
Servings: 4
Method of Preparation: Smoking

Ingredients:

2 cups whole white mushrooms

2 large yellow squash, peeled, chopped

1 cup chopped pineapple

1 cup chopped red pepper

1 cup halved strawberries

2 large zucchini, chopped

For the Dressing:

2 lemons, juiced

½ teaspoon ground black pepper

1/2 teaspoon sea salt

1 teaspoon red chili powder

1 tablespoon maple syrup

1 tablespoon orange zest

2 tablespoons apple cider vinegar

1/4 cup olive oil

Directions:

Switch on the Traeger grill, fill the grill hopper with flavored wood pellets, power the grill on by using the control panel, select 'smoke' on the temperature dial, or set the temperature to 450 degrees F and let it preheat for a minimum of 5 minutes.

Meanwhile, prepared thread vegetables and fruits on skewers alternately and then brush skewers with oil.

When the grill has preheated, open the lid, place vegetable skewers on the grill grate, shut the grill, and smoke for 20 minutes until tender and lightly charred.

Meanwhile, prepare the dressing and for this, take a small bowl, place all of its ingredients in it and then whisk until combined.

When done, transfer skewers to a dish, top with prepared dressing and then serve.

Nutrition:

Calories: 130

Fat: 2 g

Carbs: 20 g

Protein: 2 g

VEGETARIANS

Traeger Smoked Mushrooms

Preparation time: 15 minutes
Cooking time: 45 minutes
Servings: 2
Method of Preparation: Smoking

Ingredients:
4 cups whole baby portobello, cleaned
1 tbsp canola oil
1 tbsp onion powder
1 tbsp garlic, granulated
1 tbsp salt
1 tbsp pepper

Directions:
Place all the ingredients in a bowl, mix, and combine.
Set your Traeger to 180oF.
Place the mushrooms on the grill directly and smoke for about 30 minutes.
Increase heat to high and cook the mushroom for another 15 minutes.
Serve warm and enjoy!

Nutrition:
Calories 118, Total fat 7.6g, Saturated fat 0.6g, Total carbs 10.8g, Net carbs 8.3g, Protein 5.4g, Sugars 3.7g, Fiber 2.5g, Sodium 3500mg, Potassium 536mg

Grilled Zucchini Squash Spears

Preparation time: 5 minutes
Cooking time: 10 minutes
Servings: 4
Method of Preparation: Grilling

Ingredients:
4 zucchinis, medium
2 tbsp olive oil
1 tbsp sherry vinegar
2 thyme, leaves pulled
Salt to taste
Pepper to taste

Directions:
Clean zucchini cut ends off, half each lengthwise, and cut each half into thirds.
Combine all the other ingredients in a zip lock bag, medium, then add spears.
Toss well and mix to coat the zucchini.
Preheat Traeger to 350oF with the lid closed for about 15 minutes.
Remove spears from the zip lock bag and place them directly on your grill grate with the cut side down.
Cook for about 3-4 minutes until zucchini is tender and grill marks show.
Remove them from the grill and enjoy.

Nutrition:
Calories 93, Total fat 7.4g, Saturated fat 1.1g, Total carbs 7.1g, Net carbs 4.9g, Protein 2.4g, Sugars 3.4g, Fiber 2.2g, Sodium 59mg, Potassium 515mg

Grilled Asparagus & Honey-Glazed Carrots

Preparation time: 15 minutes
Cooking time: 35 minutes
Servings: 4
Method of Preparation: Grilling

Ingredients:
1 bunch asparagus, woody ends removed
2 tbsp olive oil
1 lb. peeled carrots

2 tbsp honey

Sea salt to taste

Lemon zest to taste

Directions:

Rinse the vegetables under cold water.

Splash the asparagus with oil and generously with a splash of salt.

Drizzle carrots generously with honey and splash lightly with salt.

Preheat your Traeger to 350oF with the lid closed for about 15 minutes.

Place the carrots first on the grill and cook for about 10-15 minutes.

Now place asparagus on the grill and cook both for about 15-20 minutes or until done to your liking.

Top with lemon zest and enjoy.

Nutrition:

Calories 184, Total fat 7.3g, Saturated fat 1.1g, Total carbs 28.6g, Net carbs 21g, Protein 6g, Sugars 185g, Fiber 7.6g, Sodium 142mg, Potassium 826mg

Traeger Grilled Vegetables

Preparation time: 5 minutes
Cooking time: 15 minutes
Servings: 12
Method of Preparation: Grilling

Ingredients:

1 veggie tray

1/4 cup vegetable oil

1-2 tbsp Traeger veggie seasoning

Directions:

Preheat your Traeger to 375oF.

Meanwhile, toss the veggies in oil placed on a sheet pan, large, then splash with the seasoning.

Place on the Traeger and grill for about 10-15 minutes.

Remove, serve, and enjoy.

Nutrition:

Calories 44, Total fat 5g, Saturated fat 0g, Total carbs 1g, Net carbs 1g, Protein 0g, Sugars 0g, Fiber 0g, Sodium 36mg, Potassium 116mg

Smoked Acorn Squash

Preparation time: 10 minutes
Cooking time: 2 hours
Servings: 6
Method of Preparation: Smoking

Ingredients:

3 acorn squash, seeded and halved

3 tbsp olive oil

1/4 cup butter, unsalted

1 tbsp cinnamon, ground

1 tbsp chili powder

1 tbsp nutmeg, ground

1/4 cup brown sugar

Directions:

Brush the cut sides of your squash with olive oil then cover with foil poking holes for smoke and steam to get through.

Preheat your Traeger to 225oF.

Place the squash halves on the grill with the cut side down and smoke for about 1½- 2 hours. Remove from the Traeger.

Let it sit while you prepare spiced butter. Melt butter in a saucepan then add spices and sugar stirring to combine.

Remove the foil form the squash halves.

Place 1 tbsp of the butter mixture onto each half. Serve and enjoy!

Nutrition:

Calories 149, Total 10g, Saturated fat 5g, Total carbs 14g, Net carbs 12g, Protein 2g, Sugars 2g, Fiber 2g, Sodium 19mg, Potassium 101m

Vegan Smoked Carrot Dogs

Preparation time: 10 minutes
Cooking time: 35 minutes
Servings: 2
Method of Preparation: Smoking

Ingredients:
4 carrots, thick
2 tbsp avocado oil
1/2 tbsp garlic powder
1 tbsp liquid smoke
Pepper to taste
Kosher salt to taste

Directions:
Preheat your Traeger to 425oF then line a parchment paper on a baking sheet.
Peel the carrots to resemble a hot dog. Round the edges when peeling.
Whisk together oil, garlic powder, liquid smoke, pepper and salt in a bowl, small.
Now place carrots on the baking sheet and pour the mixture over. Roll your carrots in the mixture to massage seasoning and oil into them. Use fingertips.
Roast the carrots in the Traeger until fork tender for about 35 minutes. Brush the carrots using the marinade mixture every 5 minutes.
Remove and place into hot dog buns then top with hot dog toppings of your choice.
Serve and enjoy!

Nutrition:
Calories 76, Total fat 1.8g, Saturated 0.4g, Total 14.4g, Net carbs 10.6g, Protein 1.5g, Sugar 6.6g, Fiber 3.8g, Sodium 163mg, Potassium 458mg

Stuffed Grilled Zucchini

Preparation time: 25 minutes
Cooking time: 10 minutes

Servings: 4
Method of Preparation: Grilling

Ingredients:
4 zucchinis, medium
5 tbsp olive oil, divided
2 tbsp red onion, finely chopped
1/4 tbsp garlic, minced
1/2 cup breadcrumbs, dry
1/2 cup shredded mozzarella cheese, part-skim
1/2 tbsp salt
1 tbsp fresh mint, minced
3 tbsp parmesan cheese, grated

Directions:
Halve zucchini lengthwise and scoop pulp out. Leave 1/4 -inch shell. Now brush using 2 tbsp oil, set aside, and chop the pulp.
Sauté onion and pulp in a skillet, large, then add garlic and cook for about 1 minute.
Add breadcrumbs and cook while stirring for about 2 minutes until golden brown.
Remove everything from heat then stir in mozzarella cheese, salt, and mint. Scoop into the zucchini shells and splash with parmesan cheese. Preheat your Traeger to 375oF.
Place stuffed zucchini on the Traeger grill and grill while covered for about 8-10 minutes until tender.
Serve warm and enjoy.

Nutrition:
Calories 186, Total fat 10g, Saturated fat 3g, Total carbs 17g, Net carbs 14g, Protein 9g, Sugars 4g, Fiber 3g, Sodium 553mg, Potassium 237mg

Smoked Stuffed Mushrooms

Preparation time: 15 minutes
Cooking time: 1 hour 15 minutes
Servings: 12
Method of Preparation: Smoking

Ingredients:

12-16 white mushrooms, large, cleaned and stems removed
1/2 cup parmesan cheese
1/2 cup breadcrumbs, Italian
2 minced garlic cloves
2 tbsp fresh parsley, chopped
1/4 -1/3 cup olive oil
Salt and pepper to taste

Directions:

Preheat your Traeger 375oF.
Remove mushroom very bottom stem then dice the rest into small pieces.
Combine mushroom stems, parmesan cheese, breadcrumbs, garlic, parsley, 3 tbsp oil, pepper, and salt in a bowl, large. Combine until moist.
Layer mushrooms in a pan, disposable, then fill them with the mixture until heaping. Drizzle with more oil.
Place the pan on the Traeger grill.
Smoke for about 1 hour 20 minutes until filling browns and mushrooms become tender.
Remove from Traeger and serve.
Enjoy!

Nutrition:

Calories 74, Total fat 6.1g, Saturated fat 1g, Total carbs 4.1g, Net carbs 3.7g, Protein 1.6g, Sugars 0.6g, Fiber 0.4g, Sodium 57mg, Potassium 72mg

Bacon-Wrapped Jalapeno Poppers

Preparation time: 10 minutes
Cooking time: 20 minutes
Servings: 6
Method of Preparation: Grilling

Ingredients:

6 jalapenos, Fresh
1/2 cup shredded cheddar cheese
4 oz soft cream cheese
1-1/2 tbsp Traeger veggie rub
12 bacon slices, thin cut

Directions:

Preheat your Traeger grill to 375oF.
Halve the jalapenos lengthwise then scrape membrane and seeds using a spoon. rinse them and set aside.
Meanwhile, combine cheddar cheese, cream cheese, and veggie rub in a bowl, medium stirring until incorporated fully.
Fill the jalapenos with your cheese mixture then wrap each half with a bacon slice.
Place on your grill and grill for about 15-20 minutes until bacon becomes crispy and peppers are soft.
Serve and enjoy.

Nutrition:

Calories 329, Total fat 25.7g, Saturated fat 11.4g, Total carbs 5g, Net carbs 4.6g, Protein 18.1g, Sugars 0.6g, Fiber 0.4g, Sodium 1667mg, Potassium 277mg

Roasted Green Beans with Bacon

Preparation time: 15 minutes
Cooking time: 20 minutes
Servings: 6
Method of Preparation: Grilling

Ingredients:

1-pound green beans
4 strips bacon, cut into small pieces

4 tablespoons extra virgin olive oil

2 cloves garlic, minced

1 teaspoon salt

Directions:

Fire the Traeger Grill to 4000F. Use desired wood pellets when cooking. Keep lid unopened and let it preheat for at most 15 minutes

Toss all ingredients on a sheet tray and spread out evenly.

Place the tray on the grill grate and roast for 20 minutes.

Nutrition:

Calories: 65

Fat: 5.3 g

Carbohydrates: 3 g

Protein: 1.3 g

Fiber: 0 g

Smoked Watermelon

Preparation time: 15 minutes
Cooking time: 45-90 minutes
Servings: 5
Method of Preparation: Smoking

Ingredients:

1 small seedless watermelon

Balsamic vinegar

Wooden skewers

Directions:

Slice ends of small seedless watermelons

Slice the watermelon in 1-inch cubes. Put the cubes in a container and drizzle vinegar on the cubes of watermelon.

Preheat the smoker to 225°F. Add wood chips and water to the smoker before starting preheating.

Place the cubes on the skewers.

Place the skewers on the smoker rack for 50 minutes.

Cook

Remove the skewers.

Serve!

Nutrition:

Calories: 20

Fat: 0 g

Carbohydrates: 4 g

Protein: 1 g

Fiber: 0.2 g

Grilled Corn with Honey Butter

Preparation time: 15 minutes
Cooking time: 10 minutes
Servings: 6
Method of Preparation: Grilling

Ingredients:

6 pieces corn, husked

2 tablespoons olive oil

Salt and pepper to taste

½ cup butter, room temperature

½ cup honey

Directions:

Fire the Traeger Grill to 3500F. Use desired wood pellets when cooking. Keep lid unopened to preheat until 15 minutes

Coat corn with oil and add salt and pepper

Place the corn on the grill grate and cook for 10 minutes. Make sure to flip the corn halfway through the cooking time for even cooking.

Meanwhile, mix the butter and honey on a small bowl. Set aside.

Remove corn from grill and coat with honey butter sauce

Nutrition:

Calories: 387

Fat: 21.6 g

Carbohydrates: 51.2 g

Protein: 5 g

Fiber: 0 g

Smoked Mushrooms

Preparation time: 20 minutes
Cooking time: 2 hours
Servings: 6
Method of Preparation: Smoking

Ingredients:

6-12 large Portobello mushrooms
Sea salt
black pepper
Extra virgin olive oil
Herbs de Provence

Directions:

Preheat the smoker to 200°F while adding water and wood chips to the smoker bowl and tray, respectively.

Wash and dry mushrooms

Rub the mushrooms with olive oil, salt and pepper seasoning with herbs in a bowl.

Place the mushrooms with the cap side down on the smoker rack. Smoke the mushrooms for 2 hours while adding water and wood chips to the smoker after every 60 minutes.

Remove the mushrooms and serve

Nutrition:

Calories: 106
Fat: 6 g
Carbohydrates: 5 g
Protein: 8 g
Fiber: 0.9 g

Smoked Cherry Tomatoes

Preparation time: 20 minutes
Cooking time: 1 ½ hours
Servings: 8-10
Method of Preparation: Smoking

Ingredients:

2 pints of tomatoes

Directions:

Preheat the electric smoker to 225°F while adding wood chips and water to the smoker.

Clean the tomatoes with clean water and dry them off properly.

Place the tomatoes on the pan and place the pan in the smoker.

Smoke for 90 minutes while adding water and wood chips to the smoker.

Nutrition:

Calories: 16
Fat: 0 g
Carbohydrates: 3 g
Protein: 1 g
Fiber: 1 g

Smoked and Smashed New Potatoes

Preparation time: 5 minutes
Cooking time: 8 hours
Servings: 4
Method of Preparation: Smoking

Ingredients:

1-1/2 pounds small new red potatoes or fingerlings
Extra virgin olive oil
Sea salt and black pepper
2 tbsp softened butter

Directions:

Let the potatoes dry. Once dried, put in a pan and coat with salt, pepper, and extra virgin olive oil.

Place the potatoes on the topmost rack of the smoker.

Smoke for 60 minutes.

Once done, take them out and smash each one

Mix with butter and season

Nutrition:
Calories: 258
Fat: 2.0 g
Carbohydrates: 15.5 g
Protein: 4.1 g
Fiber: 1.5 g

Smoked Brussels Sprouts

Preparation time: 15 minutes
Cooking time: 45 minutes
Servings: 6
Method of Preparation: Smoking

Ingredients:
1-1/2 pounds Brussels sprouts
2 cloves of garlic minced
2 tbsp extra virgin olive oil
Sea salt and cracked black pepper

Directions:
Rinse sprouts
Remove the outer leaves and brown bottoms off the sprouts.
Place sprouts in a large bowl then coat with olive oil.
Add a coat of garlic, salt, and pepper and transfer them to the pan.
Add to the top rack of the smoker with water and woodchips.
Smoke for 45 minutes or until reaches 250°F temperature.
Serve

Nutrition:
Calories: 84
Fat: 4.9 g
Carbohydrates: 7.2 g
Protein: 2.6 g
Fiber: 2.9 g

Apple Veggie Burger

Preparation time: 10 minutes
Cooking time: 35 minutes
Servings: 6
Method of Preparation: Smoking

Ingredients:
3 tbsp ground flax or ground chia
1/3 cup of warm water
1/2 cups rolled oats
1 cup chickpeas, drained and rinsed
1 tsp cumin
1/2 cup onion
1 tsp dried basil
2 granny smith apples
1/3 cup parsley or cilantro, chopped
2 tbsp soy sauce
2 tsp liquid smoke
2 cloves garlic, minced
1 tsp chili powder
1/4 tsp black pepper

Directions:
Preheat the smoker to 225°F while adding wood chips and water to it.
In a separate bowl, add chickpeas and mash. Mix together the remaining ingredients along with the dipped flax seeds.
Form patties from this mixture.
Put the patties on the rack of the smoker and smoke them for 20 minutes on each side.
When brown, take them out, and serve.

Nutrition:
Calories: 241
Fat: 5 g
Carbohydrates: 40 g
Protein: 9 g
Fiber: 10.3 g

Smoked Tofu

Preparation time: 10 minutes
Cooking time: 41 hour and 30 minutes
Servings: 4
Method of Preparation: Smoking

Ingredients:
400g plain tofu
Sesame oil

Directions:
Preheat the smoker to 225°F while adding wood chips and water to it.
Till that time, take the tofu out of the packet and let it rest
Slice the tofu in one-inch thick pieces and apply sesame oil
Place the tofu inside the smoker for 45 minutes while adding water and wood chips after one hour.
Once cooked, take them out and serve!

Nutrition:
Calories: 201
Fat: 13 g
Carbohydrates: 1 g
Protein: 20 g
Fiber: 0 g

Easy Smoked Vegetables

Preparation time: 15 minutes
Cooking time: 1 ½ hour
Servings: 6
Method of Preparation: Smoking

Ingredients:
1 cup of pecan wood chips
1 ear fresh corn, silk strands removed, and husks, cut corn into 1-inch pieces
1 medium yellow squash, 1/2-inch slices
1 small red onion, thin wedges
1 small green bell pepper, 1-inch strips
1 small red bell pepper, 1-inch strips
1 small yellow bell pepper, 1-inch strips
1 cup mushrooms, halved
2 tbsp vegetable oil
Vegetable seasonings

Directions:
Take a large bowl and toss all the vegetables together in it. Sprinkle it with seasoning and coat all the vegetables well with it.
Place the wood chips and a bowl of water in the smoker.
Preheat the smoker at 100°F or ten minutes.
Put the vegetables in a pan and add to the middle rack of the electric smoker.
Smoke for thirty minutes until the vegetable becomes tender.
When done, serve, and enjoy.

Nutrition:
Calories: 97
Fat: 5 g
Carbohydrates: 11 g
Protein: 2 g

Zucchini with Red Potatoes

Preparation time: 15 minutes
Cooking time: 4 hours
Servings: 4
Method of Preparation: Smoking

Ingredients:
2 zucchinis, sliced in 3/4-inch-thick disks
1 red pepper, cut into strips
2 yellow squash, sliced in 3/4-inch-thick disks
1 medium red onion, cut into wedges
6 small red potatoes, cut into chunks
Balsamic Vinaigrette:
1/3 cup extra virgin olive oil
1/4 teaspoon salt

1/4 cup balsamic vinegar

2 tsp Dijon mustard

1/8 teaspoon pepper

Directions:

For Vinaigrette: Take a medium-sized bowl and blend together olive oil, Dijon mustard, salt, pepper, and balsamic vinegar.

Place all the veggies into a large bowl and pour the vinaigrette mixture over it and evenly toss.

Put the vegetable in a pan and then smoke for 4 hours at a temperature of 225°F.

Serve and enjoy the food.

Nutrition:

Calories: 381

Fat: 17.6 g

Carbohydrates: 49 g

Protein: 6.7 g

Fiber: 6.5 g

Shiitake Smoked Mushrooms

Preparation time: 15 minutes

Cooking time: 45 minutes

Servings: 4-6

Method of Preparation: Smoking

Ingredients:

4 Cup Shiitake Mushrooms

1 tbsp canola oil

1 tsp onion powder

1 tsp granulated garlic

1 tsp salt

1 tsp pepper

Directions:

Combine all the ingredients together

Apply the mix over the mushrooms generously.

Preheat the smoker at 180°F. Add wood chips and half a bowl of water in the side tray.

Place it in the smoker and smoke for 45 minutes.

Serve warm and enjoy.

Nutrition:

Calories: 301

Fat: 9 g

Carbohydrates: 47.8 g

Protein: 7.1 g

Fiber: 4.8 g

Coconut Bacon

Preparation time: 10 minutes

Cooking time: 30 minutes

Servings: 2

Method of Preparation: Smoking

Ingredients:

3 1/2 cups flaked coconut

1 tbsp pure maple syrup

1 tbsp water

2 tbsp liquid smoke

1 tbsp soy sauce

1 tsp smoked paprika (optional)

Directions:

Preheat the smoker at 325°F.

Take a large mixing bowl and combine liquid smoke, maple syrup, soy sauce, and water.

Pour flaked coconut over the mixture. Add it to a cooking sheet.

Place in the middle rack of the smoker.

Smoke it for 30 minutes and every 7-8 minutes, keep flipping the sides.

Serve and enjoy.

Nutrition:

Calories: 1244

Fat: 100 g

Carbohydrates: 70 g

Protein: 16 g

Fiber: 2 g

Garlic and Herb Smoke Potato

Preparation time: 5 minutes
Cooking time: 2 hours
Servings: 6
Method of Preparation: Smoking

Ingredients:
1.5 pounds bag of Gemstone Potatoes
1/4 cup Parmesan, fresh grated
For the Marinade
2 tbsp olive oil
6 garlic cloves, freshly chopped
1/2 tsp dried oregano
1/2 tsp dried basil
1/2 tsp dried dill
1/2 tsp salt
1/2 tsp dried Italian seasoning
1/4 tsp ground pepper

Directions:
Preheat the smoker to 225°F.
Wash the potatoes thoroughly and add them to a sealable plastic bag.
Add garlic cloves, basil, salt, Italian seasoning, dill, oregano, and olive oil to the zip lock bag. Shake.
Place in the fridge for 2 hours to marinate.
Next, take an Aluminum foil and put 2 tbsp of water along with the coated potatoes. Fold the foil so that the potatoes are sealed in
Place in the preheated smoker.
Smoke for 2 hours
Remove the foil and pour the potatoes into a bowl.
Serve with grated Parmesan cheese.

Nutrition:
Calories: 146
Fat: 6 g
Carbohydrates: 19 g
Protein: 4 g
Fiber: 2.1 g

Smoked Baked Beans

Preparation time: 15 minutes
Cooking time: 3 hours
Servings: 12
Method of Preparation: Smoking

Ingredients:
1 medium yellow onion diced
3 jalapenos
56 oz pork and beans
3/4 cup barbeque sauce
1/2 cup dark brown sugar
1/4 cup apple cider vinegar
2 tbsp Dijon mustard
2 tbsp molasses

Directions:
Preheat the smoker to 250°F. Pour the beans along with all the liquid in a pan. Add brown sugar, barbeque sauce, Dijon mustard, apple cider vinegar, and molasses. Stir. Place the pan on one of the racks. Smoke for 3 hours until thickened. Remove after 3 hours. Serve

Nutrition:
Calories: 214
Fat: 2 g
Carbohydrates: 42 g
Protein: 7 g
Fiber: 7 g

Smoked Cauliflower

Preparation Time: 15 Minutes
Cooking time: 10 Minutes
Servings: 3-4
Method of Preparation: Smoking

Ingredients:
1 Head of cauliflower

1 Cup of parmesan cheese
1 Tablespoon of olive oil
2 Crushed garlic cloves
¼ Teaspoon of Paprika
½ Teaspoon of salt
½ Teaspoon of pepper
Directions:
Start your Wood Pellet smoker grill with the lid open for about 4 to 5 minutes
Set the temperature on about 180°F and preheat with the lid closed for about 10 to 15 minutes
Cut the cauliflower into florets of medium-sized; then place the cauliflower right on top of the grate and mix all the ingredients except for the cheese
After about 1 hour, remove the cauliflower; then turn the smoker grill on high for about 10 to 15 minutes
Brush the cauliflower with the mixture of the ingredients and place it on a sheet tray
Place the cauliflower back on the grate for about 10 minutes
Sprinkle with the parmesan cheese
Serve and enjoy your smoked cauliflower!

Nutrition:
Calories: 60
Fat: 3.6g
Carbohydrates: 3.1g
Dietary Fiber: 1g
Protein: 4g

Smoked Peppers

Preparation Time: 5 minutes
Cooking time: 20 Minutes
Servings: 4
Method of Preparation: Smoking

Ingredients:
1 Bag of pearl onions, of about 14.4 oz
1 Bag of 1 lb. of small sweet peppers
Cooking sprays, like butter or olive oil
1 Pinch of Garlic salt
1 Pinch of Black pepper
¼ Teaspoon of steak seasoning
Directions:
Preheat your wood pellet smoker grill to a temperature of about 350° F
Spray the rack of your wood pellet smoker grill with cooking spray and cut the tops of the peppers into half; then remove the seeds
Spray the peppers with cooking spray and cover with the garlic salt, the black pepper, and the seasoning; then place on top of the rack
Smoke the peppers for about 15 to 20 minutes
Serve and enjoy!

Nutrition:
Calories: 62
Fat: 3.6g,
Carbohydrates: 0g
Dietary Fiber: 1.4g
Protein: 1g

Smoked Aubergines

Preparation Time: 10 Minutes
Cooking time: 30 Minutes
Servings: 3
Method of Preparation: Smoking

Ingredients:
2 Medium whole aubergine
2 Medium spring onions
2 Teaspoons of toasted sesame seeds
4 Teaspoons of miso paste
2 Teaspoons of soy sauce
1 Teaspoon of sesame oil
1 Garlic clove
1 Inch of fresh ginger, cube
Directions:

Add the miso, the soy, and the sesame oil to a bowl; then crush a garlic clove

Grate the ginger and stir with the help of a teaspoon until you get a paste

Slice the aubergine into half; then score the flesh to create a pattern of diamond shape

Add the miso paste on top of the aubergine

Brush to add the miso concoction to the aubergine flesh

through diagonal scoring of the aubergine

Let the paste to rest for about 30 minutes

Place the aubergine with the side up over indirect heat at a temperature of about 320°F

Smoke for about 30 minutes

Add a few cherry woods pellets to the coals for any extra flavor.

Turn the aubergine over onto direct heat and cook for about 60 seconds

Serve and enjoy your dish!

Nutrition:

Calories: 112

Fat: 6g

Carbohydrates: 8g

Dietary Fiber: 4 g

Protein: 5g

Smoked Mackerel

Preparation Time: 15 Minutes

Cooking time: 30 Minutes

Servings: 9

Method of Preparation: Smoking

Ingredients:

½ Teaspoon of Garam Masala

1 Pinch of dried red chili flakes

1 Tablespoon of softened butter

3 and ½oz of smoked mackerel fillets

To prepare the raita

2 Tablespoons of Greek-style plain yogurt

1 Tablespoon of roughly chopped fresh mint

Half a lime, only use the juice

½ Thinly sliced halved cucumber

6 Roughly chopped radishes

1 Pinch of salt

Directions:

Start by making the raita and to do that, combine the yogurt with the mint and 1 squeeze of lime juice in a medium bowl and season it with 1 pinch of salt

Add in the cucumber and the radishes; then cover and put in the refrigerator until you are ready to use it

Preheat the charcoal grill to a high heat and line a baking pan with a kitchen foil.

In a medium bowl, combine the Garam Masala with the chili and the butter; then spread the butter over the mackerel

Place the fillets over the baking tray and place it on the smoker and close the smoker with a lid

Smoke the mackerel for about 30 minutes

Remove the mackerel from the smoker; then set it aside for about 5 minutes

Serve and enjoy your mackerel with the raita!

Nutrition:

Calories: 283

Fat: 23.4 g

Carbohydrates: 2g

Protein: 20g

Dietary Fiber 0.1 g

Grilled Sweet Potatoes

Preparation Time: 30 minutes

Cooking time: 30 mins

Servings: 4

Method of Preparation: Grilling

Ingredients:

Potato Ingredients:

2 lbs. chopped sweet potatoes

4 tbsps. extra virgin olive oil

½ tsp. salt

For the dressing:

¼ c. chopped cilantro

1 tsp. lime zest

2 tbsps. fresh lemon juice

¼ c. extra virgin olive oil

1 tsp. salt

Directions:

Preheat the grill to a high temperature.

Place potatoes in a medium bowl and pour the olive oil and salt over the top. Toss to coat.

To make the dressing, combine the ingredients into a medium-sized bowl and whisk together thoroughly.

Arrange the potatoes onto the grill and cook for 6 minutes on each side.

Remove potatoes from the grill and place them in the bowl with the dressing. Coat by tossing and serve.

Nutrition:

Calories: 160,

Fat: 11 g,

Carbohydrates: 16 g,

Protein: 1 g

Grilled Yellow Squash

Preparation Time: 30 minutes

Cooking time: 20 mins

Servings: 8

Method of Preparation: Grilling

Ingredients:

4 medium Yellow squash

½ c. extra virgin olive oil

2 crushed garlic cloves

Salt

pepper

Directions:

Preheat the grill for medium heat.

Using a medium pan, heat olive oil and add garlic cloves.

Cook over medium heat until the garlic becomes fragrant and sizzle.

Brush the slices of squash with garlic oil. Then season with salt and pepper.

Grill squash slices until they reach the desired tenderness, about 5 to 10 minutes per side. Occasionally turn and brush with additional garlic oil.

Nutrition:

Calories: 87

 Fat: 7 g

Carbohydrates: 6 g

Protein: 2 g

Traeger Marinated Chicken Kabobs

Preparation time: 45 minutes
Cooking time: 12 minutes
Servings: 6
Method of Preparation: Grilling

Ingredients:
Marinade
1/2 cup olive oi
2 tbsp white vinegar
1 tbsp lemon juice
1-1/2 tbsp salt
1/2 tbsp ground pepper
2 tbsp fresh chives, chopped
1-1/2 tbsp thyme, chopped
2 tbsp Italian parsley, chopped
1 tbsp minced garlic
Kabobs
1-1/2 lb. chicken breast
12 crimini mushrooms
1 each orange, red and yellow bell pepper
Serve with
Naan bread

Directions:
Mix all the marinade ingredients then toss the chicken and mushrooms until well coated.
Place in the fridge to marinate for 30 minutes.
Meanwhile, soak the skewers in water. And preheat your Traeger to 4500F.
Assemble the kabobs and grill for 6 minutes on each side. Set aside.
Heat up the naan bread on the grill for 2 minutes. serve and enjoy.

Nutrition:
Calories 165, Total fat 5g, Saturated fat 2g, Total carbs 1g, Net carbs 1g Protein 0g, Sugars 0g, Fiber 0g, Sodium 582mg

Bacon-Wrapped Jalapeño Poppers

Preparation time: 15 min
Cooking time: 40 min
Servings: 8 to 12
Method of Preparation: Grilling

Ingredients:
12 large jalapeño peppers
8 oz cream cheese, softened
1 cup pepper jack cheese, shredded
Juice of 1 lemon1/2 tsp garlic powder
1/4 tsp kosher salt
1/4 tsp ground black pepper
12 bacon slices, cut in half

Directions:
Preheat pellet grill to 400°F.
Slice jalapeños in half lengthwise. Remove seeds and scrape sides with a spoon to remove the membrane.
In a medium bowl, mix cream cheese, pepper jack cheese, garlic powder, salt, and pepper until thoroughly combined.
Use a spoon or knife to place the cream cheese mixture into each jalapeño half. Make sure not to fill over the sides of the jalapeño half.
Wrap each cheese-filled pepper with a half slice of bacon. If you can't get a secure wrap, then hold bacon and pepper together with a toothpick.
Place assembled poppers on the grill and cook for 15-20 minutes or until bacon is crispy.

Remove from grill, allow to cool, then serve and enjoy!

Nutrition:

Calories: 78.8

Fat: 7.2 g

Cholesterol: 19.2 mg

Carbohydrate: 1 g

Fiber: 0.2 g

Sugar: 0.7 g

Protein: 2.5 g

Bacon-wrapped Chicken Tenders

Preparation time: 25 minutes

Cooking time: 30 minutes

Servings: 6

Method of Preparation: Grilling

Ingredients:

1/2 tbsp Italian seasoning

1/2 tbsp salt

1/2 tbsp black pepper

1 tbsp paprika

1 tbsp garlic powder

1 tbsp onion powder

1lb. chicken tenders

10 strips bacon

1/3 cup brown sugar

1 tbsp chili powder

Directions:

Preheat your Traeger to 4500F.

In a small mixing bowl, mix seasoning, salt, pepper, paprika, garlic powder, and onion powder.

Sprinkle the mixture over all sides of the chicken tenders until well coated.

Wrap the bacon around the chicken tenders and tuck in the ends.

Mix sugar and chili powder in a bowl and sprinkle over the bacon-wrapped chicken.

Place the chicken on the grill and cook for 30 minutes or until chicken and bacon are cooked through.

Broil the chicken in a broiler for a few minutes to crisp up the bacon if you desire.

Serve and enjoy.

Nutrition:

Calories 301, Total fat 17g, Saturated fat 2g, Total carbs 1g, Net carbs 1g Protein 35g, Sugars 0.1g, Fiber 0g

Traeger Smoked Italian Meatballs

Preparation time: 15 minutes

Cooking time: 1 hour 5 minutes

Servings: 6

Method of Preparation: Smoking

Ingredients:

2 lb. beef, ground

2 slices white bread

1/2 cup whole milk

1 tbsp salt

1/2 tbsp onion powder

1/2 tbsp minced garlic

2 tbsp Italian seasoning

1/4 tbsp black pepper

Directions:

In a mixing bowl, mix all the ingredients until well combined using your hands. Turn on your Traeger and set it to smoke then line a baking sheet with parchment paper.

Roll golf size meatballs using your hands .and place them on the baking dish. Place the baking dish in the Traeger and smoke for 35 minutes.

Increase the Traeger heat to 3250F and cook for 30 more minutes or until the internal temperature reaches 1600F.

Serve when hot

Nutrition:

Calories 453, Total fat 27g, Saturated fat 10g, Total carbs 7g, Net carbs 7g Protein 0g, Sugars 2g, Fiber 0g, Sodium 550mg

Traeger Steak Kabobs

Preparation time: 15 minutes
Cooking time: 10 minutes
Servings: 6
Method of Preparation: Grilling

Ingredients:

3 lb. steak

2 small zucchinis

1 onion

2 small yellow squash

Salt and pepper

1 cup teriyaki sauce

3 tbsp sesame seeds, toasted

Directions:

Preheat your Traeger to 4000F.

Cut the steak and veggies into skewable pieces.

Place the meat and veggies on the skewers then sprinkle with salt and pepper.

Place the skewers on the grill and cook for 5 minutes per side.

Remove the skewers, drizzle teriyaki sauce and top with sesame seeds.

Serve when hot. Enjoy.

Nutrition:

Calories 727, Total fat 44g, Saturated fat 17g, Total carbs 15g, Net carbs 13g Protein 64g, Sugars 10g, Fiber 2g, Sodium 2011mg

Traeger Apple cake

Preparation time: 15 minutes
Cooking time: 45 minutes
Servings: 12
Method of Preparation: Grilling

Ingredients:

Cake

1/2 cup canola oil

1-1/2 cup brown sugar

1 egg

1 cup sour cream

1 tbsp baking soda

1/2 tbsp baking soda

1/2 tbsp baking powder

1-1/2 tbsp vanilla

2-1/2 cups flour

2 apples, finely diced.

Streusel

1 stick butter

1/2 cup brown sugar

1/2 cup flour

1/2 cup oats

1/2 tbsp cinnamon

Glaze

2 cups powdered sugar

1 tbsp apple cinnamon blend

3 tbsp milk

Directions:

Preheat your Traeger to 3250F.

Add the cake ingredients except for the apples in a blender and pulse until well-combined fold in the diced apples.

Spread the mixture on a 9x13 baking pan.

Mix the streusel ingredients using hands until crumbly then pour the mixture over the cake mixture.

Place the baking pan at the top rack of your Traeger to create a space between the cake pan and the fire.

Bake for 45 minutes or until the tester comes out with moist crumbs only.

Let rest for 10 minutes before serving.

Nutrition:

Calories 452, Total fat 21g, Saturated fat 8g, Total carbs 61g, Net carbs 59g Protein 5g, Sugars 34g, Fiber 2g, Sodium 207mg

Traeger Beef Pot Pie

Preparation time: 25 minutes

Cooking time: 60 minutes

Servings: 8

Method of Preparation: Grilling

Ingredients:

1 pie crust

Pot Pie

2 cups potatoes, diced

3 cups leftover pot roast

1 cup corn

1 cup carrots

1/2 cup peas

1/2 cup green beans

Gravy

1/4 cup butter +2 tbsp

1/4 cup flour

3 cups beef broth

1/4 tbsp sherry

1/2 tbsp onion powder

1/8 tbsp garlic powder

1/4 thyme

Egg Wash

1 egg yolk

1 tbsp water

Directions:

Preheat your Traeger to 3500F.

Take the potatoes and drizzle with some oil then sprinkle with salt. Microwave them for 4 minutes. Place the pot pie ingredients in a cast iron pan.

Melt butter in a nonstick skillet, then whisk in flour until there are no lumps.

Stir cook the mixture for 7 minutes over medium heat. Whisk in broth, sherry, onion powder, garlic powder, and thyme.

Pour the mixture over the meat and vegetables. Top everything with a pie crust and slits for vents. Whisk together the egg wash ingredients and brush the mixture at the top of the bowl.

Place the pie in the Traeger, close the lid, and cook for 1 hour or until the internal temperature reaches 1650F. Cover the pie with a foil if it gets too much dark.

Let rest for 10 minutes before serving.

Nutrition:

Calories 371, Total fat 20g, Saturated fat 8g, Total carbs 33g, Net carbs 29g Protein 16g, Sugars 5g, Fiber 4g, Sodium 671mg

Traeger Apple Crisp

Preparation time: 20 minutes

Cooking time: 1 hours

Servings: 15

Method of Preparation: Grilling

Ingredients:

Apple

10 apples, washed, peeled and cored

1/2 cup four

1 cup dark brown sugar

1/2 tbsp cinnamon

1/2 cup butter

Crisp

3 cups oatmeal, old fashioned

1-1/2 cups flour

1-1/2 cups salted butter

1-1/2 tbsp cinnamon

Cups brown sugar

Directions:

Preheat your Traeger to 3500F.

Slice the apples into cubes then toss with flour, sugar, and cinnamon

Spray cooking spray on a 10x12 foil grill pan, then place the apples in it place the butter randomly on the apples.

In a mixing bowl, mix the crisp ingredients until well combined. Place the mixture over the apples. Place the grill pan at the hottest part of the Traeger and cook while checking every 20 minutes.

Remove the pan from the Traeger when the edges are bubbly, the topping is golden brown and the apples are tender.

Let rest for 25 minutes before serving.

Nutrition:

Calories 528, Total fat 26g, Saturated fat 16g, Total carbs 75g, Net carbs 70g Protein 4g, Sugars 51g, Fiber 5g, Sodium 209mg

Berry Cobbler

Preparation time: 15 minutes
Cooking time: 35 minutes
Servings: 8
Method of Preparation: Grilling

Ingredients:

Fruit Filling

3 cups berries, mixed (blueberries, blackberries, raspberries)

1 cup brown sugar

1 lemon juice

1 tbsp lemon zest

1 tbsp vanilla extract

1 pinch salt

Cobbler Topping

1-1/2 cups flour, all-purpose

3 tbsp granulated sugar

1-1/2 tbsp baking powder

1/2 tbsp salt

8 tbsp cold butter

1/2 cup sour cream

2 tbsp sugar

Directions:

Fire up the Traeger to smoke setting for 5 minutes with the lid open or until the fire has been established, then preheat it to 3500F with the lid closed

Combine berries, sugar, juice, zest, vanilla, and salt in a mixing bowl until the fruits are well coated.

Place the fruit mixture in an 8x8 aluminum pan. Make cobbler topping by mixing all-purpose flour, brown sugar, baking powder, and salt in a mixing bowl. Cut the butter in the flour into pea-size pieces.

Stir in sour cream until the dough starts to come together. Pinch the dough into small pieces placing them on top of the fruits until well covered.

Top with sugar if you desire.

Put the grill pan on the grill grate and cook for 35 minutes or until the top is golden brown.

Carefully remove the pan from the Traeger and let rest for a few minutes to Serve.

Nutrition:

Calories 371, Total fat 13g, Saturated fat 8g, Total carbs 60g, Net carbs 58g Protein 3g, Sugars 39g, Fiber 2g, Sodium 269mg

Traeger Smoked Mac and Cheese

Preparation time: 2 minutes
Cooking time: 1 hours
Servings: 8
Method of Preparation: Grilling

Ingredients:
1/2 cup salted butter
1/3 cup flour
6 cups whole milk
1/2 tbsp salt
1/2 tbsp dry mustard
A dash of Worcestershire
White sauce
noodles
1 lb. small shells, cooked in saltwater
2 cups cheddar jack cheese
2 cups white cheddar, smoked
1 cup ritz, crushed

Directions:
Startup the Traeger and set it to smoke with the lid open. Let it run for 10 minutes then turn the grill up to 3250F with the lid closed.

Meanwhile, melt butter in a saucepan over medium heat. Whisk in flour, reduce heat and continue whisking for 6 minutes or until it turns into light tan color.

Stir in milk, salt, dry mustard, and Worcestershire. increase the heat to medium and cook while stirring until the sauce has thickened.

Stir in white sauce, noodles, small shells, and all cheeses in 1 cup in a baking dish sprayed with cooking spray.

Top with ritz and the remaining cheese. Place the baking dish in the Traeger and bake for 30 minutes.

Nutrition:

Calories 628, Total fat 42g, Saturated fat 24g, Total carbs 38g, Net carbs 37g Protein 25g, Sugars 11g, Fiber 1g, Sodium 807mg

Smoked Bananas Foster Bread Pudding

Preparation time: 1 hour
Cooking time: 2 hours 15 minutes
Servings: 8 to 10
Method of Preparation: Smoking

Ingredients:
1 loaf (about 4 cups) brioche or challah, cubed to 1 inch cubes
3 eggs, lightly beaten
2 cups of milk
2/3 cups sugar
2 large bananas, peeled and smashed
1 tbsp vanilla extract
1 tbsp cinnamon
1/4 tsp nutmeg
1/2 cup pecans
Rum Sauce

Ingredients:
1/2 cup spiced rum
1/4 cup unsalted butter
1 cup dark brown sugar
1 tsp cinnamon
5 large bananas, peeled and quartered

Directions:
Place pecans on a skillet over medium heat and lightly toast for about 5 minutes, until you can smell them.

Remove from heat and allow to cool. Once cooled, chop pecans.

Lightly butter a 9" x 13" baking dish and evenly layer bread cubes in the dish.

In a large bowl, whisk eggs, milk, sugar, mashed bananas, vanilla extract, cinnamon, and nutmeg until combined.

Pour egg mixture over the bread in the baking dish evenly. Sprinkle with chopped pecans. Cover with aluminum foil and refrigerate for about 30 minutes.

Preheat pellet grill to 180°F. Turn your smoke setting to high, if applicable.

Remove foil from dish and place on the smoker for 5 minutes with the lid closed, allowing bread to absorb smoky flavor.

Remove dish from the grill and cover with foil again. Increase your pellet grill's temperature to 350°F.

Place dish on the grill grate and cook for 50-60 minutes until everything is cooked through and the bread pudding is bubbling.

1.   In a saucepan, while pudding cooks heat up butter for rum sauce over medium heat. When the butter begins to melt, add the brown sugar, cinnamon, and bananas. Sauté until bananas begin to soften.

2.   Add rum and watch. When the liquid begins to bubble, light a match, and tilt the pan. Slowly and carefully move the match towards the liquid until the sauce lights. When the flames go away, remove skillet from heat.

3.   If you're uncomfortable lighting the liquid with a match, just cook it for 3-4 minutes over medium heat after the rum has been added.

4.   Keep rum sauce on a simmer or reheat once it's time to serve.

5.   Remove bread pudding from the grill and allow it to cool for about 5 minutes.

6.   Cut into squares, put each square on a plate and add a piece of banana then drizzle rum sauce over the top. Serve on its own or a la mode and enjoy it!

Nutrition:

Calories: 274.7

Fat: 7.9 g

Cholesterol: 10 mg

Carbohydrate: 35.5 g

Fiber: 0.9 g

Sugar: 24.7 g

Protein: 4 g

Grilled Pound Cake with Fruit Dressing

Preparation time: 20 min

Cooking time: 50 min

Servings: 12

Method of Preparation: Grilling

Ingredients:

1 buttermilk pound cake, sliced into 3/4-inch slices

1/8 cup butter, melted

1 1/2 cup whipped cream

1/2 cup blueberries

1/2 cup raspberries

1/2 cup strawberries, sliced

Directions:

Preheat pellet grill to 400°F. Turn your smoke setting to high, if applicable.

Brush both sides of each pound cake slice with melted butter.

Place directly on the grill grate and cook for 5 minutes per side. Turn 90° halfway through cooking each side of the cake for checkered grill marks.

You can cook a couple of minutes longer if you prefer deeper grill marks and smoky flavor.

Remove pound cake slices from the grill and allow it to cool on a plate.

Top slices with whipped cream, blueberries, raspberries, and sliced strawberries as desired. Serve and enjoy!

Nutrition:
Calories: 222.1
Fat: 8.7 g
Cholesterol: 64.7 mg
Carbohydrate: 33.1 g
Fiber: 0.4 g
Sugar: 20.6 g
Protein: 3.4 g

Grilled Pineapple with Chocolate Sauce

Preparation time: 10 min
Cooking time: 25 min
Servings: 6 to 8
Method of Preparation: Grilling

Ingredients:
1 pineapple
8 oz bittersweet chocolate chips
1/2 cup spiced rum
1/2 cup whipping cream
2 tbsp light brown sugar

Directions:
Preheat pellet grill to 400°F.

De-skin the pineapple and slice pineapple into 1 in cubes.

In a saucepan, combine chocolate chips. When chips begin to melt, add rum to the saucepan. Continue to stir until combined, then add a splash of the pineapple's juice.

Add in whipping cream and continue to stir the mixture. Once the sauce is smooth and thickening, lower heat to simmer to keep warm.

Thread pineapple cubes onto skewers. Sprinkle skewers with brown sugar.

Place skewers on the grill grate. Grill for about 5 minutes per side, or until grill marks begin to develop.

Remove skewers from grill and allow to rest on a plate for about 5 minutes. Serve alongside warm chocolate sauce for dipping.

Nutrition:
Calories: 112.6
Fat: 0.5 g
Cholesterol: 0
Carbohydrate: 28.8 g
Fiber: 1.6 g
Sugar: 0.1 g
Protein: 0.4 g

Nectarine and Nutella Sundae

Preparation time: 10 min
Cooking time: 25 min
Servings: 4
Method of Preparation: Grilling

Ingredients:
2 nectarines, halved and pitted
2 tsp honey
4 tbsp Nutella
4 scoops vanilla ice cream
1/4 cup pecans, chopped
Whipped cream, to top
4 cherries, to top

Directions:
Preheat pellet grill to 400°F.

Slice nectarines in half and remove the pits.

Brush the inside (cut side) of each nectarine half with honey.

Place nectarines directly on the grill grate, cut side down. Cook for 5-6 minutes, or until grill marks develop.

Flip nectarines and cook on the other side for about 2 minutes.

Remove nectarines from the grill and allow it to cool.

Fill the pit cavity on each nectarine half with 1 tbsp Nutella.

Place 1 scoop of ice cream on top of Nutella. Top with whipped cream, cherries, and sprinkle chopped pecans. Serve and enjoy!

Nutrition:

Calories: 90

Fat: 3 g

Cholesterol: 0

Carbohydrate: 15g

Fiber: 0

Sugar: 13 g

Protein: 2 g

Cinnamon Sugar Donut Holes

Preparation time: 10 min

Cooking time: 35 min

Servings: 4

Method of Preparation: Grilling

Ingredients:

1/2 cup flour

1 tbsp cornstarch

1/2 tsp baking powder

1/8 tsp baking soda

1/8 tsp ground cinnamon

1/2 tsp kosher salt

1/4 cup buttermilk

1/4 cup sugar

1 1/2 tbsp butter, melted

1 egg

1/2 tsp vanilla

Topping Ingredients:

2 tbsp sugar

1 tbsp sugar

1 tsp ground cinnamon

Directions:

Preheat pellet grill to 350°F.

In a medium bowl, combine flour, cornstarch, baking powder, baking soda, ground cinnamon, and kosher salt. Whisk to combine.

In a separate bowl, combine buttermilk, sugar, melted butter, egg, and vanilla. Whisk until the egg is thoroughly combined.

Pour wet mixture into the flour mixture and stir. Stir just until combined, careful not to overwork the mixture.

Spray mini muffin tin with cooking spray.

Spoon 1 tbsp of donut mixture into each mini muffin hole.

Place the tin on the pellet grill grate and bake for about 18 minutes, or until a toothpick can come out clean.

Remove muffin tin from the grill and let rest for about 5 minutes.

In a small bowl, combine 1 tbsp sugar and 1 tsp ground cinnamon.

1.   Melt 2 tbsp of butter in a glass dish. Dip each donut hole in the melted butter, then mix and toss with cinnamon sugar. Place completed donut holes on a plate to serve.

Nutrition:

Calories: 190

Fat: 17 g

Cholesterol: 0

Carbohydrate: 21 g

Fiber: 1 g

Sugar: 8 g

Protein: 3 g

Pellet Grill Chocolate Chip Cookies

Preparation time: 20 min
Cooking time: 45 min
Servings: 12
Method of Preparation: Grilling

Ingredients:

1 cup salted butter, softened

1 cup of sugar

1 cup light brown sugar

2 tsp vanilla extract

2 large eggs

3 cups all-purpose flour

1 tsp baking soda

1/2 tsp baking powder

1 tsp natural sea salt

2 cups semi-sweet chocolate chips, or chunks

Directions:

Preheat pellet grill to 375°F.

Line a large baking sheet with parchment paper and set aside.

In a medium bowl, mix flour, baking soda, salt, and baking powder. Once combined, set aside.

In stand mixer bowl, combine butter, white sugar, and brown sugar until combined. Beat in eggs and vanilla. Beat until fluffy.

Mix in dry ingredients, continue to stir until combined.

Add chocolate chips and mix thoroughly.

Roll 3 tbsp of dough at a time into balls and place them on your cookie sheet. Evenly space them apart, with about 2-3 inches in between each ball.

Place cookie sheet directly on the grill grate and bake for 20-25 minutes, until the outside of the cookies is slightly browned.

Remove from grill and allow to rest for 10 minutes. Serve and enjoy!

Nutrition:
Calories: 120
Fat: 4
Cholesterol: 7.8 mg
Carbohydrate: 22.8 g
Fiber: 0.3 g
Sugar: 14.4 g
Protein: 1.4 g

Delicious Donuts on a Grill

Preparation time: 5 minutes
Cooking time: 10 Minutes
Servings: 6
Method of Preparation: Grilling

Ingredients:

1-1/2 cups sugar, powdered

1/3 cup whole milk

1/2 teaspoon vanilla extract

16 ounces of biscuit dough, prepared

Oil spray, for greasing

1 cup chocolate sprinkles, for sprinkling

Directions:

Take a medium bowl and mix sugar, milk, and vanilla extract.

Combine well to create a glaze.

Set the glaze aside for further use.

Place the dough onto the flat, clean surface.

Flat the dough with a rolling pin.

Use a ring mold, about an inch, and cut the hole in the center of each round dough.

Place the dough on a plate and refrigerate for 10 minutes.

Open the grill and install the grill grate inside it. Close the hood.

1.   Now, select the grill from the menu, and set the temperature to medium.

2.   Set the time to 6 minutes.

3.   Select start and begin preheating.

4. Remove the dough from the refrigerator and coat it with cooking spray from both sides.
5. When the unit beeps, the grill is preheated
6. place the adjustable amount of dough on the grill grate.
7. Close the hood, and cook for 3 minutes.
8. After 3 minutes, remove donuts and place the remaining dough inside.
9. Cook for 3 minutes.
10. Once all the donuts are ready, sprinkle chocolate sprinkles on top.
11. Enjoy.

Nutrition:
Calories: 400
Total Fat: 11g
Saturated Fat: 4.2g
Cholesterol: 1mg
Sodium: 787mg
Total Carbohydrate: 71.3g
Dietary Fiber 0.9g
Total Sugars: 45.3g
Protein: 5.7g

Smoked Pumpkin Pie

Preparation time: 10 minutes
Cooking time: 50 minutes
Servings: 8
Method of Preparation: Smoking

Ingredients:
1 tbsp cinnamon
1-1/2 tbsp pumpkin pie spice
15 oz can pumpkin
14 oz can sweetened condensed milk
2 beaten eggs
1 unbaked pie shell
Topping: whipped cream

Directions:
Preheat your smoker to 325oF.

Place a baking sheet, rimmed, on the smoker upside down, or use a cake pan.

Combine all your ingredients in a bowl, large, except the pie shell, then pour the mixture into a pie crust.

Place the pie on the baking sheet and smoke for about 50-60 minutes until a knife comes out clean when inserted. Make sure the center is set. Remove and cool for about 2 hours or refrigerate overnight.

Serve with a whipped cream dollop and enjoy it!

Nutrition:
Calories: 292
Total Fat: 11g
Saturated Fat: 5g
Total Carbs: 42g
Net Carbs: 40g
Protein: 7g
Sugars: 29g
Fiber: 5g
Sodium: 168mg

Wood Pellet Smoked Nut Mix

Preparation time: 15 minutes
Cooking time: 20 minutes
Servings: 8-12
Method of Preparation: Smoking

Ingredients:
3 cups mixed nuts (pecans, peanuts, almonds, etc.)
1/2 tbsp brown sugar
1 tbsp thyme, dried
1/4 tbsp mustard powder
1 tbsp olive oil, extra-virgin

Directions:
Preheat your pellet grill to 250oF with the lid closed for about 15 minutes.

Combine all ingredients in a bowl, large, then transfer into a cookie sheet lined with parchment paper.

Place the cookie sheet on a grill and grill for about 20 minutes.

Remove the nuts from the grill and let cool.

Serve and enjoy.

Nutrition:

Calories: 249

Total Fat: 21.5g

Saturated Fat: 3.5g

Total Carbs: 12.3g

Net Carbs: 10.1g

Protein: 5.7g

Sugars: 5.6g

Fiber: 2.1g

Sodium: 111mg

Grilled Peaches and Cream

Preparation time: 15 minutes

Cooking time: 8 minutes

Servings: 8

Method of Preparation: Grilling

Ingredients:

4 halved and pitted peaches

1 tbsp vegetable oil

2 tbsp clover honey

1 cup cream cheese, soft with honey and nuts

Directions:

Preheat your pellet grill to medium-high heat.

Coat the peaches lightly with oil and place on the grill pit side down.

Grill for about 5 minutes until nice grill marks on the surfaces.

Turn over the peaches then drizzle with honey.

Spread and cream cheese dollop where the pit was and grill for additional 2-3 minutes until the filling becomes warm.

Serve immediately.

Nutrition:

Calories: 139

Total Fat: 10.2g

Saturated Fat: 5g

Total Carbs: 11.6g

Net Carbs: 11.6g

Protein: 1.1g

Sugars: 12g

Fiber: 0g

Sodium: 135mg

Smoked Peach Parfait

Preparation time: 20 minutes

Cooking time: 35-45 minutes

Servings: 4

Method of Preparation: Smoking

Ingredients:

4 barely ripe peaches, halved and pitted

1 tablespoon firmly packed brown sugar

1-pint vanilla ice cream

3 tablespoons honey

Directions:

Preheat your smoker to 200 degrees Fahrenheit

Sprinkle cut peach halves with brown sugar

Transfer them to smoker and smoke for 33-45 minutes

Transfer the peach halves to dessert plates and top with vanilla ice cream

Drizzle honey and serve!

Nutrition:

Calories: 309

Fats: 27g

Carbs: 17g

Fiber: 2g

Grilled Fruit and Cream

Preparation time: 15 minutes
Cooking time: 10 minutes
Servings: 4
Method of Preparation: Grilling

Ingredients:
2 apricots, halved
1 nectarine, halved
2 peaches, halved
¼ cup blueberries
½ cup raspberries
2 tablespoons honey
1 orange, peel
2 cups cream
½ cup balsamic vinegar

Directions:
Preheat your smoker to 400 degrees F, lid closed
Grill peaches, nectarines, apricots for 4 minutes, each side
Place pan on the stove and turn on medium heat
Add 2 tablespoons honey, vinegar, orange peel
Simmer until medium-thick
Add honey and cream in a bowl and whip until it reaches a soft form
Place fruits on serving plate and sprinkle berries, drizzle balsamic reduction
Serve with cream and enjoy!

Nutrition:
Calories: 230
Fats: 3g
Carbs: 35g
Fiber: 2g

Apple Pie Grill

Preparation time: 20 minutes
Cooking time: 30 minutes
Servings: 4
Method of Preparation: Grilling

Ingredients:
¼ cup of sugar
4 apples, sliced
1 tablespoon cornstarch
1 teaspoon cinnamon, ground
1 pie crust, refrigerator, soften in according to the directions on the box
½ cup peach, preserves

Directions:
Preheat your smoker to 375 degrees F, the closed lid
Take a bowl and add cinnamon, cornstarch, apples and keep it on the side
Place piecrust in pie pan and spread preserves, place apples
Fold crust slightly
Place pan on your smoker (upside down), smoke for 30-40 minutes
Once done, let it rest
Serve and enjoy!

Nutrition:
Calories: 160
Fats: 1g
Carbs: 35g
Fiber: 1g

Fall Season Apple Pie

Preparation time: 15 mins
Cooking time: 1 hour
Servings: 8
Method of Preparation: Grilling

Ingredients:
8 C. apples, peeled, cored and sliced thinly
¾ C. sugar
1 tbsp. fresh lemon juice
1 tsp. ground cinnamon
¼ tsp. ground nutmeg

2 whole frozen pie crusts, thawed
¼ C. apple jelly
2 tbsp. apple juice
2 tbsp. heavy whipping cream

Directions:

Set the temperature of Traeger Grill to 375 degrees F and preheat with closed lid for 15 mins.

In a bowl, add the apples, sugar, lemon juice, flour, cinnamon, and nutmeg and mix well.

Roll the pie crust dough into two (11-inch) circles.

Arrange 1 dough circle into a 9-inch pie plate.

Spread the apple jelly over dough evenly and top with apple mixture.

Dampen the edges of dough crust with apple juice.

Cover with the top crust, pressing the edges together to seal.

Trim the pastry, and flute the edges.

With a sparing knife, make several small slits in the top crust.

Brush the top of the pie with the cream.

Place the pie pan onto the grill and cook for about 50-60 mins.

Remove from the grill and place the pie onto a wire rack to cool slightly.

Serve warm.

Nutrition:

Calories: 419
Carbohydrates: 79.5g
Protein: 2.2g
Fat: 12.3g
Sugar: 54.2g
Sodium: 214mg
Fiber: 6.1g

Sweet Tooth Carving Rhubarb Crunch

Preparation time: 15 mins
Cooking time: 1 hour
Servings: 8
Method of Preparation: Grilling

Ingredients:

1 C. oatmeal
1 C. flour
1 C. brown sugar
½ C. butter, melted
¼ tsp. salt
4 C. raw rhubarb, chopped finely
1 C. white sugar
2 tbsp. cornstarch
1 C. cold water
1 tsp. vanilla extract

Directions:

Set the temperature of Traeger Grill to 350 degrees F and preheat with closed lid for 15 mins.

In a bowl, add oatmeal, flour, brown sugar, butter and salt and mix until well combined.

In a pan, add white sugar, cornstarch, cold water and vanilla extract and cook until sugar is dissolves, stirring continuously.

Place half of the four mixture into a 9x12-inch pan and top with chopped rhubarb evenly.

Place sugar mixture over rhubarb evenly and top with remaining flour mixture.

Place the pan onto the grill and cook for about 1 hour.

Remove from grill and place the crunch onto a wire rack to cool in the pan for about 10 mins.

Cut into desired-sized slices and serve warm.

Nutrition:

Calories: 382
Carbohydrates: 66.3g
Protein: 3.7g
Fat: 12.5g
Sugar: 43.5g
Sodium: 164mg
Fiber: 2.6g

North American Pot Pie

Preparation time: 15 mins
Cooking time: 1 hour 25 mins
Servings: 10
Method of Preparation: Grilling

Ingredients:

2 tbsp. cornstarch
2 tbsp. water
3 C. chicken broth
1 C. milk
3 tbsp. butter
1 tbsp. fresh rosemary, chopped
1 tbsp. fresh thyme, chopped
Salt and freshly ground black pepper, to taste
2¾ C. frozen chopped broccoli, thawed
3 C. frozen peas, thawed
3 C. chopped frozen carrots, thawed
1 frozen puff pastry sheet

Directions:

Set the temperature of Traeger Grill to 375 degrees F and preheat with closed lid for 15 mins.

In a small bowl, dissolve cornstarch in water. Set aside.

In a pan, add broth, milk, butter and herbs over medium heat and bring to a boil.

Add the cornstarch mixture and stir to combine well.

Stir in salt and black pepper and remove from the heat.

In a large bowl, add the vegetables and milk sauce and mix well.

Transfer mixture into a cast iron skillet.

With the puff pastry, cover the mixture and cut excess from edges.

Place the skillet onto the grill and cook for about 80 mins.

Remove the pan from grill and set aside for about 15 mins before serving.

Cut the pie into desired-sized portions and serve.

Nutrition:

Calories: 257
Carbohydrates: 26.1g
Protein: 7.6g
Fat: 14g
Sugar: 5.8g
Sodium: 408mg
Fiber: 4.7g

Decadent Chocolate Cheesecake

Preparation time: 20 mins
Cooking time: 1 hour 10 mins
Servings: 8
Method of Preparation: Grilling

Ingredients:

For Base:
1 C. chocolate wafer crumbs
2 tbsp. butter, melted
For Filling:
4 oz. unsweetened baking chocolate, chopped
16 oz. cream cheese, softened
¾ C. white sugar
2 eggs
1 tsp. vanilla extract
For Topping:
¼ C. heavy cream
2 oz. unsweetened baking chocolate, chopped finely
¼ C. white sugar
1 tbsp. unsalted butter

Directions:

Set the temperature of Traeger Grill to 325 degrees F and preheat with closed lid for 15 mins.

For base: in a bowl, mix together wafer crumbs and melted butter.

Line an 8-inch springform pan with parchment paper.

Place the crumb mixture in the bottom of prepared springform pan and gently, press to fit.

Place the pan onto the grill and cook for about 10 mins.

Remove the pan from grill and set aside to cool.

For filling: in a microwave-safe bowl, add chocolate and microwave on High for about 1-2 mins or until melted, stirring after every 30 seconds.

Remove from microwave and set aside to cool slightly.

In another bowl, add cream cheese and sugar and beat until light and fluffy.

Add the eggs, one at a time, beating well after each addition.

Add melted chocolate and vanilla extract and mix well.

Place filling mixture over cooled base evenly and cook onto the grill for about 45-50 mins.

Remove the cheesecake from grill and place onto a wire rack to cool.

For topping: in a heavy-bottomed pan, place heavy cream over medium-low heat and cook until heated through.

Add chocolate, sugar and butter and cook until sugar dissolves, stirring continuously.

Remove the pan from heat and set aside to cool slightly.

Pour chocolate mixture over the cooled cheesecake evenly.

Refrigerate for at least 4 hours before serving.

Nutrition:
Calories: 489
Carbohydrates: 43.2g
Protein: 9.4g
Fat: 35.4g
Sugar: 29.6g
Sodium: 271mg
Fiber: 4g

Traditional English Mac n' Cheese

Preparation time: 15 mins
Cooking time: 1 hour 20 mins
Servings: 12
Method of Preparation: Grilling

Ingredients:
2 lb. elbow macaroni
¾ C. butter
½ C. flour
1 tsp. dry mustard
1½ C. milk
2 lb. Velveeta cheese, cut into ½-inch cubes
Salt and freshly ground black pepper, to taste
1½ C. cheddar cheese, shredded
2 C. plain dry breadcrumbs
Paprika, to taste

Directions:
Set the temperature of Traeger Grill to 350 degrees F and preheat with closed lid for 15 mins.

In a large pan of lightly salted boiling water, cook the macaroni for about 7-8 mins.

Drain the macaroni well and transfer into a large bowl.

Meanwhile, in a medium pan, melt 8 tbsp. of butter over medium heat.

Slowly, add flour and mustard, beating continuously until smooth.

Cook for about 2 mins, beating continuously.

Slowly, add milk, beating continuously until smooth.

Reduce the heat to medium-low and slowly, stir in Velveeta cheese until melted.

Stir in salt and black pepper and remove from heat.

Place cheese sauce over cooked macaroni and gently, stir to combine.

Place the macaroni mixture into greased casserole dish evenly and sprinkle with cheddar cheese.

In a small frying pan, melt remaining 4 tbsp. of butter.

Stir in breadcrumbs and remove from heat.

Place breadcrumbs mixture over cheddar cheese evenly and sprinkle with paprika lightly.

Arrange the casserole dish onto the grill and cook for about 45-60 mins, rotating the pan once halfway through.

Serve hot.

Nutrition:

Calories: 914

Carbohydrates: 99.9g

Protein: 37.2g

Fat: 42.3g

Sugar: 12g

Sodium: 1600mg

Fiber: 4.1g

Satisfying Veggie Casserole

Preparation time: 15 mins

Cooking time: 3 hours

Servings: 10

Method of Preparation: Grilling

Ingredients:

5 tbsp. olive oil, divided

6 C. onions, sliced thinly

1 tbsp. fresh thyme, chopped and divided

Salt and freshly ground black pepper, to taste

1 tbsp. unsalted butter

1¼ lb. Yukon gold potatoes, peeled and 1/8-inch thick slices

½ C. heavy cream

2¼ lb. tomatoes, cut into ¼-inch thick slices

¼ cup black olives, pitted and sliced

Directions:

In a large cast iron pan, heat 3 tbsp. of oil and over high heat and cook onions, 1 tsp. of thyme, salt and black pepper for about 5 mins, stirring occasionally.

Add the butter and cook over medium heat for about 15 mins.

Reduce the heat to low and cook for about 10 mins.

Set the temperature of Traeger Grill to 350 degrees F and preheat with closed lid for 15 mins.

Meanwhile, in a bowl, add potatoes slices, cream, 1 tsp. of thyme, salt and black pepper and toss to coat.

In another bowl, add tomato slices, salt and black pepper and toss to coat.

Transfer half of the caramelized onions into a small bowl.

In the bottom of the cast iron pan, spread the remaining onion slices evenly and top with 1 layer of potatoes and tomatoes.

Drizzle with 2 tbsp. of cream from potato mixture and 1 tbsp. of olive oil.

Sprinkle with a little salt, black pepper and ½ tsp. of thyme.

Spread remaining caramelized onions on top, followed by potatoes, tomatoes and olives.

Drizzle with remaining cream from the potatoes and remaining tbsp. of olive oil.

Sprinkle with a little salt, black pepper and remaining ½ tsp. of thyme.

With a piece of foil, cover the cast iron pan tightly.

Place the pan onto the grill and cook for about 2 hours.

Remove from grill and uncover the cast iron pan.

Now, set the temperature of Traeger Grill to 450 degrees F.

Place the cast iron pan, uncovered onto the grill and cook for about 25-30 mins.

Remove from grill and serve hot.

Nutrition:

Calories: 158

Carbohydrates: 14.8g

Protein: 2.3g

Fat: 11.1g

Sugar: 5.8g

Sodium: 65mg

Fiber: 3.2g

Potluck Favorite Baked Beans

Preparation time: 15 mins
Cooking time: 3 hours 5 mins
Servings: 10
Method of Preparation: Grilling

Ingredients:

1 tbsp. butter

½ of red bell pepper, seeded and chopped

½ of medium onion, chopped

2 jalapeño peppers, chopped

2 (28-oz.) cans baked beans, rinsed and drained

8 oz. pineapple chunks, drained

1 C. BBQ sauce

1 C. brown sugar

1 tbsp. ground mustard

Directions:

Set the temperature of Traeger Grill to 220-250 degrees F and preheat with closed lid for 15 mins.

In a non-stick skillet, melt butter over medium heat and sauté the bell peppers, onion and jalapeño peppers for about 4-5 mins.

Remove from heat and transfer the pepper mixture into a bowl.

Add the remaining ingredients and stir to combine.

Transfer the mixture into a Dutch oven.

Place the Dutch oven onto the grill and cook for about 2½-3 hours.

Remove from grill and serve hot.

Nutrition:

Calories: 364

Carbohydrates: 61.4g

Protein: 9.4g

Fat: 9.8g

Sugar: 23.5g

Sodium: 1036mg

Fiber: 9.7g

Amazing Irish Soda Bread

Preparation time: 15 mins
Cooking time: 1½ hours
Servings: 10
Method of Preparation: Grilling

Ingredients:

4 C. flour

1 C. raisins

½ C. sugar

1 tbsp. caraway seeds

2 tsp. baking powder

1 tsp. baking soda

¾ tsp. salt

1¼ C. buttermilk

1 C. sour cream

2 eggs

Directions:

Set the temperature of Traeger Grill to 350 degrees F and preheat with closed lid for 15 mins.

Grease a 9-inch round cake pan.

Reserve 1 tbsp. of flour in a bowl.

In a large bowl, mix together remaining flour, raisins, sugar, caraway seeds, baking powder, baking soda and salt.

In another small bowl, add buttermilk, sour cream and eggs and beat until well combined.

Add egg mixture into flour mixture and mix until just moistened.

With your hands, knead the dough until sticky.

Place the dough into the prepared pan evenly and cut a 4x¾-inch deep slit in the top.

Dust the top with reserved flour.

Place the pan onto the grill and cook for about 1½ hours or until a toothpick inserted in the center comes out clean.

Remove from grill and place the pan onto a wire rack to cool for about 10 mins.

Carefully, invert the bread onto the wire rack to cool completely before slicing.

Cut the bread into desired-sized slices and sere.

Nutrition:

Calories: 340

Carbohydrates: 63g

Protein: 8.6g

Fat: 6.6g

Sugar: 20.3g

Sodium: 361mg

Fiber: 2.2g

Native Southern Cornbread

Preparation time: 15 mins

Cooking time: 20 mins

Servings: 8

Method of Preparation: Grilling

Ingredients:

2 tbsp. butter

1½ C. all-purpose flour

1½ C. yellow cornmeal

2 tbsp. sugar

3 tsp. baking powder

¾ tsp. baking soda

¾ tsp. salt

1 C. whole milk

1 C. buttermilk

3 large eggs

3 tbsp. butter, melted

Directions:

Set the temperature of Traeger Grill to 400 degrees F and preheat with closed lid for 15 mins.

In a 13x9-inch baking dish, place 2 tbsp. of butter.

Place the baking dish onto grill to melt butter and heat up the pan.

In a large bowl, mix together flour, cornmeal, sugar, baking powder, baking soda and salt.

In another bowl, add milk, buttermilk, eggs and melted butter and beat until well combined.

Add the egg mixture into flour mixture and mix until just moistened.

Carefully, remove the heated baking dish from grill.

Place the bread mixture into heated baking dish evenly.

Place the pan onto the grill and cook for about 20 mins or until a toothpick inserted in the center comes out clean.

Remove from grill and place the pan onto a wire rack to cool for about 10 mins.

Carefully, invert the bread onto the wire rack to cool completely before slicing.

Cut the bread into desired-sized slices and sere.

Nutrition:

Calories: 302

Carbohydrates: 42.4g

Protein: 8.7g

Fat: 10.4g

Sugar: 6.4g

Sodium: 467mg

Fiber: 2.3g

RECIPE INDEX

A

Amazing Irish Soda Bread **155**
Apple Pie Grill 150
Apple Veggie Burger 131
Apricot BBQ Smoked Pork Tenderloin 77
Aromatic Herbed Rack of Lamb 82

B

Backyard Cookout Sausages 79
Bacon-wrapped Chicken Tenders 139
Bacon-Wrapped Jalapeno Poppers 128
Bacon-Wrapped Jalapeño Poppers 138
Bacon-Wrapped Sausages in Brown Sugar 90
Baked Cheesy Corn Pudding 116
Baked Cornbread with Honey Butter 24
Baked Pulled Pork Stuffed Potatoes 27
Baked Steelhead 104
Baked Wild Sockeye Salmon 29
Balsamic Smoked Pork Chops 72
Banana Walnut bread 28
Barbeque Sauce 37
BBQ Baby Back Ribs 93
BBQ Chicken 53
BBQ Half Chickens 43
BBQ Honey Pork Belly 74
BBQ Oysters 96
BBQ St. Louis-Style Ribs 72
BBQ-Seasoned Chicken Breast 62
Beautiful Christmas Ham 79
Beef Tenderloin with Cherry Tomato Vinaigrette 65
Berry Cobbler 142
Bourbon Whiskey Sauce 38
Brown Sugar Baked Pork Belly 77
Brown Sugar Lamb Chops 89
Brown Sugared Bacon Cinnamon Rolls 26

Butter Braised Green Beans 119
Butter-Sugar Glazed BBQ Pork Ribs 76

C

Cajun Smoked Chicken Wings 58
Cajun Style Grilled Corn 107
Carne Asada Marinade 39
Cauliflower with Parmesan and Butter 115
Cheesy Lamb Burgers 84
Chicken Brined with Lemon 61
Chicken Cordon Bleu 50
Chicken Fajitas on a Wood Pellet Grill 51
Chicken Marinade 38
Chicken Tortillas with Tzatziki Sauce 53
Chicken, Applewood Smoked 59
Chile Verde Braised Pork Shoulder 75
Chinese BBQ Pork 91
Chocolate Pecan Bourbon Pie 32
Cinnamon Sugar Donut Holes 146
Citrus Salmon 100
Classic Apple Pie 30
Cocoa-Rubbed Steak for Two 64
Coconut Bacon 133
Crab Legs on the Grill 105
Crazy Delicious Lobster Tails 103
Crispy Maple Bacon Brussels Sprouts 110
Crusty Artisan Dough Bread 30

D

Decadent Chocolate Cheesecake 152
Delicious Donuts on a Grill 147
Deliciously Spicy Rack of Lamb 81

E

Easy Smoked Vegetables 132
Easy-to-Prepare Lamb Chops 80
Elegant Lamb Chops 80
Enticing Mahi-Mahi 101

F
Fajita Favorite Pork Shoulder 78
Fall Season Apple Pie 150
Fancy Gathering's Lamb Shoulder 83
Feisty Roasted Cauliflower 113
Flavor-Bursting Prawn Skewers 102
Foolproof Lamb Chops 81

G
Garlic and Herb Smoke Potato 134
Garlic and Rosemary Potato Wedges 112
Garlic Parmesan Chicken Wings 45
Garlicky Grilled Rack of Lamb 71
Garlic-Mustard Roasted Prime Rib 68
Glazed Smoked Chicken 60
Grapefruit Juice Marinade 39
Green Beans with Bacon 113
Grilled Artichokes 118
Grilled Asparagus & Honey-Glazed Carrots 125
Grilled Asparagus with Wild Mushrooms 117
Grilled Beef Short Ribs 66
Grilled Bloody Mary Flank Steak 63
Grilled Broccoli 111
Grilled Carrots and Asparagus 122
Grilled Cherry Tomato Skewers 108
Grilled Clams with Garlic Butter 105
Grilled Corn on The Cob with Parmesan and Garlic 117
Grilled Corn with Honey Butter 129
Grilled Fruit and Cream 150
Grilled Lamb and Apricot Kabobs 69
Grilled Lamb Burgers 85
Grilled Lamb Leg 70
Grilled Lamb Sandwiches 86
Grilled Peaches and Cream 149
Grilled Pineapple with Chocolate Sauce 145
Grilled Potato Salad 121
Grilled Pound Cake with Fruit Dressing 144

Grilled Scallions 118
Grilled Shrimp 96
Grilled Stuffed Turkey Breast 71
Grilled Sugar Snap Peas 122
Grilled Sweet Potatoes 137
Grilled Yellow Squash 137
Grilled Zucchini 121
Grilled Zucchini Squash 120
Grilled Zucchini Squash Spears 125

H
Halibut in Parchment 99
Hellfire Chicken Wings 42
Herb Roasted Turkey 40
Holiday Dinner Leg of Lamb 82

J
Jerk Shrimp 97
Juicy BBQ Ribs 73
Juicy Smoked Salmon 94

K
Kahluá Coffee Brownies 31
Kale Chips 123
Korean Chicken Wings 44

L
Lamb Breast 88
Lamb Chops 86
Lamb Ribs Rack 87
Lamb Shank 87
Lamb Skewers 89
Leg of a Lamb 87
Lemon Chicken Breast 46
Lemon Garlic Scallops 98
Lemon Pepper Pork Tenderloin 91
Lively Flavored Shrimp 102
Lobster Tails 98
Louisiana Hot Apple-Smoked Turkey 55

M

Maple and Bacon Chicken 48

N

Native Southern Cornbread 156
Nectarine and Nutella Sundae 145
No-Fuss Tuna Burgers 102
North American Pot Pie 152

O

Omega- Rich Salmon 100

P

Paprika Chicken 48
Peach Blueberry Cobbler 28
Pellet Grill Chocolate Chip Cookies 147
Peppercorn Tuna Steaks 94
Pizza dough roll 29
Pork Dry Rub 37
Potluck Favorite Baked Beans 155

Q

Quick Yeast Dinner Rolls 24

R

Red Chile and Lime Shortbread Cookies 31
Roasted Breaded Rack of Lamb 70
Roasted Butternut Squash 115
Roasted Green Beans with Bacon 128
Roasted Parmesan Cheese Broccoli 107
Roasted Root Vegetables 123
Roasted Sheet Pan Vegetables 115
Roasted Shrimp Mix 106
Roasted Vegetable Medley 108
Rosemary Orange Chicken 46

S

S'Mores Dip with Candied Pecans 25
Satisfying Veggie Casserole 154
Seared Rib-Eye Steaks 67
Seared Strip Steak with Butter 67
Seared Tuna Steaks 106
Shiitake Smoked Mushrooms 133

Simple but Delicious Fish Recipe 105
Simplest Pork Belly 78
Smoked Acorn Squash 126
Smoked and Smashed New Potatoes 130
Smoked Aubergines 135
Smoked Baked Beans 134
Smoked Baked Kale Chips 119
Smoked Balsamic Potatoes and Carrots 120
Smoked Bananas Foster Bread Pudding 143
Smoked -Bean Salad 118
Smoked Beef Brisket with Mop Sauce 66
Smoked Brussels Sprouts 131
Smoked Cauliflower 134
Smoked Cherry BBQ Sauce 35
Smoked Cherry Tomatoes 130
Smoked Chicken 59
Smoked Chicken Drumsticks 49
Smoked Cornish Chicken in Wood Pellets 52
Smoked Cranberry Sauce 34
Smoked Deviled Eggs 109
Smoked Garlic Sauce 35
Smoked Garlic White Sauce 36
Smoked Healthy Cabbage 111
Smoked Hummus 116
Smoked Lamb Shoulder Chops 88
Smoked Mackerel 136
Smoked Mushroom Sauce 33
Smoked Mushrooms 130
Smoked Peach Parfait 149
Smoked Peppers 135
Smoked Pickles 119
Smoked Pumpkin Pie 148
Smoked Rib-Eye Caps 64
Smoked Sausages 92
Smoked Soy Sauce 35
Smoked Sriracha Sauce 34
Smoked Stuffed Mushrooms 128
Smoked Tofu 132

Smoked Tomahawk Steak 63
Smoked Tomato and Mozzarella Dip 112
Smoked Tomato Cream Sauce 33
Smoked Watermelon 129
Smoked Whole Chicken 57
Smoked Whole Chicken with Carolina Glaze 58
Smoked Whole Duck 50
Smokey Fried Chicken 47
Smokey Roasted Cauliflower 109
Spiced Tomahawk Steaks 65
Spicy & Tangy Lamb Shoulder 83
Spicy BBQ Chicken 43
Spicy Braised Lamb Shoulder 69
Spicy Chicken Thighs 62
Spicy Chipotle Chicken Kabobs 54
Spicy Smoked StLouis Ribs 74
Spicy Turkey Cheeseburgers 56
Steak Marinade 39
Steak Sauce 38
Steak Skewers with Cherry BBQ Sauce 66
Stuffed Grilled Zucchini 127
Stuffed Shrimp Tilapia 94
Super-Tasty Trout 101
Sweet and Hot BBQ Ribs 90
Sweet Jalapeño Cornbread 110
Sweet Pull-Apart Rolls 27
Sweet Sriracha BBQ Chicken 49
Sweet Tooth Carving Rhubarb Crunch 151

T
Take and Bake Pepperoni Pizza 30
Teriyaki Smoked Shrimp 97
Teriyaki Wings 44
Texas Barbeque Rub 37
Texas-Style Brisket Rub 37
Togarashi Smoked Salmon 95

Traditional English Mac n' Cheese 153
Traeger Apple cake 140
Traeger Apple Crisp 141
Traeger Beef Pot Pie 141
Traeger Braised BBQ Ribs 76
Traeger Grilled Pork Chops 75
Traeger Grilled Vegetables 126
Traeger Marinated Chicken Kabobs 138
Traeger Smoked Italian Meatballs 139
Traeger Smoked Mac and Cheese 143
Traeger Smoked Mushrooms 125
Traeger Smoked Queso 73
Traeger Soft Gingerbread Cookie 26
Traeger Steak Kabobs 140
Traeger Stuffed Burgers 85
Turkey Breast 41
Turkey Legs 40
Twice- Baked potatoes with Smoked Gouda and grilled scallions 32
Twice-Baked Spaghetti Squash 29

V
Vegan Smoked Carrot Dogs 127
Vegetable Sandwich 114
Vegetable Skewers 124

W
Whole Maple-Smoked Turkey 56
Whole Vermillion Snapper 104
Wild Turkey Egg Rolls 52
Wine Braised Lamb Shank 84
Wine Infused Salmon 99
Wood Pellet Smoked Nut Mix 148

Y
Yummy Buttery Clams 103

Z
Zucchini with Red Potatoes 132